THE DEAD SEA SCRIPTURES

THE DEAD SEA
SCRIPTURES

In English Translation
With Introduction and Notes by
THEODOR H. GASTER

Doubleday Anchor Books
Doubleday & Company, Inc.
Garden City, New York, 1957

To the Memory of
the Men of Qumran

*Ye that did cleave unto the Lord your God
are alive every one of you this day.*

DEUTERONOMY 4.4.

JACKET AND TYPOGRAPHY BY EDWARD GOREY

Library of Congress Catalog Card Number 56–10680

PREFACE

The purpose of this book is to provide a complete and reliable translation of the celebrated Dead Sea Scrolls, insofar as the original Hebrew texts have yet been published. Everything that is sufficiently well preserved to make connected sense has been included. Mere fragments, however, have been left out, because there is no point in rendering disjointed (and often incomplete) sentences wrested from their contexts. Furthermore, no translation is offered of the Dead Sea Scroll of Isaiah or of the other more fragmentarily preserved Biblical manuscripts. The contents of the Bible are readily available in English, and the special contribution of the Dead Sea Scrolls in this field is of interest only to scholars.

This book is addressed to laymen. It is not intended as an independent scholarly contribution to the problem (or problems) of the Scrolls, nor as a survey of, or introduction to, the current controversy about them. It is concerned only with what the Scrolls themselves have to say, not with what has been or is being said about them. The Introduction therefore confines itself to providing background material for an understanding of the documents, but does not venture into any detailed discussion of the various theories that have been advanced concerning their date, the possibility of recognizing historical allusions, and the like.

The present writer holds the view that:

(a) The texts here presented were composed at various dates between about 170 B.C. and 68 A.D.

(b) They were conserved in the library of an Essene monastery or meeting-house at Qumran, but represent the religious repertoire of the Essene Brotherhood as a whole.

Some elements of this literature may even have been inherited by the Essenes from earlier sources.

(c) The Dead Sea Scrolls and the religious movement which they depict help us to reconstruct the spiritual climate of early Christianity and throw light especially on the mission of John the Baptist and on the constitution of the primitive Church. But the Scrolls contain no anticipation of, or parallel to distinctive Christian doctrines, e.g. Incarnation, Vicarious Atonement or Communion.

(d) The religious brotherhood represented by the Scrolls did *not* believe, as has been supposed, in a martyred Messianic 'Teacher of Righteousness' who reappeared posthumously to his disciples and whose Second Coming was awaited. The title 'Teacher of Righteousness' (more correctly, 'true exponent of the Law') designates an office, not a particular person. The passage of the texts on which the sensational theory has been based has been misunderstood. The Brotherhood indeed looked forward to the advent of a prophetic and priestly Teacher before the Final Era, but this was not the Second Coming of a martyred Christ.

(e) It is unsafe at present to draw historical conclusions from the texts or to speculate about historical allusions in them.

More than to all the foregoing, however, the writer adheres to the view that the Dead Sea Scrolls should be regarded as something more than the subject matter of a scholarly controversy. For those who will read them sympathetically, they possess value in their own right as conveying the religious message of men who gave up the world and were able to find God in a wilderness, simply because they preferred nakedness to motley and because they realized that, in the larger analysis, crucifixion can itself be resurrection.

The translation of the non-literary documents (e.g. *The Manual of Discipline*) aims to reproduce the original in idiomatic English. The same liberties have been taken in breaking up the sequences of the Hebrew sentences, rendering copulas by punctuation-marks, and the like as would readily be permitted—even expected—in any version of a modern work. These renderings, therefore, are not to be regarded as slavish 'ponies', while at the same time they stick strictly to the letter of the text.

In the case of the hymns, a different technique has had to be adopted. The hymns are written in the style of the Biblical Psalms; but to the composer this style was a conscious archaism, while it fell on the ears of the reciters with the same effect as does the language of the Anglican Prayerbook or the King James' Version upon the modern churchgoer. The only feasible way of reproducing this effect is to fall back on 'Biblical English'. Readers who may be irritated or impeded by the 'howbeits' and 'whiloms' and the like need only to be reminded that the original reciters were, in all probability, just as much put out by the plethora of rare and recondite words and by the artificial manipulation of Biblical 'tags' in which the authors indulged. But to smooth this out would be to lose the flavor; it would be like trying to make Lyly talk the language of Housman. And, after all, do not the English Bible and the Prayerbook Psalter *have* to retain the infuriating 'Selah', even though no one has the faintest idea what it means?

For the benefit of those who may wish to use this book alongside of the original texts, I should like to point out that the translations have been made in all cases from the facsimile plates, not from the editors' transcriptions. This means that in a few instances I have read faint traces or ambiguous spellings somewhat differently.

Then, too, it should be pointed out that in rendering the innumerable Biblical 'tags' that are interwoven in all the texts, I have not simply fallen back on the standard English versions. The original authors often understood the Scriptural passages in a way quite different from ours, and more often they deliberately manipulated them to produce effective phrases and tropes. In all cases I have carefully consulted the Ancient Versions (especially the Aramaic Targum and the Syriac Peshitta) in order, if possible, to recover from those sources traces of the tradition that the authors may have followed. Not infrequently, this has provided the clue to expressions that would otherwise be obscure; but it means that in translating the 'tags' I have had perforce to render them somewhat unrecognizable to those brought up on the English Bible. This is especially so in the case of the Hymns, where the impression that is made on a reader familiar with the Hebrew Scriptures can scarcely be reproduced. For even measure, however, I have cited in the notes all the main Scriptural passages from which the writers borrowed. The reader must be warned, nonetheless, that these will have to be turned up in the Hebrew Bible. (It is for that reason that they are cited according to the Hebrew rather than the English numeration.)

Finally, I should like to say that I propose later to publish my detailed notes on the original texts. These will explain—and, I hope, justify—to the initiated the principles and technical basis of my renderings, especially in the more difficult passages.

T.H.G.

CONTENTS

Introduction

Almost everyone has heard by now of the ancient Hebrew writings that have been found during recent years in caves near the Dead Sea. Almost everyone has been moved by the assertion of scholars that they come from the very community in which 'John the Baptist taught and Jesus learned'. And almost everyone has been intrigued by the much-publicized claim that they reveal to us a long-lost forerunner of Christianity—a sect which believed in a martyred 'Teacher of Righteousness' who would eventually reappear to the faithful. Thus far, however, very few people have had a chance of reading the documents themselves, for the simple reason that no complete translation of them has yet appeared in a form accessible to the layman.

This book is designed to supply that need. It offers renderings of all the principal and intelligibly preserved documents retrieved from the Dead Sea caves, together with that of a related text (the so-called *Zadokite Document*) which was discovered, nearly fifty years ago, in an old synagogue at Cairo. Moreover, it does not gear these renderings to any particular theory, but allows the documents to raise their own voice and give their own testimony amid the din and hubbub of current controversy about them.

I

We do not yet know for certain who wrote the Dead Sea Scrolls, when and where. Attempts have been made to date them by palaeography—that is, by the form (or forms) of script which they employ—and by detecting in them allusions to known persons or events. Neither method, however, has thus far yielded conclusive results. Palaeography could determine, at best, the time when our actual manuscripts were penned, but not when their contents were originally composed. Moreover, as things are, most of the ancient documents used for purposes of comparison or contrast are themselves of uncertain date, are executed in a wide variety of media (stone, sherds and papyrus) and are the products of widely different environments, so that they scarcely represent a single linear development of Hebrew script. And as to the alleged historical allusions, the difficulty here is that even if the passages in question do indeed possess specific reference, most of them are so vague and ambiguous that they can be pegged with equal plausibility to any number of different persons and events all the way from the third to the first century B.C., if not also slightly later.[1]

In these circumstances, it seems best at present to leave in abeyance the question of ultimate origin and to start from the situation that existed at the time the documents were cached in the caves. That situation is that, whenever, wherever and by whomever they may have been composed, they had come to be accepted as the literature or religious repertoire of an ascetic, 'protestant' and 'puritan' Jewish community that lived in the Desert of Judah—more precisely, on the western shore of the Dead Sea—during the early years of the Common Era; that is, in the very area and at the very time in which John the Baptist 'came for witness, that he might bear witness of the light'. It is this fact that gives them today their main interest and importance. They recover for us what may best be described as the backdrop of the stage on which the first act of the Christian drama was performed.

The community of which we have been speaking—estimated by a contemporary writer as more than four thousand in number—lived in a series of encampments, and one of these, accommodating some two hundred persons, was situated in the forbidding ravine of Qumran, at the northern end of the Dead Sea. It was clustered around a central building located about a kilometer away from the cave in which the principal scrolls were discovered by an Arab boy in 1947. This building has now been excavated, and on the evidence of coins found within it, it has been established that it was occupied continuously (except for a break, due to earthquake, between about 31 B.C. and 5 B.C.) from, approximately, 125 B.C. until 68 A.D. Now, this latter date coincides with the entry into the area of the Tenth Roman Legion which had been despatched thither to suppress the First Jewish Revolt. It is therefore a very plausible conjecture that the building was abandoned when the troops drew near, and that the manuscripts of its library (several of which may have been, of course, considerably older and originally composed in quite different places) were then cached for safekeeping in the surrounding caves.

Various and ingenious attempts have been made to identify the community with one or other of the Jewish sects known to have existed at the time. It has been pointed out, for instance, that many of the beliefs and practices described in the Scrolls bear a striking similarity to those associated by the first-century writers Philo and Josephus with an ascetic brotherhood known as the Essenes and that, according to Pliny the Elder (23–79 A.D.), the Essenes indeed lived in this area at the period in question. For the moment, however, we may postpone consideration of such theories and, without prejudging the issue, allow the texts to describe for themselves the community whose 'scriptures' they were.

Insofar as basic principles, constitution and practice are concerned, our principal sources of information are the *Book of the Order* (or *Manual of Discipline*) and the complementary *Zadokite Document;* while for the beliefs and religious concepts we may draw mainly upon the more personal and less academic *Book of Hymns* (or *Psalms of Thanksgiving*).

II

We are introduced by the Dead Sea Scrolls to a group of people who believed that they constituted the true and ideal Congregation of Israel, the small remnant that had stayed faithful to the traditional Covenant and that was thereby ensuring the continuance of God's people and the eventual cleansing of His land from the stain of guilt. The Covenant, it was held, had been maintained and preserved throughout history only by a succession of such pious 'remnants'.

The members of the community conceived of themselves as repeating in a later age the experience of their remote forefathers in the days of Moses. When they left the cities and villages and repaired to the desert, they pictured themselves as going out into the wilderness to receive a new Covenant. What was envisaged, however, was no 'New Testament' in the Christian sense of the term, no abrogation or substitution of the old Covenant, but simply a new affirmation of it. This was in accordance with the traditional Jewish view that the eternal Covenant is periodically reaffirmed and that the Pact concluded at Sinai was itself but a re-articulation of that which God had previously made, in their several generations, with Abraham, Isaac and Jacob.

To emphasize this basic idea and to bring out more clearly its sense of continuity with previous 'remnants', the community made a point of applying to itself a series of titles, styles and epithets charged with significant historical associations. It spoke of itself as 'the elect' or 'rightfully chosen', in reference especially to the election of Israel at Mount Sinai. It called its priests 'the sons of Zadok', in reference to the foremost priestly family in the time of David (cf. II Sam. 8.17) and to those whom the prophet Ezekiel had designated, in his visions of the future restored Temple, as the only legitimate priests (Ez. 40.46; 43.19; 44.15; 48.11). It described its sojourn in the forbidding desert as exile in 'the wilderness of Damascus', thereby dramatizing it as the fulfillment of the prophet Amos' prediction that God would cause His people to 'go into exile beyond Damascus' (Am. 5.27). And it regarded itself as the militia of God—a kind of Salvation Army—ready, like its ancestors under Moses and Joshua, to do battle for His name and to drive out the heathen from His land—in this case, from the whole earth. (Indeed, it sometimes called its adherents 'the volunteers'—a name with distinctly military overtones; and it even drew up an elaborate plan of campaign for 'Armageddon'!)

There was, however, one crucial difference between this

community and its remote prototype: it was not waiting to receive the Law; it already possessed it. Its aim was simply to assert that Law, to deliver it from the realm of darkness in which it had become engulfed. The Torah—that is, the Divine Teaching (or Guidance) as revealed to Moses—had, it was held, been successively garbled and perverted by 'false expositors'. The community's main purpose was to exemplify and promulgate the true interpretation. It based that interpretation on a kind of 'apostolic succession', begun by the prophets and continued by a series of inspired leaders each of whom was known as 'the correct expositor' or 'right-teacher' (*not* 'Teacher of Righteousness', as many scholars have rendered it)—that is, the *orthodox* expounder of the Word.[2] The 'right-teacher' was probably in every case a *priest*,[3] his title being derived from Moses' farewell blessing upon the priestly tribe of Levi: 'They have observed Thy word and kept Thy covenant. They shall *teach* Jacob Thine ordinances, and Israel Thy Law' (Deut. 33.9–10).

Just as Israel had been led of old by these prophets and teachers, so, it was held, a new Prophet and a new Teacher (perhaps, indeed, one and the same person) would arise at the end of the present era to usher in the Golden Age, when the scattered hosts of Israel would be gathered in, a duly anointed high priest and a duly anointed king ('the Messiahs [anointed] of Aaron and Israel') installed, and 'the earth filled with the knowledge of the Lord like the waters which cover the sea'. The concept was derived directly from the words of Moses in Deuteronomy 18.15–18: 'The Lord thy God will raise up unto thee a prophet from the midst of thee, of thy brethren, like unto me; unto him ye shall hearken . . . The Lord hath said unto me . . . "I will raise them up a prophet from among their brethren, like unto thee; and I will put My words in his mouth, and he shall speak unto them all that I shall command him"'. Indeed, it is significant that on a small fragment found in one of the caves, that very passage heads a list of Scriptural quotations justifying the Messianic ideas of the community, and that it is there associated with the words of Moses' final Blessing which we have just seen to be the source of the technical term, 'teacher'!

III

But even if the Torah be correctly expounded by prophet and teacher, men, it was held, can and will receive it only if they be correctly attuned. And that attunement comes—if we may mix the metaphor—through inner 'enlightenment'. The community considered itself, therefore, not only the remnant of Israel but also the specially 'enlightened'. Over and over again in the *Book of Hymns* thanks are rendered to God for 'illumining the face' of his servant or for shining His light in His servant's heart. The acquisition of that light, however, was not attributed to any sudden, spontaneous act of grace. Rather was it the result of man's own voluntary exercise of that power of discernment which God placed in every creature at the moment of its creation. All things, it was affirmed—even the sun and moon and stars —had been endowed by God with sensate knowledge, though the choice of using it or ignoring it had been left, in the case of man, to his individual will. If he heeded the gift, he achieved harmony with the eternal cosmic scheme and broke the trammels of his mortality. Automatically, he was embraced in the communion of eternal things; he became one with the great forces of the universe, with what we would call Nature, and with the non-mortal beings of the celestial realm—the 'holy ones' who stood for ever in direct converse with God. He achieved, in short, what mystics term the 'unitive state'.

It was this state that the members of the community claimed for themselves. This was the ultimate goal of their entire spiritual adventure; the aim and *raison d'être* of the Torah and of the disciplined life which it enjoined. They held that by virtue of their 'enlightenment' they were members not only of the consecrated earthly brotherhood but *eo ipso* also of the Eternal Communion. As one of their psalmists puts it, they walked for ever 'in uplands unbounded' and knew that 'there is hope for that which is molded of clay to have converse with things everlasting'.

This is not, as all too many scholars have supposed, a mere belief in bodily resurrection or a mere hope for the survival of the soul in some cloudland of bliss. Rather is it the sound mystic sense that, given the right spiritual posture, given the victory over that darkness which is set before him along with the light, man may live even on earth in a dimension of eternity.

IV

It would be a mistake to suppose that the Dead Sea Covenanters were inspired only by recollection of things past or that they betook themselves to the desert simply because they were unsettled by political turbulence or disgusted by the venality of the Jerusalemitan priests. They were swept also by other winds. One of these was a widespread and well-attested contemporary belief that the great cycle of the ages was about to complete its revolution. This belief was based on a conception, which can in fact be traced to remote Indian antiquity, that existence consists not in linear progressive development—that is, in 'history' —but in a constant cyclic repetition of primordial and archetypal events. When major upheavals occurred, it was promptly supposed that the cycle was nearing its end, that the Great Year was at hand, and that cosmos was about to revert to chaos. The primal elements, restrained and regulated at the beginning of the world, would again be unleashed; all things would dissolve in an overwhelming deluge or be burned in that everlasting fire which rages in the depths of the earth. Then the cycle would begin again; a new world would be brought to birth.

For men, this theory posed the immediate problem of escape, and Religion answered that problem by the postulate that 'righteousness delivereth from death' and that 'the just shall live by his faith'. There was a sense in which, if he could not be delivered from the body of this death, man could at least be released from the trammels of this life. He could immerse himself in eternal things, divorce himself from the temporal and the mundane and, reversing the old adage, find that in the midst of death he was in fact in life.

The men of Qumran lived at a time of such 'cyclic crisis'. It is writ large in the pseudepigraphic literature of the two centuries immediately preceding the Common Era, and its fading echo may be heard in John the Baptist's cry that 'the Kingdom of Heaven is at hand'. It was escape from the inexorable cycle, release not from sin but from mortality, that these men were also seeking. The desert to which they repaired was not simply the Desert of Judah; it was also the mystic's Desert of Quietude—what John Tauler called 'The Wilderness of Godhead, into which He leads all who are to receive this inspiration of God, now or in eternity'. In that wilderness, they would not merely receive a renewal of the Covenant; they would also have the vision of the Burning Bush. Removed from men, they would acquire an unobstructed view of the divine. Thirsting in an inhospitable wild, they would drink the unfailing waters of God's grace. Shorn of earthly possessions, theirs would be the poverty of the mystics—that poverty which Evelyn Underhill has described as 'complete detachment from all finite things'. Burned by the scorching sun, they would see the *semplice lume* of Dante, the 'infused brightness' of Saint Teresa, and by that light they would not be dazzled. They would achieve an intimacy, a communion with the eternal, unchanging things, such as one can achieve only in a desert or on a sea. And in this experience they would reproduce and concentrate within themselves the drama of the cosmic cycle, the dissolving of the old order and the birth of the new.

It is impossible for anyone who reads the *Book of Hymns* sensitively and sympathetically not to apprehend, behind the cliché-ridden language, the tortuous and barely grammatical sentences, the incessant filching of Scriptural 'tags', the movement of these deep mystic currents; and they too must be taken into account.

In strange juxtaposition with these rarefied speculations, however, the community also took a severely practical view of what was going to happen when the time for the world's renewal fell due. Even if individual men escaped the impending doom, general doom there still would be, and a good deal of evil would still remain to be destroyed. The destruction would come by means of a forty years' war waged by 'the sons of light',[4] aided by the celestial hosts,[5] against 'the sons of darkness'. In three campaigns they would win; in three, lose. At last, at the seventh encounter, God would triumph over Belial. This would be the Day of Vengeance. Thereafter all things would be renewed.[6] The Era of Divine Favor[7] (in contrast to the Era of Wrath)[8] would be ushered in. God's light would shine sevenfold strong.[9] He would reaffirm the Covenant with the faithful, and engrave His Law on their hearts.

V

Concerning the practical organization of the community, we are particularly well-informed both by the *Manual of Discipline* and by the so-called *Zadokite Document*.

Children had to undergo a ten-year period of study in the provisions and institutions of the Covenant and in a manual known as the *Book of Study*. At twenty years of age, they were eligible for membership. Every candidate was examined publicly regarding his intellectual capacity and his moral character. If he passed the test, he underwent a year's probation, but was permitted no share in the community's resources nor was he admitted to the common table. At the end of the probationary year, he came up again for review. If his conduct were deemed satisfactory, he then served a further probation of one year within the community itself. He had to place all his property in trust with an 'overseer', but he himself was not yet permitted to enjoy the resources of the group or to dine with them. Only after this second year could he become fully enrolled, and then only by general vote, and after swearing an oath of allegiance.

No one under twenty-five could occupy a communal office, and no one under thirty could be reckoned as head of a family or hold rank in the community's military establishment.

The supreme authority in all doctrinal and economic matters was vested in the priests, assisted by the levites. In any group of ten men, if one of them happened to be a priest, he was not to move to another place, and every such group was to have an 'expounder of the law' to whom reference could be made at any time of day or night.

There was a general 'council' to which any member of the community might be elected. This served as a kind of parliament for purposes of deliberation, but it did not determine matters of doctrine, which were left to the priests.

For administrative purposes, there was also a kind of presbytery, consisting of three priests and twelve especially qualified laymen. These 'presbyters' were known as 'the men of (special) holiness', and they had to undergo a year's probation before appointment.

Every member of the community was assigned a special rank, which was reviewed from year to year, promotions or demotions being determined by general vote. It may be questioned, however, whether such rank was really a matter of individual status rather than of class. At all events, we hear in the documents of clear distinctions between priests, 'men of (special) holiness', 'dignitaries' (literally, 'men of repute'), 'men eligible for summons to the assembly', and 'heads of families'. Moreover, there is frequent reference to admission to or rejection from 'the purity', and this would seem, in the various contexts, to refer most naturally to the different degrees or levels of purity credited to various strata within the total group. Josephus, it may be observed, speaks of four such degrees as having been recognized among the Essenes.

All goods and wages were placed in a common pool, administered by an 'overseer' or 'superintendent'. A similar officer presided over the allocation of communal tasks and duties.

Members of the community dined together, the food being first blessed by the priest. Everyone sat in order of rank or class, the priest occupying first place. They also met together regularly for prayer and study, and were obliged to spend one third of all the nights of the year in such spiritual exercise.

Breaches of the rules were punished by temporary ostracism and exclusion from normal rations of food. Repeated offenses, or acts amounting to repudiation of the basic Covenant, entailed irrevocable expulsion.

A quorum of ten seems to have been required, in accordance with normal Jewish practice, in order to constitute a 'congregation' or conventicle. Members of the community were encouraged to discuss matters of law and doctrine for their mutual instruction and edification, but they were forbidden to indulge in theological disputation with 'disreputable persons' (literally, 'men of corruption')—that is, to all intents and purposes, with outsiders.

To form an idea of the temper and complexion of this strange community, one could scarcely do better than to compare it with the Waldensian Brotherhood as described (albeit with an overtone of polemic) by Bernard Gui in the early fourteenth century. From the viewpoint of religious psychology, the comparison is, indeed, both arresting and illuminating.

In both cases we have a group in revolt against the doctrinal degeneration and material venality of the established 'church', and in both cases the schism takes the form not of innovation or reformulation but of a return to the true but corrupted 'apostolic' tradition.

In both cases, the schismatics constitute not merely a spiritual fellowship of faith, but a concrete social organism. The Waldensians, like the Dead Sea Covenanters, 'eat and drink at common meals'. They do not own private property, but, on admission to the sect, 'sell all they possess and give the price to the common fund'.

They hold annual conventions for the transaction of communal affairs, just as the *Manual of Discipline* prescribes annual 'reviews'. The more advanced members of the sect are called 'the perfect'—exactly like 'the men of perfect conduct' of the *Manual*, and, like them, they serve as guides, preachers and 'apostles' of the sect.

Members of the brotherhood are forbidden to lie or to swear oaths. They call themselves 'the poor', a name which recalls the fact that in the Aramaic dialect of the early

Palestinian Christians—that is, the same dialect as would have been spoken at Qumran—the word for 'poor' also bore the specific sense of 'ascetic'.

Finally, the Waldensians claimed to be the most ancient of all Christian sects, 'going back to the time of the early Fathers'; and to this we may find a telling parallel in Philo's statement that 'our lawgiver Moses formed countless disciples into a fellowship called Essenes'.

VI

Having now reviewed the basic beliefs and institutions of the community, we are ready to answer the burning question: *Do the Dead Sea Scrolls restore to us a long-lost forerunner of Christianity?*

The answer is, Yes and No.

Yes, in the sense that they furnish a picture of the religious and cultural climate in which John the Baptist conducted his mission and in which Jesus was initially reared. They portray for us, in vivid but authentic colors, the environment whose spiritual idiom John and Jesus spoke, whose concepts they developed and transmuted and whose religious ideas served largely as the seedbed of the New Testament. They also mirror a form of religious organization many elements of which were adopted by the primitive Church.

No, in the sense that what we have in these documents is, as it were, but the rude clay as yet unmolded by Christian hands. There is in them no trace of any of the cardinal theological concepts—the incarnate Godhead, Original Sin, redemption through the Cross, and the like—which make Christianity a distinctive faith.

The affinities between the thought and language of the Dead Sea Scrolls and that of the New Testament may best be gauged by a representative list of examples:

1. The members of the community styled themselves 'the elect' or 'the elect of God'. Compare Titus 1.1: 'Paul, a servant of God, and an apostle of Jesus Christ, according to the faith of God's elect'; or I Peter 1.1: 'Peter, an apostle

of Jesus Christ to the elect who are sojourners of the Dispersion'.

2. The truth of God, as revealed in His law, is constantly called the Light. Compare John 1.7–9: '[John] came for witness, that he might bear witness of the light . . . There was the true light, which lighteth every man, coming into the world'; John 8.12: 'I am the light of the world'.

3. The 'enlightened' members of the community describe themselves as 'Sons of Light'. Compare John 12.36: 'While ye have the light, believe on the light, that ye may become sons of light'; Ephesians 5.8: 'Walk as children of light'.

4. In the *Book of Hymns,* the faithful frequently declare that they stand in the eternal congregation of God, hold direct converse with Him, and 'share the lot of the holy beings'. Compare Ephesians 2.19: 'Ye are no more strangers and sojourners, but ye are fellow-citizens with the holy ones (E.V. saints), and of the household of God'.

5. A basic tenet is the doctrine of the 'remnant'—the belief that the community constitutes the true 'relic' of Israel, faithful to the Covenant. Compare Romans 11.3–5: 'Lord, they have killed Thy prophets, they have digged down thine altars: and I am left alone, and they seek my life. But what saith the answer of God . . . ? Once I left for myself seven thousand men that bowed not the knee to Baal. Even so then at this present time also there is a remnant by the election of grace'.

6. The spiritual leader of the community is called 'teacher' or 'right-teacher'. In John 3.2, Jesus is hailed as the teacher sent by God—that is, as the teacher who, it was held, would arise in the last days. So, too, in John 16.13, the incarnate Spirit of Truth is described as one 'who shall guide you unto all the truth', and these words are an almost perfect translation of the term rendered 'right-teacher', for Hebrew has only one expression for 'teacher' and 'guide'.

7. In the *Manual of Discipline,* it is said that, if the community abide by the prescribed rules, it will be a veritable 'temple of God, a true holy of holies'. Compare I Corinthians 3.16–17: 'Know ye not that ye are a temple of God, and that the Spirit of God dwelleth in you? If any man destroy the temple of God, him shall God destroy, for the

temple of God is holy, which temple ye are'. (A similar
sentiment may be found also in Ephesians 2.20–22.)

8. In the same *Manual of Discipline* there is a long passage describing the Two Ways, viz. of good and evil, light
and darkness, which God sets before every man. The idea
is indeed a commonplace of ancient Iranian and later
Jewish thought, but it is interesting to note the development
of the same basic imagery in the familiar picture of the wide
and strait gates in Matthew 7.13f. and Luke 13.23f.

9. The Prophet that is to arise at the end of days, in accordance with the promise in Deut. 18.18, was, as we have
seen, a key figure in the religious doctrine of the Dead Sea
Scrolls. Compare, then, Matthew 17.10f. and Mark 9.11f.,
where Jesus is asked whether Elijah should not have pre-
ceded his coming. Compare also John 6.14: 'Then those
men, when they had seen the miracle that Jesus did, said,
This is of a truth that prophet that should come into the
world'. And note that Stephen, when arraigned before the
council, quotes the very passage of Deuteronomy in evidence of the true character of Jesus (Acts 7.37).

10. The *Manual of Discipline* quotes the famous words
of Isaiah (40.3), 'Prepare in the desert a highway', in token
of the fact that the final apocalyptic age is at hand. In John
1.23, the Baptist quotes exactly the same passage in exactly
the same content.

11. The community is often styled 'God's plantation'
(after Isa. 60.21). So, in I Timothy 3.6, a novice is called a
'neophyte'—literally, one 'newly planted'.

12. The river (or lake) of fire graphically portrayed in
one of the *Hymns* as destined to burn up the wicked (cf.
Dan. 7.10f.), finds its counterpart in Revelation 19.20;
20.10, 14f.; 21.8, suggesting that this was a standard element of the current eschatological 'nightmare'.

These, it must be emphasized, are but a few of the many
parallels that could be quoted. One might refer also to the
use of the same literary devices both in the Scrolls and in
the New Testament, e.g. the stereotyped catalog of vices
in the *Manual of Discipline* (col. iv) on the one hand and
in such passages as Galatians 5.19f.; Romans 1.29f.; 13.13;
Colossians 3.5, 8 on the other. Or one might adduce some

striking *verbal* analogues, as when the Fourth Gospel speaks of 'men from beneath' (8.23) or of a 'son of perdition' (17.12), both of which curious expressions occur in the *Hymns;* or when John 1.3 is found in virtually the same words at the end of one of those same compositions!

Especially illuminating in this respect is a comparison of the Dead Sea Scrolls with the General Epistle of James, the earliest of all the epistles contained in the New Testament. It is now generally agreed that this document, addressed to 'the twelve tribes in the dispersion', was written between 40 A.D. and 50 A.D., that its author was James, the 'brother' of Jesus, who occupied a leading position among the Jewish Christians in Jerusalem (Acts 12.17; 15.13; 21.18); and that it represents the outlook of what has been called 'the church of the circumcision'—that is, the circle of Jews who were ready to accept the general teachings of Jesus and his call to regeneration but were not prepared to view them through the prism of Pauline philosophy and doctrine. In other words, this Epistle bespeaks the standpoint of men who were neither normative Jews nor normative Christians, but who were sufficiently attuned by their own 'zeal for the Kingdom' and their own non-conformist attitude to find the new gospel attractive rather than repellent. In such a group, we may assume *a priori*, the teachings of the Dead Sea Scrolls would have struck a sympathetic chord. The fact is, however, that it is possible to detect in the Epistle of James several direct echoes of ideas and expressions prominent in the Qumran texts.

Thus, when James says[10] (1.12), 'Blessed is the man that hath stood the trial, for when he hath stood the test, he shall receive the crown of life which the Lord hath promised to them that love him', we are reminded at once of the many references to the 'trial' that occur in the *Manual of Discipline* (e.g. viii, 4) and in the *Book of Hymns* (e.g. ii, 35; ix, 6ff.; viii, 26ff.; xi, 19ff.) and more particularly of the statement in the former (iv, 7-8) that the faithful will receive a diadem of glory and a robe of beauty.

Again, when the author speaks (1.14) of men who are

'hooked and trapped by their lusts' (for that is what the Greek words really mean), we cannot but recall the passages in the *Hymns* (iii, 26; v, 8) where exactly the same metaphor is used to describe the enticement of the unwary. And when James declares (1.17) that 'every good endowment and every perfect gift is from above, coming down from the Father of Lights', his words find a striking counterpart in that curious compound expression 'Light-Perfection' which the Qumran documents employ (e.g. *Hymns*, iv, 6; xviii, 29) to describe the special endowment of the faithful. Nor, further, can we fail to recall that, according to the *Manual of Discipline* (iii, 20), control over the 'sons of righteousness' is 'in the hand of the Prince of Lights'.

In 2.2–4, James advises the brethren not to respect wealth: 'If there come unto your assembly a man with a gold ring, in goodly apparel, and there come also a poor man in vile raiment, they are not to say to the one, Sit here in a good place, and to the other, Stand there, or sit under my footstool'. Now, the Greek word rendered 'assembly' is *synagōgē*, and this is the regular translation in the Septuagint Version of the Scriptures of the Hebrew word *'edah*, which is the term used in the Dead Sea Scrolls to denote the community as a whole, and which in its Syriac counterpart was actually used by the early Palestinian Christians as the equivalent of 'the Church' in the larger sense. When we bear in mind the specific precept in the *Manual of Discipline* that all members of the community are to be graded by intelligence and character alone, and when we remember that the Hebrew and Aramaic words for 'seat' (viz. *môshab* and *mêthbâ*) also mean 'status' and that 'to stand without' was common Hebrew idiom for 'be excluded from society', it becomes clear that James is echoing this injunction, and not referring specifically to the seating arrangements in a synagogue.

Finally—to omit other examples—attention may be drawn to the curious passage (4.5) where the author of the Epistle declares: 'Do ye think that the scripture saith in vain, "The spirit which [God] made to dwell in us lusteth to envy"?'[12] The passage is curious because there is in fact no such statement in Scripture. But is James really referring to Holy Writ?

The *Manual of Discipline* (iv, 9ff.) suggests the answer. There we are told that the spirit of wrongdoing which God has set before man alongside that of truth 'tends to greed . . . wickedness, falsehood, pride, presumption . . . zeal for arrogance (or, arrogant zeal)'. May not *this* be 'the scripture' to which allusion is made?

On the strength of these comparisons we may perhaps not unreasonably conclude that the Dead Sea Scrolls indeed open a window upon the little community of Jewish Christians clustered around James in Jerusalem. These men may have been originally the urban brethren of the hardier souls that betook themselves to Qumran and to other camp-settlements in the Desert of Judah. For the *Zadokite Document* provides expressly for urban as well as camp communities; while of the Essenes, with whom they may be identical, Josephus states (*War*, II, viii, 4) that they also lived in the cities.

The possibility is increased by a number of significant statements made about James by Hegesippus, the historian of the Jews, who wrote during the latter half of the second century C.E. 'Because of his exceeding righteousness', we are informed, 'James was named the Righteous'; and once, when the scribes urged him to preach against Jesus, they addressed him pointedly as 'Thou Righteous One, to whom we are all bound to listen'. Does not this sound uncommonly like a reflection of the title 'Teacher of Righteousness' (or, True Expounder of the Law) which occurs so frequently in the Scrolls and in the *Zadokite Document* as that of the spiritual instructor of the Brotherhood? And is it not equally significant that, according to this same Hegesippus, James habitually eschewed the use of oil and wore linen garments only—two of the characteristic traits which Josephus (*War*, II, viii, 3, 5) attributes to the Essenes?

VII

But it is not only in the realm of ideas and doctrines that the Dead Sea Scrolls present affinities to early Christianity. No less arresting are certain parallels between the organization of the community and that of the primitive Church.

It is significant, for instance, that some of the terms used to
define its several constituent elements, though themselves
derived ultimately from the Old Testament, possess in the
Palestinian Aramaic dialect of the early Christians exactly
the same quasi-technical sense as denoting parts of the
ecclesiastical organization. A case in point is the term employed to denote the deliberative assembly (viz. *'eṣah*); in
Palestinian Aramaic (where, significantly, it is a loanword)
this means specifically the council of the church or synagogue: it is used in the Scriptures as the rendering of the
Greek *synhedrion*, more familiar to us in the Hebraized
form, *sanhedrin*. Similarly, the word used to denote the
total congregation (viz. *'edah*), though borrowed from the
Old Testament, was likewise adopted in Syriac as the regular term for 'church'. In other words, the technical vocabulary of the early Palestinian Church seems to reproduce
that used by the Dead Sea Covenanters to describe their
own organization.

Again, the Dead Sea Scrolls might at last clear up the
vexed problem of the distinction between bishops and presbyters in the primitive church, for in these documents the
administrative officers of the community consist not only
of *mebaqqerim*, or 'overseers'—the exact equivalent of the
Greek *episkopos*, whence our 'bishop'—but also of the
twelve good laymen and true who assisted the three priests
and in whom we may very well see the counterpart of the
Christian 'presbyters'.

Then, too, it is worth pointing out that the rule requiring
all 'who perform communal service' to be at least twenty-
five years old, and all 'heads of families' and military officers
to be at least thirty survived in the Church in the statement
of the Council of Hippo (393 A.D.) that no one is to be ordained under twenty-five, and in the Neo-Caesarean and
Maronite rules that no presbyter may be under thirty.

VIII

On the other hand, it must be stated emphatically—particularly in view of recent exaggerated claims—that the
Dead Sea Covenanters (or whatever we may choose to call

this community) were in no sense Christians and held none of the fundamental theological doctrines of the Christian faith.

It has been asserted, for instance, that the several references in the Scrolls to the 'right-teacher' all refer to a single historical Teacher of Righteousness—a prototype of Jesus—and that a passage in one of them which speaks of his having been 'persecuted' but having subsequently 'appeared' to the community on the Day of Atonement foreshadows the Christian doctrine of the suffering and resurrected Saviour. Even, however, if the interpretation were correct (which is very doubtful), this would still be poles apart from the Christian belief that the crucified Master was God incarnate Who by His passion removed a sinfulness inherent in man through a pristine fall from grace. Of this basic doctrine of Christianity there is not a shred or trace in the Dead Sea Scrolls.

Other essential doctrines also are missing. There is, here, for instance, no vestige of the idea of Original Sin. On the contrary, the idea is affirmed constantly in the *Book of Hymns* that every man is endowed at birth with the charisma of knowledge and discernment and that any sinfulness which he incurs is due only to his individual neglect of these gifts and to his individual submission to, or entrapment by, the domination of the evil impulse (Belial). Moreover, because sin is individual and not the inherited lot of man, and because it is incurred by his own personal disposition, it can be removed also by his own individual experience. Once he 'sees the light' by the exercise of his own God-given powers, he is out of darkness. In such a system, since there is no concept of original, universal sin, there is obviously no place for universal vicarious atonement. Men suffer their individual crucifixions and resurrections; there is no Calvary.

Again, there is no Communion. Certain scholars, to be sure, have tried to find a prototype of the Eucharist in the description given, in a fragment of the *Manual of Discipline* (or an analogous document), of a banquet attended by 'the Messiah'. But this interpretation is untenable for several reasons. First, the 'Messiah' in question is no

divine eschatological figure. He is simply the duly anointed
king of Israel *at any future epoch*. The aim of the passage
—which the reader can examine for himself on p. 310—is
simply to indicate that, as in normative Jewish law, the
sacred seed of Aaron has precedence over all laymen.
Accordingly, it is affirmed, even if the anointed king—what
we should call 'a crowned head'—should happen to be present at a meal, he and his retinue are not to take their seats
until the high priest and *his* priestly retinue have done so,
and it is still to be left to the priest to pronounce the customary benediction over the food.

Second, it is to be observed that this rule is not laid down
as one of the regulations of our particular community, but
forms part of a code promulgated for 'the whole Congregation of Israel in future times'. Accordingly, on any showing, it affords no testimony to the current beliefs or practices of the men of Qumran.

Third, this document does not refer to any banquet 'at
the end of days', as some scholars have supposed, the
Hebrew words so rendered being a common idiom for 'the
future, hereafter'.

Fourth—and, perhaps, most important—even if, for argu-
ment's sake, this document *did* refer to a divine eschatological Messiah attending a banquet with his disciples, it would
still not be a eucharist in the Christian sense, for there is
not the slightest suggestion that the bread and wine were
regarded as his flesh and blood or that consumption of them
had any redemptive power. At most, it would be an *agape*,
or love-feast'.[13]

IX

In order to get this whole question into the right per-
spective, it should be observed that just as many things
in the Dead Sea Scrolls as can be paralleled from the New
Testament can be paralleled equally well from the Apocry-
pha and Pseudepigrapha of the Old Testament—that is,
from the non-canonical Jewish 'scriptures' that were circu-
lating between 200 B.C. and 100 A.D.—and from the earlier
strata of the Talmud. Moreover, many of them find place

also in the ancient doctrines of such sects as the Mandaeans of Iraq and Iran and the Samaritans, so that even if they have not come down to us through *Jewish* channels, we can still recognize in them part of the common Palestinian thought and folklore of the time. Accordingly, to draw from the New Testament parallels any inference of special relationship is misleading.

The point can best be illustrated by a few pertinent examples.

1. The Brethren called themselves 'the sons of light'. The title is familiar from the New Testament (Luke 16.8; John 12.36; I Thess. 5.5). But it is common also among the Mandaeans of Iraq and Iran as a name for those celestial beings with whom, indeed, the men of the Brotherhood claimed to stand in a single communion.

2. The Brethren also affected the name of 'the Elect'. This, too, is especially familiar to us from the New Testament. But it is also a common style among the Mandaeans; while the Manichaeans (who share many of their ideas) likewise call themselves 'the chosen' (*vičidagan*).

3. Another common title of the Brethren was 'God's plantation' (cf. *Hymns*, vi, 15; viii, 6.10). This, of course, was derived from the Bible (Isa. 60.21). But it is likewise a common image in pseudepigraphic literature (e.g. *Psalms of Solomon* 14.3-4; *Odes of Solomon* 38.18-21), and it is also very frequent among the Mandaeans (e.g. Lidzbarski, *Mandäische Liturgien*, 149, 190, 194ff.; *Right Ginza* II, iv, *init.*).

4. The Brethren claimed that they were especially 'enlightened' or 'endowed with insight'. Exactly the same claim—expressed by exactly the same Semitic word—is made by the Mandaeans; while among the Manichaeans, the lay member of the community (*nigōšag*) was known as 'the man with insight'. Moreover, the Brethren sometimes described this special illumination by the strange compound word *Ôr-Tôm*—literally, 'Light-Perfection', and this was simply a play on the Biblical Urim and Thummim of the high priest. The light in question, it may be added, seems often to be identified with the Law (*Torah*), and this idea, too, is found in pseudepigraphic literature (e.g. in the

Testament of Levi, written between 109 and 106 B.C.)
and in the Talmud (e.g. Berachôth 17a).

5. The Brethren held that the deeds of men are divided
between the dominion of God, which is light, and that of
Belial, which is darkness (*Manual,* iv). Here again we have
a concept familiar enough from the New Testament and
one which, at a far earlier date, dominated Iranian religion.
But the fact is that by the second century B.C. it had already
percolated into Jewish thought. The *Testament of Levi* says
explicitly (5.30): 'Choose either the light or the darkness,
either the Law of the Lord or the works of Beliar (i.e.,
Belial); while in the *Testament of Joseph,* Belial is called
'the spirit of darkness'.

6. The *Manual of Discipline* says that the faithful will
receive a crown of glory (*kelîl kabôd;* iv, 7). Peter and
James, it is true, use a similar image; but in Mandaean
thought the 'lustrous crown' plays an extremely important
role and is frequently mentioned in the hymns of the sect
(e.g. Lidzbarski, *Mandäische Liturgien,* 4f., 29, 108, 177,
243); and in the pseudepigraphic *Odes of Solomon,* there
is a reference (9.11) to the 'crown of truth'.

The correspondence between the ideas of the Brotherhood and those that obtained generally in Palestine during
the Graeco-Roman age and that survive sporadically
among the more 'exotic' sects is especially striking in the
field of eschatology—that is, the lore about the Last Things.

1. The concept of a 'final conflagration', to which we
have already alluded (above, p. 7), occurs frequently in
the Third Book of the *Sibylline Oracles,* a basically Jewish
compilation dating about 140 B.C. The Jews appear to have
adopted it from Gentile sources (although there is a fore-
gleam of it in Isa. 34.9–10), for it was held by Zeno and
the Stoics and dominated the Roman-Oriental world from
the first century B.C. until the third century C.E.

2. The idea, articulated especially in the Qumran text
called *The War of the Sons of Light and the Sons of Darkness,* that the world is at present in the clutches of Belial,
but that he will ultimately be defeated, occurs again, not
only in the New Testament (Matthew 24.5–12), but even

more explicitly in the *Testament of Levi* (5.27) and in the *Sybilline Oracles* (ii, 165f.). The apocalyptic war (mentioned also in *Hymns* iii, 29ff.; 35–36; 34–35)—an idea derived ultimately from the Biblical prophets (Isa. 13.9; Zech. 14.2)—is likewise commonplace in pseudepigraphic writings (e.g. *Syriac Apocalypse of Baruch,* 70.7–10) and in the Talmud; while the notion that angels too will fight finds an echo in the *Slavonic Book of Enoch* 17.1, where they are described as 'the armed troops of heaven'—a play, of course, on the expression 'heavenly host'.

3. The picture which is painted in Hymn No. 5 of the world travailing in the throes of new birth is admirably illustrated by the fact that the Messianic turmoil preceding the final Golden Age is called in the Talmud (Shab. 118a; Sanh. 98b) 'the birth-pangs of the Messiah' (cp. Matthew 24.8; Mark 13.8–9; I Thess. 5.3).

4. The final age is called 'the Time of Favor' (*Hymns* xv, 15; frag. ix, 8), evidently in contrast to 'the Time of Anger' mentioned in the *Zadokite Document* (1.5). This accords remarkably with the Samaritan idea that Jewish history is divided into periods of 'Favor' (*Rahûtâ*) and 'Turning Away' of God's Face (*Fanûtâ*). Similarly, when the day of God's eventual triumph is termed 'the Day of Vengeance', the expression (based on Deut. 32.35, as read in the Samaritan and Greek Septuagint recensions, and in a fragment from Qumran itself) accords with one of the most prominent technical terms of the Samaritan faith.

5. The doctrine that all things will be renewed (*Hymns* xi, 13f.; xiii, 11–12) is again part and parcel of Oriental thought at the time, and cannot be compared exclusively with Matthew's well-known reference (19.28) to the eventual 'regeneration'. The pseudepigraphic *Testament of Abraham,* and likewise *The Book of Jubilees* (1.29) speak of a renewal of the world after seven millennia; while the concept of a periodic renewal was also a favorite doctrine of Neo-Pythagoreanism, which enjoyed a great vogue in Roman society in the second and first centuries B.C. An allusion to this idea, it may be added, occurs in the very ancient form of the Jewish doxology (*Kaddish*) which is recited after a funeral, for God is there extolled as 'He

who will hereafter renew the world and quicken the dead'.

6. One of the *Hymns* states (vii, 24) that God's light will eventually shine sevenfold strong. The basic idea has, of course, good Old Testament authority (Isa. 60.19), but it is interesting to observe that, according to the Talmud (Sanh. 91b), the light of the Messianic sun will be seven times as powerful as usual.

7. Finally, the important concept of the New Covenant to be concluded with the faithful at the end of the present era is admirably illustrated by the standard Samaritan tenet that God's bond with Israel has already been concluded on no less than seven occasions, viz. with Noah in the rainbow; with Abraham in circumcision; with Moses in the Sabbath; with the Two Tablets of the Ten Commandments; with the Passover; with the Covenant of Salt (Num. 18.19); and with the Covenant of Priesthood with Phineas (Num. 25.12f.).

X

Just as unfortunate as the attempts to 'Christianize' the Scrolls are the attempts unduly to 'historicize' them—that is, to detect in them precise and specific historical allusions.

In order to emphasize that what was happening or about to happen both to themselves and to the world was but the fulfillment of Biblical prophecy, the Brotherhood made use of a kind of figurative geography, based on the Scriptures. It spoke of its own voluntary withdrawal from the normative forms of Jewish life as 'exile in the desert of Damascus', in allusion to the words of God in the Book of Amos (5.27): 'I will cause you to go into exile beyond Damascus'. Conversely, the future regeneration of Israel was depicted as a return from 'the wilderness of the peoples' (cp. Ez. 20.35) to the 'Desert of Judah'. The prime enemy—the representative of Belial or the Evil One—was styled Gog, originally the name of a northern power whose doom had been foretold by the prophet Ezekiel (chaps. 38–39). Alternatively, and more often, the hostile forces were described as Kittians (or Kittaeans), a term which originally denoted the inhabitants of Kition, in Cyprus (cp. Gen. 10.4), but which came later to be used in an extended sense—rather like 'Huns' or 'Tartars'—of 'barbarians' in general and was applied in the Hellenistic age to the 'Macedonians' of the Alexandrian Empire, and in the Roman age to the Romans themselves. *The War of the Sons of Light and the Sons of Darkness*, a text which describes the final apocalyptic conflict, refers to 'Kittians of Assyria' and 'Kittians of Egypt', where nothing more is meant than the heathen population of either land, the doom of which had long since been foretold (cf. Zech. 10.10–11, etc.).

There is no need to take such references literally and consequently to set off on a wild goose-chase after historical identifications. The figurative use of names, always designed to evoke traditional associations, is commonplace in most cultures; we need think only of such terms as 'Parnassus', 'Mecca', 'Babylon', or 'Waterloo' in current English parlance.

There was likewise a figurative use of *personal* names. Wicked priests who opposed the 'teacher of righteousness'—himself a priest—were described as a 'house of Absalom', in reference to the Biblical Absalom's treason against his own father, David. Schismatics were referred to fancifully as 'the house of Peleg' (cp. Gen. 10.25), simply because the Hebrew word *p-l-g* means 'divide'. Such designations should deceive no one; it is quite futile to go casting around among the records of the Hellenistic or Roman periods of Jewish history for a particular villain called Absalom. The name must be treated simply like 'Attila', 'Machiavelli', 'Benedict Arnold', or 'Quisling' in modern speech.

Unfortunately, however, the true understanding of the Scrolls has been compromised (or, at least, embarrassed) by the understandable eagerness of scholars to peg them to a definite date, and under this impulse there has arisen an almost frenetic tendency to read specific historical reference into these purely figurative names. Consequently, the literature on the subject is cluttered up with all kinds of ingenious, but usually very forced, attempts to give them specific setting in the Hellenistic or Roman periods. It has been assumed, for instance, that the 'Kittians of Assyria'

and the 'Kittians of Egypt' are necessarily the Seleucid and
Ptolemaic empires; that the sect really migrated, allegedly
in the face of the Roman troops, from the western shores of
the Dead Sea to the region of Damascus; and that 'the
house of Absalom' may have been that of an Absalom mentioned casually in the First Book of the Maccabees (11.70;
13.11) or of the son of John Hyrcanus I who bore that name
(Josephus, *Ant.*, XIV, 4.4; *War*, I, 154)!

Nowhere has this 'historicizing' tendency (or aberration)
played more havoc than in the attempts which have been
made to weld the several references to 'the teacher of righteousness' into a single consistent biography, and to reconstruct from the collateral allusions to a 'wicked priest' and
a 'man of lies' who persecuted him a specific historical situation. All sorts of characters (Onias, Menelaus, Antiochus
Epiphanes, Alexander Jannaeus, John Hyrcanus, Mattathias,
the father of Judas Maccabaeus—even Jesus, John the
Baptist, and Paul) have been proposed to fill these several
roles. If, however, we look at the data without prejudice
or preconception, it is pretty apparent that the 'teacher of
righteousness' denotes a continuing office rather than a
particular individual, and that the various allusions to him
are not in fact to one and the same person.

In the *Zadokite Document*, for example, we are told that
God raised up a 'teacher of righteousness' some twenty
years after the beginning of a 390-year period of His dis-
pleasure, calculated from the capture of Jerusalem by
Nebuchadnezzar. This evidently refers to Nehemiah or—
perhaps more probably, seeing that he was a priest—to
Ezra. On the other hand, we are told in the same document
(ix, 29ff.) that 'about forty years will elapse from the
death of the teacher of righteousness until all who have
taken up arms and relapsed in the company of the Man
of Falsehood are finally destroyed'. Here, obviously, the
reference is to a *future* teacher, one who will arise to occupy
the traditional office in advance of that forty-year period
of 'Messianic woes' of which we indeed read in Talmudic
and later rabbinic literature. This figure is, in fact, a
prototype of the Arabic *Mahdi*—a title which likewise
means 'guide'.

Similarly, if we go soberly through the several references to the 'teacher of righteousness' in the *Commentary on Habakkuk,* it soon becomes apparent that the author is simply citing a number of incidents which might illustrate the prophet's words. There is no compelling reason why they should be taken to constitute a connected historical narrative. Thus, when he interprets the verse (1.13), 'Why do ye look on, ye traitors, and keep silent when the wicked confounds one more righteous than he?' as referring to 'the "house of Absalom" and the men of their company who kept silent when charges were brought against the teacher of righteousness, and who did not come to his aid against the man of lies', he may be referring to an historical incident which involved one particular 'teacher of righteousness'; while when he speaks (in the comment on 2.15) of such a teacher's having once been vexed by a wicked priest who attempted (apparently) to usurp his office, he may be referring to quite a different person living at quite a different period. Similarly, too, the allusion (in *The Manual of Discipline for the Future Congregation of Israel*) to the presence of a 'messiah' at a communal banquet is no evidence, as has been somewhat sensationally supposed, that the Brotherhood believed in a single Christ-like Teacher of Righteousness who had suffered martyrdom but whose Second Coming was expected. For the plain fact is that the term 'messiah' there means simply 'anointed king'. The text in question gives the protocol which is to be observed in the future dispensation, and its whole point is to emphasize that even an anointed king will then have to yield place to an anointed priest at public gatherings!

This is not to say, of course, that specific and identifiable allusions (such as that to Demetrius Eucerus in the *Commentary on Nahum*) are not of crucial importance in dating the several documents. It is simply to warn against the tendency to string such allusions together into a consistent narrative and then to draw from that synthetic narrative far-reaching historical and doctrinal conclusions. What we have to realize is that the commentators were merely fitting a stock set of masks ('the righteous man', 'the wicked man', 'the foreign invader') upon a stock set of characters ('the teacher of righteousness', 'the wicked priest', 'the Kittians'), differently identified at different epochs.

* * * *

The archaeologists tell us that the Dead Sea caves are hot and dark. The same might be said of the controversy which has raged around their contents. At this point, however, it might be healthy to stand back a little from the din and furor and clouds of dust and try to appreciate the scriptures of the Brotherhood simply from the point of view of what they offer to religious thought and insight. They represent an experience which has been repeated often enough in history—the experience of the typical nonconformist who combines, by a strange and wonderful alchemy, an inner quietude with an outer fanaticism, and whose sense of God is a sense of burning fire as well as of radiant light. It may be true that the documents which have come down to us are not great literary masterpieces. Nevertheless they are the testimonies of men who, like their greater forebear, stood in the cleft of a rock and saw the glory of God passing by.

NOTES

Introduction

1. These efforts turn mainly on two assumptions, viz. (a) that various characters described respectively as 'the Teacher of Righteousness', 'the Wicked Priest', and 'the Man of Lies' are particular individuals that can be identified; and (b) that a people called the Kittians may be identified as either the Macedonian Greeks of the Alexandrian Empire or as the Romans. Details of the various theories are set forth in Millar Burrows' *The Dead Sea Scrolls*, in H. H. Rowley's *The Zadokite Fragments and the Dead Sea Scrolls*, and in Edmund Wilson's more popular presentation in *The Scrolls from the Dead Sea*. At the moment, it may be said, the darkness of the Dead Sea caves has not yet been dissipated, and scholars are really in the position of eager readers guessing the solution of a serialized 'whodunit' before the final installment has been published!

2. It may be observed that the Hebrew word for 'teacher' derives from the same verbal root as the word 'Torah'. The 'right-teacher' is therefore, in this context, 'the man who expounds the Torah aright'.

3. First: only a priest would have had uncontested authority so to lay down the law. Second, our documents say specifically, over and over again, that the rules and standards of the community were determined of old by 'the sons of Zadok, *the priests*'. Third: the *Manual of Discipline* affirms expressly that '*the priests* alone are to have authority in all judicial and economic matters'. Fourth: the Prophetic Teacher who will arise at the end of the present era and usher in the Mes-

sianic Age is invariably associated in Jewish tradition
with either Elijah or Phinehas or even Melchizedek, *all
of whom were priests*.

4. See pp. 13, 21.

5. *Hymns*, iii, 35–36; vi, 29th; x, 34–35.

6. *Hymns*, xi, 13f.; xiii, 11–12.

7. *Hymns*, xv, 15; frag. 9.8.

8. *Zadokite Document*, i, 5.

9. *Hymns*, vii, 24.

10. Where necessary, quotations have been translated
    afresh from the Greek, in order to bring out the cor-
    respondences more clearly.

11. Literally, 'well'. The Revised Standard Version misses
    the point by taking this to mean simply, 'please'.

12. Some scholars try to get over the difficulty by taking
    the words 'to envy' as meaning 'jealously', and by con-
    struing 'the spirit' as accusative rather than nomina-
    tive, i.e., '[God] yearns jealously over the spirit which
    He planted in us'. But even this yields no Scriptural
    quotation. Moreover, it dulls the point of the succeed-
    ing, 'But he giveth more grace'. Surely, this means that
    God balances man's propensity to envy by ever in-
    creasing His own grace.

13. We may safely leave out of serious consideration the
    alleged occurrence in this text of a phrase reading, 'If
    [God] begets the Messiah'. This bizarre statement rests
    on nothing more substantial than an arbitrary reading
    of a faded word and an even more capricious restora-
    tion of a lacuna. Such a statement, it need scarcely be
    observed, would be utterly preposterous to a com-
    munity of Jews committed to belief in the Torah and
    in the traditional doctrines of their faith. This whole
    document, in fact, has been egregiously misunder-
    stood.

THE SERVICE
OF GOD

Rules of the Brotherhood

They that loved the synagogues of the pious fled from them, as sparrows that fly from their nest.

They wandered in deserts that their lives might be saved from harm.

PSALMS OF SOLOMON 17.15–16.

INTRODUCTION Because the Brotherhood regarded itself as the true Congregation of Israel, charged with the specific task of maintaining the Law and Covenant of God in an age of apostasy and confusion, of bringing men back to the True Way before the Final Judgment overtook them, and of fighting the ultimate battle against the heathen, it organized itself into what may fairly be described as a 'church'. Such an organization requires a formal set of principles and a constitution, and these are set forth in the two documents known respectively as *The Manual of Discipline* and *The Zadokite Document*.

The former is contained in one of the scrolls discovered at Qumran in 1947. The latter, on the other hand, has been known for several years from two twelfth-century copies found by the late Solomon Schechter, in 1896–97, in the Ezra synagogue at Old Cairo (Fostat), where they formed part of the *genizah,* or repository of discarded manuscripts. Although published as far back as 1910, it was not until the Qumran texts came to light that the true character of this document and its relation to the Dead Sea Brotherhood were made manifest. That relation is immediately apparent as soon as it is read alongside of the *Manual;* and it has been confirmed by the fact that a fragment of an earlier copy has actually been found in one of the caves at Qumran.

Both documents are in the nature of compilations. They

are, so to speak, communal 'commonplace books' in which
several different formulations of the Code and Principles
have been bound up together. This is especially apparent
in the case of the *Manual* from a long interpolation reciting the doctrine of the Two Instincts of Man (cols. iii—iv)
and headed explicitly 'For the use of the Instructor' (literally, 'him who would bring others to the inner vision'),
shewing that this section was originally the 'prompt-book'
for a sermon. In the case of the *Zadokite Document,* a clear
distinction can be recognized between the initial portion,
which is in the nature of a homiletical discourse about the
history of the Brotherhood and the doctrine of the Remnant,
and the subsequent sections which recite the actual rules
of the order.

Both documents were intended *for the Brotherhood as
a whole,* not specifically for its Qumran 'chapter'. The
Zadokite Document makes this particularly plain by distinguishing between the rules which are to obtain 'in cities'
and those which are to obtain 'in camps'—a distinction
clarified by Josephus' statement that the Essenes had communities in many cities.

The major interest of these documents lies in their correspondence with what Josephus and Philo tell us about
the organization of the Essenes. There is basically the same
system of probation and initiation; the same order of
'degrees of purity'; the same communal ownership of
property; the same communal meals; the same system of
'overseers'; the same provision against blasphemy and the
like; and the same rule about speaking in public sessions;
not to mention several lesser points of similarity. There
are, of course, differences; and these have led several
scholars to caution against too ready an identification of
the Brotherhood with the Essenes. One must remember,
however, that Josephus and Philo are describing conditions
as they obtained in the first century C.E., whereas our
documents may reflect an earlier state of affairs and
even ascend to the Hasidim (Pious Ones) of Maccabean
times, who were the spiritual forerunners of the Essenes.

One point of difference that has frequently been adduced
is that, among the Essenes, men were initiated once for

good, whereas—so it is contended—the *Manual* prescribes an annual repetition. This, however, rests on a misreading of what the *Manual* actually says; for the fact is that it does not prescribe an annual *initiation* but only an annual *review of conduct* with a view to upgrading or downgrading the members in the various 'degrees of purity'.

No less interesting, and perhaps more exciting, than their connection with the Essenes are the many parallels which these texts afford with the organization of the primitive Christian Church. The community calls itself by the same name ('*edah*) as was used by the early Christians of Palestine to denote the Church. The same term is employed to designate its legislative assembly as was used by that community to denote the council of the Church. There are twelve 'men of holiness' who act as general guides of the community—a remarkable correspondence with the Twelve Apostles. These men have three superiors, answering to the designation of John, Peter and James as the three pillars of the Church (Galatians 2.9f.). There is a regular system of *mebaqqerîm* or 'overseers'—an exact equivalent of the Greek *episkopoi*, or 'bishops' (before they had acquired *sacerdotal* functions). And the Brotherhood describes itself as 'preparing the way in the desert'—words which John the Baptist likewise quoted from the Old Testament in defining his mission (John 1.23).

The *Manual of Discipline* and the *Zadokite Document* may be compared, in fact, with the *Didachê*, the *Didascalia Apostolorum* and the *Apostolic Constitutions*—the primary documents relating to the organization of the primitive Church. Indeed, if we get away from the Greek terminology in which the details of that organization have mostly come down to us, and if we translate it back into Hebrew or Aramaic, we shall find that it bears a quite remarkable correspondence to that found in the Qumran texts, showing that the latter reflect a type of religious organization upon which the early Christian Church was largely patterned.

A pendant to the two great codes is the fragmentary *Formulary of Blessings*.

This little document gives the protocol for the exchange of greetings ('blessings') between members of the community. These greetings are based on the Priestly Benediction in the Biblical Book of Numbers (6.24–26), the ancient words being so interpreted and elaborated in each case as to bear special application to the person addressed. The interpretations rest on the device, familiar from rabbinic literature, of reading further meaning into a Scriptural text by mentally correlating it with other passages in which the same words are used in different contexts.

Thus, the phrase, 'The Lord bless thee' is tacitly associated with such a passage as Psalm 68.26, where the word 'bless' occurs beside the expression, 'fountain of Israel'. This at once suggests the thought that the blessing is to consist in draughts from the Divine Fountain.

Similarly, the phrase, 'and keep thee' at once recalls such passages as Deut. 7.12: 'The Lord shall keep with thee the covenant', or Psalm 121.7: 'The Lord shall keep thee from all evil'. Accordingly, it evokes the idea that the blessing is to consist in maintenance of the Covenant and in protection from satanic influences.

Again, the words, 'The Lord lift up His countenance' are interpreted in the light of the various senses of the word 'lift', e.g. of lifting the soul from the pit, the sword and standard in battle, obstacles from the path.

This method of interpreting the Priestly Benediction may be admirably illustrated from the way in which it is in fact expounded in the rabbinic classic, *Sifrê*, a compilation made from earlier sources in the third century C.E.:

And keep thee: Rabbi Isaac says: This means, keep thee from the evil inclination, even as the Scripture declares, 'The Lord will be thy confidence, and will keep thy foot from being caught' (Prov. 3.26). Another explanation is that the words mean, keep thee from the demons, even as the Scripture says, 'He giveth His angels charge over thee, to keep thee from all evil' (Ps. 91.11). Yet another explanation is that they mean that God will keep unto thee the covenant made with thy fathers, as it is said, 'The Lord thy God will keep for thee the covenant and the mercy which

He swore unto thy fathers' (Deut. 7.12). Or again, the words may be taken to mean that God will keep (in mind) for thee the appointed consummation, as the Scripture says: 'Watchman (Heb. Keeper), what of the night? Watchman, what of the night? Saith the Watchman (i.e. He who keeps the time in mind), 'Morning cometh, though now it be night' (Is. 21.11–12). Lastly, the words may be referred to God's keeping thy soul at the hour of death, even as the Scripture says, 'The soul of my lord shall be bound up (i.e. kept tight) in the bond of life' (I Sam. 25.29); or of His keeping thy feet from hell, as it is said, 'He will keep the feet of His pious ones' (I Sam. 2.9).

The same compilation, it may be added, also records interpretations of the words, 'The Lord make His face to shine upon thee and be gracious unto thee', which are in perfect agreement with those given in our little document:

Be gracious unto thee: This means, give thee grace in the sight of all creatures . . . or, give thee the grace of knowledge and understanding and intelligence and instruction and wisdom . . . or, again, grace thee with study of the Torah.

In prescribing the greetings ('blessings') of the priests in general and of the high priest in particular, our document adopts yet another device. It plays on the various outward symbols of the priestly office. Thus, since the priest ministered in the 'holy place', the blessing is invoked upon him that he may minister hereafter in the celestial 'holy place'; since the high priest wore a crown or mitre, it is invoked upon him that he be crowned by God with the diadem of eternal honor. Since the priest normally received the first portion of the offerings, he is saluted with the hope that he may enjoy 'the first portion of delights'; and since he is a ministrant at the altar, that he may 'share the lot of the ministering angels'. (This last, it may be observed, likewise has a remarkable parallel in *Sifrê.* 'When Torah issues from the priests' mouths', we read, 'God speaks of them as if they were ministering angels' [*Korah*, §119]).

Our text bears the title 'For the *Maskil*'. The same title recurs in the *Manual of Discipline* in the passage dealing with the two spirits which God has placed in every man (cols. iii–iv). It is not quite certain what the Hebrew word *Maskil* means in these contexts. Formally, it can denote either (a) one endowed with inner vision, or (b) one who seeks to impart such vision to others.* If it bears the latter sense, it is possible that both our present text and the passage in the *Manual* were originally designed as 'model sermons' for the religious instructors of the community. Indeed, we may even venture the conjecture that they were expository discourses designed to accompany readings from the Law; our present document being geared to that section of the Book of Numbers which includes the Priestly Benediction, and the passage in the *Manual* to some such 'lesson' as Deut. 11.26ff. ('Behold I set before you this day a blessing and a curse'). Josephus tells us explicitly that among the Essenes such expositions were a regular feature of the sabbath services.

The text of this document is very fragmentary, and in some cases the rubrics indicating to whom a particular blessing is addressed are missing. But the tenor of the blessing itself usually indicates who is intended. In this matter I have followed the suggestions of the original editors. For the rest, my restorations (indicated by brackets) are based on a recognition of that underlying method of Scriptural exegesis which has been outlined above.

---

* The word occurs in this latter sense in Dan. 12.3 where, however, it is commonly rendered 'they that are wise'.

The Manual of Discipline

Of the Commitment (i, 1–15)

Everyone who wishes to join the community must pledge
himself to respect God and man; to live according to the
communal rule; to seek God [   ]; to do what is good
and upright in His sight, in accordance with what He has
commanded through Moses and through His servants the
prophets; to love all that He has chosen and hate all that
He has rejected; to keep far from all evil and to cling to
all good works; to act truthfully and righteously and justly
on earth and to walk no more in the stubbornness of a
guilty heart[1] and of lustful eyes,[2] doing all manner of evil;
to bring into a bond of mutual love all who have declared
their willingness to carry out the statutes of God; to join
the formal community of God; to walk blamelessly before
Him in conformity with His various laws and dispositions;
to love all the children of light,[3] each according to his
stake in the formal community of God; and to hate all the
children of darkness, each according to the measure of his
guilt, which God will ultimately requite.

All who declare their willingness to serve God's truth
must bring all of their mind, all of their strength, and all
of their wealth into the community of God,[4] so that their
minds may be purified by the truth of His precepts, their
strength controlled by His perfect ways, and their wealth
disposed in accordance with His just design. They must
not deviate by a single step from carrying out the orders

of God at the times appointed for them; they must neither advance the statutory times nor postpone the prescribed seasons.[5] They must not turn aside from the ordinances of God's truth[6] either to the right or to the left.

Of initiation   (i, 16–ii, 18)

Moreover, all who would join the ranks of the community must enter into a covenant in the presence of God to do according to all that He has commanded and not to turn away from Him through any fear or terror[7] or through any trial to which they may be subjected through the domination of Belial.[8]

When they enter into that covenant, the priests and the levites are to pronounce a blessing upon the God of salvation and upon all that He does to make known His truth; and all that enter the covenant are to say after them, Amen, amen.[9]

Then the priests are to rehearse the bounteous acts of God as revealed in all His deeds of power, and they are to recite all His tender mercies towards Israel; while the levites are to rehearse the iniquities of the children of Israel and all the guilty transgressions and sins that they have committed through the domination of Belial. And all who enter the covenant are to make confession after them, saying, We have acted perversely, we have transgressed, we have sinned, we have done wickedly, ourselves and our fathers before us, in that we have gone counter to the truth. God has been right to bring His judgment upon us and upon our fathers.[10] Howbeit, always from ancient times He has also bestowed His mercies upon us, and so will He do for all time to come.

Then the priests are to invoke a blessing on all that have cast their lot with God,[11] that walk blamelessly in all their ways; and they are to say: MAY HE BLESS THEE with all good and KEEP THEE from all evil, and ILLUMINE thy heart with insight into the things of life, and GRACE THEE with knowledge of things eternal, and LIFT UP HIS gracious COUNTENANCE TOWARDS THEE to grant thee peace everlasting.[12]

The levites, on the other hand, are to invoke a curse on

all that have cast their lot with Belial, and to say in response: Cursed art thou for all thy wicked guilty works. May God make thee a thing of abhorrence at the hands of all who would wreak vengeance, and visit thine offspring with destruction at the hands of all who would mete out retribution. Cursed art thou, beyond hope of mercy. Even as thy works are wrought in darkness, so mayest thou be damned in the gloom of the fire eternal.[13] May God show thee no favor when thou callest, neither pardon to forgive thine iniquities. May He lift up an angry countenance towards thee, to wreak vengeance upon thee. May no man wish thee peace of all that truly claim their patrimony.[14]

And all that enter the covenant shall say alike after them that bless and after them that curse, Amen, amen.

Thereupon the priests and the levites shall continue and say: Cursed be every one that hath come to enter this covenant[15] with the taint of idolatry in his heart and who hath set his iniquity as a stumblingblock before him[16] so that thereby he may defect, and who, when he hears the terms of this covenant, blesses himself in his heart, saying, May it go well with me, for I shall go on walking in the stubbornness of my heart! Whether he satisfy his passions or whether he still thirst for their fulfillment,[17] his spirit shall be swept away and receive no pardon. The anger of God and the fury of His judgments shall consume him as by fire unto his eternal extinction, and there shall cleave unto him all the curses threatened in this covenant. God shall set him apart for misfortune, and he shall be cut off from the midst of all the children of light in that through the taint of his idolatry[18] and through the stumblingblock of his iniquity he has defected from God. God will set his lot among those that are accursed for ever! And all who have been admitted to the covenant shall say after them in response, Amen, amen.

Of the annual review (ii, 19–25)

The following procedure is to be followed year by year so long as Belial continues to hold sway.

The priests are first to be reviewed in due order, one

after another, in respect of the state of their spirits. After
them, the levites shall be similarly reviewed, and in the
third place all the laity[19] one after another, in their thousands, hundreds, fifties and tens. The object is that every
man in Israel may be made aware of his status in the community of God in the sense of the ideal, eternal society,[20]
and that none may be abased below his status nor exalted
above his allotted place. All of them will thus be members
of a community founded at once upon true values and upon
a becoming sense of humility, upon charity and mutual
fairness—members of a society truly hallowed, partners in
an everlasting communion.[21]

Of those who are   (ii, 25–iii, 12)
to be excluded

Anyone who refuses to enter the (ideal) society of God
and persists in walking in the stubbornness of his heart
shall not be admitted to this community of God's truth.
For inasmuch as his soul has revolted at the discipline entailed in a knowledge of God's righteous judgments, he has
shown no real strength in amending his way of life, and
therefore cannot be reckoned with the upright. The mental,
physical and material resources of such a man are not to be
introduced into the stock of the community, for such a
man 'plows in the slime of wickedness'[22] and 'there are
stains on his repentance'. He is not honest in resolving
the stubbornness of his heart. On paths of light he sees but
darkness. Such a man cannot be reckoned as among those
essentially blameless. He cannot be cleared by mere cere-
monies of atonement, nor cleansed by any waters of ablution, nor sanctified by immersion in lakes or rivers, nor
purified by any bath. Unclean, unclean he remains so long
as he rejects the government of God and refuses the discipline of communion with Him. For it is only through the
spiritual apprehension of God's truth that man's ways can
be properly directed. Only thus can all his iniquities be
shriven so that he can gaze upon the true light of life.
Only through the holy spirit can he achieve union with
God's truth and be purged of all his iniquities.[23] Only by

a spirit of uprightness and humility can his sin be atoned.
Only by the submission of his soul to all the ordinances of
God can his flesh be made clean. Only thus can it really
be sprinkled with waters of ablution. Only thus can it really
be sanctified by waters of purification. And only thus can
he really direct his steps to walk blamelessly through all
the vicissitudes of his destiny in all the ways of God in
the manner which He has commanded, without turning
either to the right or to the left and without overstepping
any of God's words. Then indeed will he be acceptable
before God like an atonement-offering which meets with
His pleasure, and then indeed will he be admitted to the
covenant of the community for ever.

Of the two spirits in man   (iii, 13–iv, 26)

This is for the man who would bring others to the inner
vision,[24] so that he may understand and teach to all the
children of light the real nature of men, touching the
different varieties of their temperaments with the distinguishing traits thereof, touching their actions throughout
their generations, and touching the reason why they are
now visited with afflictions and now enjoy periods of wellbeing.

All that is and ever was comes from a God of knowledge.[25]
Before things came into existence He determined the plan
of them; and when they fill their appointed roles, it is in
accordance with His glorious design that they discharge
their functions. Nothing can be changed. In His hand lies
the government of all things. God it is that sustains them
in their needs.

Now, this God created man to rule the world, and appointed for him two spirits after whose direction he was
to walk until the final Inquisition.[26] They are the spirits of
truth and of perversity.

The origin of truth lies in the Fountain of Light, and
that of perversity in the Wellspring of Darkness. All who
practice righteousness are under the domination of the
Prince of Lights,[27] and walk in ways of light; whereas
all who practice perversity are under the domination of the

Angel of Darkness and walk in ways of darkness. Through the Angel of Darkness,[28] however, even those who practice righteousness are made liable to error. All their sin and their iniquities, all their guilt and their deeds of transgression are the result of his domination; and this, by God's inscrutable design, will continue until the time appointed by Him. Moreover, all men's afflictions and all their moments of tribulation are due to this being's malevolent sway.[29] All of the spirits that attend upon him are bent on causing the sons of light to stumble. Howbeit, the God of Israel and the Angel of His truth[30] are always there to help the sons of light. It is God that created these spirits of light and darkness and made them the basis of every act, the [instigators] of every deed and the directors of every thought. The one He loves to all eternity, and is ever pleased with its deeds; but any association with the other He abhors, and He hates all its ways to the end of time.

This is the way those spirits operate in the world. The enlightenment of man's heart, the making straight before him all the ways of righteousness and truth, the implanting in his heart of fear for the judgments of God, of a spirit of humility, of patience, of abundant compassion, of perpetual goodness, of insight, of perception, of that sense of the Divine Power that is based at once on an apprehension of God's works and a reliance on His plenteous mercy, of a spirit of knowledge informing every plan of action, of a zeal for righteous government, of a hallowed mind in a controlled nature, of abounding love for all who follow the truth, of a self-respecting purity which abhors all the taint of filth, of a modesty of behavior coupled with a general prudence and an ability to hide within oneself the secrets of what one knows[31]—these are the things that come to men in this world through communion with the spirit of truth.[32] And the guerdon of all that walk in its ways is health and abundant well-being, with long life and fruition of seed along with eternal blessings and everlasting joy in the life everlasting, and a crown of glory[33] and a robe of honor,[34] amid light perpetual.

But to the spirit of perversity belong greed, remissness in right-doing, wickedness and falsehood, pride and presumption, deception and guile, cruelty and abundant insolence, shortness of temper and profusion of folly, arrogant passion, abominable acts in a spirit of lewdness, filthy ways in the thralldom of unchastity, a blasphemous tongue, blindness of eyes, dullness of ears, stiffness of neck and hardness of heart, to the end that a man walks entirely in ways of darkness and of evil cunning.[35] The guerdon of all who walk in such ways is multitude of afflictions at the hands of all the angels of destruction,[36] everlasting perdition through the angry wrath of an avenging God, eternal horror and perpetual reproach, the disgrace of final annihilation in the Fire, darkness throughout the vicissitudes of life in every generation, doleful sorrow, bitter misfortune and darkling ruin—ending in extinction without remnant or survival.

It is to these things that all men are born, and it is to these that all the host of them are heirs throughout their generations. It is in these ways that men needs must walk and it is in these two divisions, according as a man inherits something of each, that all human acts are divided throughout all the ages of eternity. For God has appointed these two things to obtain in equal measure until the final age.

Between the two categories He has set an eternal enmity. Deeds of perversity are an abomination to Truth, while all the ways of Truth are an abomination to perversity; and there is a constant jealous rivalry between their two regimes, for they do not march in accord. Howbeit, God in His inscrutable wisdom has appointed a term for the existence of perversity, and when the time of Inquisition comes, He will destroy it for ever. Then truth will emerge triumphant for the world, albeit now and until the time of the final judgment it go sullying itself in the ways of wickedness owing to the domination of perversity. Then, too, God will purge all the acts of man in the crucible of His truth, and refine for Himself all the fabric of man, destroying every spirit of perversity from within his flesh and cleansing him by the holy spirit from all the effects of wickedness. Like waters of purification He will sprinkle upon him the spirit of truth,[37] to cleanse him of all the abominations of falsehood and of all pollution through the spirit of filth; to

the end that, being made upright, men may have understanding of transcendental knowledge and of the lore of the
sons of heaven,[38] and that, being made blameless in their
ways, they may be endowed with inner vision. For them has
God chosen to be the partners of His eternal covenant, and
theirs shall be all mortal glory.[39] Perversity shall be no
more, and all works of deceit shall be put to shame.

Thus far, the spirits of truth and perversity have been
struggling in the heart of man. Men have walked both in
wisdom and in folly. If a man casts his portion with truth,
he does righteously and hates perversity; if he casts it with
perversity, he does wickedly and abominates truth. For God
has apportioned them in equal measure until the final age,
until 'He makes all things new'.[40] He foreknows the effect
of their works in every epoch of the world, and He has made
men heirs to them that they might know good and evil.
But [when the time] of Inquisition [comes], He will determine the fate of every living being in accordance with
which of the [two spirits he has chosen to follow].

Of social relations   (v, 1–7)

This is the rule for all the members of the community—
that is, for such as have declared their readiness to turn
away from all evil and to adhere to all that God in His good
pleasure has commanded.

They are to keep apart from the company of the froward.

They are to belong to the community in both a doctrinal
and an economic sense.

They are to abide by the decisions of the sons of Zadok,[41]
the same being priests that still keep the Covenant, and of
the majority of the community that stand firm in it. It is by
the vote of such that all matters doctrinal, economic and
judicial are to be determined.

They are concertedly and in all their pursuits to practise truth, humility, righteousness, justice, charity and de-
cency, with no one walking in the stubbornness of his
own heart or going astray after his heart or his eyes or
his fallible human mind.

Furthermore, they are concertedly to remove the im-

purity of their human mold, and likewise all stiffnecked-
ness.

They are to establish in Israel a solid basis of truth.

They are to unite in a bond indissoluble for ever.

They are to extend forgiveness to all among the priesthood that have freely enlisted in the cause of holiness,
and to all among the laity that have done so in the cause
of truth, and likewise to all that have associated themselves with them.[42]

They are to make common cause both in the struggle
and in the upshot of it.

They are to regard as felons all that transgress the law.

Of the obligation of holiness   (v, 7–20)

And this is the way in which all those ordinances are
to be applied on a collective basis.

Everyone who is admitted to the formal organization*
of the community is to enter into a covenant in the presence of all fellow-volunteers in the cause and to commit
himself by a binding oath[43] to abide with all his heart and
soul by the commandments of the Law of Moses, as that
Law is revealed to the sons of Zadok—that is, to the priests
who still keep the Covenant and seek God's will—and to
a majority of their co-covenanters who have volunteered
together to adhere to the truth of God and to walk according to His pleasure.

He that so commits himself is to keep apart from all
froward men that walk in the path of wickedness; for such
men are not to be reckoned in the Covenant inasmuch as
they have never sought nor studied God's ordinances in
order to find out on what more arcane points they may
guiltily have gone astray, while in regard to the things
which stand patently revealed they have acted high-handedly. They have thus incurred God's angry judgment and
caused Him to take vengeance upon them with all the
curses threatened in the Covenant[44] and to wreak great
judgments upon them that they be finally destroyed without remnant.

* Heb. 'council'.

No one is to go into water in order to attain the purity
of holy men.[45] For men cannot be purified except they
repent their evil. God regards as impure all that transgress
His word. No one is to have any association with such a
man either in work or in goods, lest he incur the penalty
of prosecution. Rather is he to keep away from such a
man in every respect, for the Scripture says: 'Keep away
from every false thing' [Exodus 23.7].[46] No member of
the community is to abide by the decision of such men
in any matter of doctrine or law. He is not to eat or drink
of anything that belongs to them nor to receive anything
from them except for cash, even as it is written: 'Desist
from man whose breath is in his nostrils, for as what is he
reckoned?' [Isaiah 2.22].[47] All that are not reckoned in the
Covenant must be put aside, and likewise all that they
possess. A holy man must not rely on works of vanity, and
vanity is what all of them are that have not recognized
God's Covenant. All that spurn His word will God blast
out of the world. All their actions are as filth before Him,
and He regards all their possessions as unclean.

Of the examination   (v, 20–24)
of initiants

When a man enters the covenant, minded to act in
accordance with all the foregoing ordinances and formally
to ally himself to the holy congregation, inquiry is to be
made concerning his temper in human relations and his
understanding and performance in matters of doctrine.
This inquiry is to be conducted jointly by the priests who
have undertaken concertedly to uphold God's Covenant
and to supervise the execution of all the ordinances which
He has commanded, and by a majority of the laity who
have likewise undertaken concertedly to return to that
Covenant. Every man is then to be registered in a particular rank, one after the other, by the standard of his understanding and performance. The object is that each person
will be rendered subject to his superior. Their spiritual
attitudes and their performance are to be reviewed, however, year by year, some being then promoted by virtue

of their [improved] understanding and the integrity of their conduct, and others demoted for their waywardness.

Of accusations and grudges   (v, 24–vi, 1)

When anyone has a charge against his neighbor, he is to prosecute it truthfully, humbly and humanely. He is not to speak to him angrily or querulously or arrogantly or in any wicked mood.[48] He is not to bear hatred [towards him in the inner recesses] of his heart. When he has a charge against him, he is to proffer it then and there* and not to render himself liable to penalty by nursing a grudge. Furthermore, no man is to bring a charge publicly against his neighbor except he prove it by witnesses.

Of communal duties   (vi, 1–8)

This is the procedure which all members of the community are to follow in all dealings with one another, wherever they dwell.

Everyone is to obey his superior in rank[49] in all matters of work or money. But all are to dine together, worship together and take counsel together.[50]

Wherever there be ten men[51] who have been formally enrolled in the community, one who is a priest is not to depart from them. When they sit in his presence, they are to take their places according to their respective ranks; and the same order is to obtain when they meet for common counsel.

When they set the table for a meal or prepare wine to drink, the priest is first to put forth his hand to invoke a blessing on the first portion of the bread or wine.[52]

Similarly, wherever there be ten men who have been formally enrolled in the community, there is not to be absent from them one who can interpret the Law[53] to them at any time of day or night, for the harmonious adjustment of their human relations.

The general members of the community are to keep

* Heb. 'on the selfsame day'.

awake for a third of all the nights of the year reading
book(s),* studying the Law and worshiping together.[54]

Of the General Council   (vi, 8–13)

This is the rule covering public sessions.

The priests are to occupy the first place. The elders are
to come second; and the rest of the people are to take
their places according to their respective ranks. This order
is to obtain alike when they seek a judicial ruling, when
they meet for common counsel, or when any matter arises
of general concern.

Everyone is to have an opportunity of rendering his
opinion in the common council. No one, however, is to
interrupt while his neighbor is speaking, or to speak until
the latter has finished.[55] Furthermore, no one is to speak
in advance of his prescribed rank. Everyone is to speak
in turn, as he is called upon.

In public sessions, no one is to speak on any subject
that is not of concern to† the company as a whole.[56] If the
superintendent[57] of the general membereship or anyone
who is not of the same rank as the person who happens
to be raising a question for the consideration of the community, has something to say to the company, he is to
stand up and declare: I have something to say to the
company; and only if they so bid him, is he to speak.

Of postulants and novices   (vi, 13–23)

If any man in Israel wish to be affiliated to the formal
congregation of the community, the superintendent of the
general membership is to examine him as to his intelligence
and his actions and, if he then embark on a course of
training, he is to have him enter into a covenant to return
to the truth and turn away from all perversity. Then he
is to apprise him of all the rules of the community.

Subsequently, when that man comes to present himself
to the general membership, everyone is to be asked his

* Or, 'the Book (of the Law)'.
† Or, 'to the liking of'.

opinion about him, and his admission to or rejection from the formal congregation of the community is to be determined by general vote.

No candidate, however, is to be admitted to the formal state of purity enjoyed by the general membership of the community[58] until, at the completion of a full year, his spiritual attitude and his performance have been duly reviewed. Meanwhile he is to have no stake in the common funds.[59]

After he has spent a full year in the midst of the community, the members are jointly to review his case, as to his understanding and performance in matters of doctrine. If it then be voted by the opinion of the priests and of a majority of their co-covenanters to admit him to the sodality, they are to have him bring with him all his property and the tools of his profession. These are to be committed to the custody of the community's 'minister of works'. They are to be entered by that officer into an account, but he is not to disburse them for the general benefit.

Not until the completion of a second year among the members of the community is the candidate to be admitted to the common board.[*60] When, however, that second year has been completed, he is to be subjected to a further review by the general membership,[61] and if then it be voted to admit him to the community, he is to be registered in the due order of rank which he is to occupy among his brethren in all matters pertaining to doctrine, judicial procedure, degree of purity and share in the common funds. Thenceforth his counsel and his judgment are to be at the disposal of the community.

Of false, impudent and blasphemous speech (vi, 23–vii, 5)

And these are the rules to be followed in the interpretation of the law regarding forms of speech.

If there be found in the community a man who consciously lies in the matter of (his) wealth, he is to be re-

* Heb. 'drink'.

garded as outside the state of purity entailed by membership, and he is to be mulcted of one fourth of his food ration.

If a man answer his neighbor defiantly or speak brusquely so as to undermine the composure* of his fellow, and in so doing flout the orders of one who is registered as his superior [   ],† he is to be mulcted for one year.

If a man, in speaking about anything, mention that Name which is honored above all [names],§ 62 or if, in a moment of sudden stress or for some other personal reason, he curse the   (i.e., the man who reads the Book of the Law or leads worship),* 63 he is to be put out and never to return to formal membership in the community.

If a man speak in anger against one of the registered priests, he is to be mulcted for one year, placed in isolation, and regarded as outside the state of purity entailed in membership of the community. If, however, he spoke unintentionally, he is to be mulcted only for six months.

If a man dissemble about what he really knows, he is to be mulcted for six months.

If a man defames his neighbor unjustly, and does so deliberately, he is to be mulcted for one year and regarded as 'outside'.

Of fraud   (vii, 5–8)

If a man speak with his neighbor in guile or consciously practice deceit upon him, he is to be mulcted for six

---

* Heb. 'shake (or, disturb) the foundation'.

† An imperfectly preserved phrase follows in the text. Possibly, it means, 'And if his hand act wickedly against him', i.e., if he bodily assaults him.

§ I.e., the name of God.

* This, gap and all, is how the text reads in the original. It is apparent that the scribe found in the archetype (or heard from dictation?) a rare word which he did not understand fully. He therefore left a blank, but added a gloss giving the approximate sense. The word must have been a technical term for something like 'precentor' or 'deacon'.

months. If, however, he practices the deceit [unintentionally],* he is to be mulcted only for three months.

If a man defraud the community, causing a deficit in its funds, he is to make good that deficit. If he lack means to do so, he is to be mulcted for sixty days.

Of vindictiveness (vii, 8–9)

If he harbor a grudge against his neighbor without legitimate cause, he is to be mulcted for six months [supralinear correction: 'one year']. The same is to apply also to anyone who takes personal revenge on his neighbor in any respect.

Of improper speech (vii, 9)

Anyone who indulges in indecent talk is to be mulcted for three months.

Of misconduct at public sessions (vii, 9–12)

Anyone who interrupts his neighbor in a public session is to be mulcted for ten days.

Anyone who lies down and goes to sleep at a public session is to be mulcted for thirty days.

Anyone who leaves a public session gratuitously and without reason for as many as three times during one sitting is to be mulcted for ten days. If he be ordered to stay (?)† and he still leave, he is to be mulcted for thirty days.

Of indecorous acts (vii, 12–15)

If, except he be under duress (?)§, a man walk naked before his neighbor, he shall be mulcted for six months.

* There is again a blank in the original. The scribe evidently could not decipher the word in his archetype, but the sense is clear.

† This word is partly obliterated. The sense is therefore obscure.
§ Heb. uncertain.

If a man spit into the midst of a public session, he shall be mulcted for thirty days.

If a man bring out his hand from under his cloak, and so expose himself that his private parts become visible, he be mulcted for thirty days.

If a man indulge in raucous, inane laughter, he shall be mulcted for thirty days.

If a man put forth his left hand[64] to gesticulate with it in conversation, he shall be mulcted for ten days.

Of slander and incrimination (vii, 15–18)

If a man slander his neighbor, he shall be regarded as outside the communal state of purity for one year, and he shall also be mulcted. But if he slander the entire group, he is to be expelled and never to return.

If a man complain against the whole basis of the community, he is to be expelled irrevocably.

If he complain against his neighbor without legitimate cause, he is to be mulcted for six months.

Of defection (vii, 18–25)

If a man's spirit waver so far from the basis of the community that he betray the truth and walk in the stubbornness of his own heart, but if he subsequently repent, he shall be mulcted for two years. During the first, he shall be regarded as outside the communal state of purity altogether. During the second, he shall be excluded only from the communal board* and occupy a place behind all the other members. At the completion of the two years, the membership in general shall hold an enquiry about him. If it then be decided to readmit him, he shall again be registered with duly assigned rank and thereafter he too shall be called upon to render his opinion in deliberations concerning the rules.

If a man has been a formal member of the community for a full ten years, but then, through a spiritual relapse, betray the principles of the community and quit the gen-

* Heb. 'drink'.

eral body in order to walk in the stubbornness of his own heart, he is never to return to formal membership in the community. No member of the community is to associate with him either by recognizing him as of the same state of purity or by sharing property with him. Any of the members who does so shall be liable to the same sentence: he too shall be expelled.[65]

Of the appointment (viii, 1–19)
of 'presbyters'

In the formal congregation of the community there shall be twelve laymen and three priests schooled to perfection in all that has been revealed of the entire Law.[66] Their duty shall be to set the standard for the practice of truth, righteousness and justice, and for the exercise of charity and humility in human relations; and to show how, by control of impulse and contrition of spirit, faithfulness may be maintained on earth; how, by active performance of justice and passive submission to the trials of chastisement, iniquity may be cleared, and how one can walk with all men with the quality of truth and in conduct appropriate to every occasion.

So long as these men exist in Israel, the formal congregation of the community will rest securely on a basis of truth. It will become a plant evergreen. Insofar as the laymen are concerned, it will be indeed a sanctuary; and insofar as the priesthood is concerned, it will indeed constitute the basis for a true 'holy of holies'. The members of the community will be in all justice the witnesses of God's truth and the elect of His favor,[67] effecting atonement for the earth and ensuring the requital of the wicked. They will be, indeed, a 'tested bulwark' and 'a precious cornerstone' [cf. Isa. 28.16],[68] which shall never be shaken or moved from their place. As for the priesthood, they shall be a seat for the holy of holies, inasmuch as all of them will then have knowledge of the Covenant of justice and all of them be qualified to offer what will be indeed 'a pleasant savor' to the Lord. And as for the laity, they will constitute a household of integrity and truth, qualified to maintain the Covenant as an everlasting pact. They shall prove acceptable to God, so that He will shrive the earth of its guilt, bring final judgment upon wickedness, and perversity shall be no more.

When these men have undergone, with blamelessness of conduct, a two-year preparation in the fundamentals of the community, they shall be segregated as especially sacred among the formal members of the community. Any knowledge which the expositor of the law may possess but which may have to remain arcane to the ordinary layman, he shall not keep hidden from them; for in their case there need be no fear that it might induce apostasy.[69]

When these men exist in Israel, these are the provisions whereby they are to be kept apart from any consort with froward men, to the end that they may indeed 'go into the wilderness to prepare the way', i.e., do what Scripture enjoins when it says, 'Prepare in the wilderness the way . . . make straight in the desert a highway for our God' [Isa. 40.3].[70] (The reference is to the study of the Law which God commanded through Moses to the end that, as occasion arises, all things may be done in accordance with what is revealed therein and with what the prophets also have revealed through God's holy spirit.)

No member of the community—that is, no duly covenanted member—who blatantly deviates in any particular from the total body of commandments is to be permitted to come into contact with the purity enjoyed by these specially holy men or to benefit by* their counsel until his actions be free of all perversity and he has been readmitted to the common council by decision of the general membership and thereupon reinstated in his rank.

The same rule is to apply also to novices.

Of the conduct of 'presbyters'   (viii, 20–ix, 6)

These are the rules of conduct for the 'men of perfect holiness' in their dealings with one another.

If any of those that have been admitted to the degree

* Heb. 'know'.

of special sanctity—that is, to the degree of 'those that walk blamelessly in the way as God has commanded'—transgress a single word of the Law of Moses either blatantly or deviously, he is to be excommunicated and never to return. No other person in the degree of the specially holy is to have anything to do with him in the sharing either of property or of counsel.

If, however, he erred unintentionally, he is to be debarred only from that particular degree of purity and from participation in the common council. This is to be interpreted to mean that he is not to render any judgment nor is his counsel to be invited in any matter for a full two years. This holds good, however, only if, after the expiration of the full two years, his conduct be considered, in the judgment of the general membership, to be perfect alike in attendance at general assemblies, in study and in frame of mind, and if he has not meanwhile committed any further act of inadvertence. In other words, this two-year penalty is to apply only in the case of a single inadvertent error, whereas if a man acts blatantly, he is nevermore to be readmitted. In sum, it is only the man who acts by inadvertence that is to be placed on probation for two years to see whether, in the opinion of the general membership, his conduct and frame of mind have meanwhile again become blameless. If so, he may be reinstated in the body of the especially holy.

When these things obtain in Israel, as defined by these provisions, the Holy Spirit will indeed rest on a sound foundation; truth will be evinced perpetually; the guilt of transgression and the perfidy of sin will be shriven; and atonement will be made for the earth more effectively than by any flesh of burnt-offerings or fat of sacrifices. The 'oblation of the lips' will be in all justice like the erstwhile 'pleasant savor' on the altar; righteousness and integrity like that free-will offering which God deigns to accept. At that time, the men of the community will constitute a true and distinctive temple—a veritable holy of holies—wherein the priesthood may fitly foregather, and a true and distinctive synagogue made up of laymen who walk in integrity.

Of the authority of the priests   (ix, 7)

The priests alone are to have authority in all judicial and economic matters, and it is by their vote that the ranks of the various members of the community are to be determined.

Of the property of 'presbyters'   (ix, 8–11)

The property of the 'specially holy men'—that is, of 'the men that walk blamelessly'—is not to be put into a common pool with that of men who may still be addicted to deceit* and may not yet have achieved that purity of conduct which leads them to keep apart from perversity and to walk in integrity.

Until the coming of the Prophet† and of both the priestly and the lay Messiah,[71] these men are not to depart from the clear intent of the Law to walk in any way in the stubbornness of their own hearts. They shall judge by the original laws in which the members of the community were schooled from the beginning.

Of the daily conduct   (ix, 12–16)
of the faithful

These are the ordinances for the conduct of any man that seeks after inner vision, in regard alike to human relations, the regulation of affairs on specific occasions, and the appraisal of his fellow men.

He is to perform at all times the will of God, as it has been revealed.

He is to make a point of studying all extant wisdom pertinent to different circumstances and the particular ordinance that applies to the particular occasion.

---

* Heb. simply, 'men of deceit'.

† That is, the prophet foretold in Deuteronomy 18:18, 'I will raise them up a prophet from among their brethren, like unto thee [Moses]; and I will put My words in his mouth, and he shall speak unto them all that I shall command him'. See Introduction, p. 5.

He is to respect the distinctive rank accorded to the sons of Zadok and to the elect of any specific epoch by virtue of their spiritual attitudes, and to appraise them by that criterion, thus adhering to the will of God, as He has commanded.

Everyone is to be judged by the standard of his spirituality. Intercourse with him is to be determined by the purity of his deeds,* and consort with him by the degree of his intelligence. This alone is to determine the degree to which a man is to be loved or hated.

Of religious discussion (ix, 16–21)

No one is to engage in discussion or disputation with men of ill repute; and in the company of froward men everyone is to abstain from talk about† the meaning of the Law [Torah].

With those, however, that have chosen the right path everyone is indeed to discuss matters pertaining to the apprehension§ of God's truth and of His righteous judgments. The purpose of such discussions is to guide the minds of the members of the community, to give them insight into God's inscrutable wonders and truth, and to bring them to walk blamelessly each with his neighbor in harmony with all that has been revealed to them. For this is the time when 'the way is being prepared in the wilderness', and it behooves them to understand all that is happening. It is also the time when they must needs keep apart from all other men and not turn aside from the way through any form of perversity.

Of loving and hating fellow-men; and of duty to God (ix, 21–26)

And these are the regulations of conduct for every man that would seek the inner vision in these times, touching what he is to love and what he is to hate.

* Heb. 'hands' (palms).
† Heb. 'keep hidden'.
§ Heb. 'knowledge'.

He is to bear unremitting hatred towards all men of ill repute, and to be minded to keep in seclusion from them. He is to leave it to them to pursue wealth and mercenary gain, like servants at the mercy of their masters or wretches truckling to a despot.

He is to be zealous to carry out every ordinance punctiliously, against the Day of Requital.[72]

In all his emprises and in all things over which he has control he is to act in a manner acceptable to God, in accordance with what God has commanded.

He is to accept willingly whatever befalls him and to take pleasure in nothing but the will of God.

He is to make [all] the words of his mouth acceptable, and not to lust after anything that God has not commanded.

He is to watch ever for the judgment of God, and [in every vicissitude of his existence] he is to bless his Maker. Whatever befalls, he is to [recount God's glory] and to bless him [with 'the oblation of] the lips'.

The Zadokite Document

I.

Of God's vengeance   (i, 1–ii, 12)
and providence

Now listen, all right-minded men, and take note how God acts: He has a feud with all flesh and exacts satisfaction from all who spurn Him.

Whenever Israel broke faith and renounced Him, He hid His face both from it and from His sanctuary and consigned them to the sword. But whenever He called to mind the covenant which He had made with their forbears, He spared them a remnant and did not consign them to utter extinction.

So, in the Era of Anger, that era of the three hundred and ninety years,[1] when He delivered them into the hand of Nebuchadnezzar, king of Babylon, He took care of them and brought to blossom alike out of the priesthood and out of the laity that root which had been planted of old, allowing it once more to possess the land and to grow fat in the richness of its soil. Then they realized their iniquity and knew that they had been at fault. For twenty years, however, they remained like blind men groping their way,[2] until at last God took note of their deeds, how that they were seeking Him sincerely, and He raised up for them one who would teach the Law correctly,[3] to guide

them in the way of His heart and to demonstrate to future
ages what He does to a generation that incurs His anger,
that is, to the congregation of those that betray Him and
turn aside from His way.

The period in question was that whereof it is written,
'Like a stubborn heifer, Israel was stubborn' [Hos. 4.16].
It was the time when a certain scoffer arose to distil upon
Israel the waters deceptive[4] and to lead them astray in a
trackless waste, bringing low whatsoever had once been
high, diverting them from the proper paths and removing the landmarks which their forbears had set up, to
the end that through his efforts those curses cleaved to
them which had been prescribed when the Covenant was
concluded, and they were delivered to the sword. Thus
was avenged that breach of the Covenant which they had
committed in seeking smooth things and in preferring delusion and in being constantly on the watch to breach the
faith and in choosing to walk proudly and in justifying the
wicked and condemning the righteous, and in abrogating
the Covenant and annulling the pact, and in assailing the
life of the righteous and abhorring all whose conduct was
blameless, and in pursuing them with the sword, and in
raising a general clamor against them. God then grew
angry with their horde and utterly destroyed all their
throng and treated all their works as an abominable thing
unclean.

Of God's judgment on the wicked   (ii, 2–13)
and His clemency to the righteous

And now, listen to me, all who have entered the Covenant, and I will open your ears to the fate which attends
the wicked.

God loves knowledge. Wisdom and sound sense has He
posted before Him. Prudence and knowledge minister to
Him.[5] Patience attends on him and abundant forgiveness,
so that He may shrive the repentant. But also with Him
are might and power and great wrath, along with flames of
fire and all the angels of destruction[6]—appointed for them
that turn aside from His way and treat His ordinance as a

thing to be shunned, to the end that they shall be left without remnant or survival.

Never, from the very beginning of the world, has God approved such men. He has always known what their actions would be, even before the foundations of them were laid. He has anathematized whole generations on account of bloodshed, hiding His face from the land. Their end has always been pre-determined. He has always foreknown how long they would endure and the exact and precise extent of their continuance; yea, all that has happened in their several epochs throughout history, and likewise all that was to befall them.

Nevertheless, in all of their generations He has ever raised up for Himself duly designated men, so that He might provide survival for the earth and fill the face of the world with their seed. And to these has He ever revealed His holy spirit at the hands of His anointed[7] and has ever disclosed the truth; and He has clearly specified who they were. But those whom He hated He has always left to wander astray.

Of ancient sinners (ii, 14–iii, 12)

And now, children, listen to me, and I will open your eyes to see and understand how God acts, so that you may choose what He has desired and reject what He has hated, walking blamelessly in all His ways and not straying after thoughts of guilty lust or after whoring eyes. For many there be that have strayed thereby from olden times until now, and even strong heroes have stumbled thereby.

Because they walked in the stubbornness of their hearts, the Watchers of heaven fell;[8] yea, they were caught thereby because they kept not the commandments of God.

So too their sons, whose height was like the lofty cedars and whose bodies were as mountains.[9] They also fell.

So too 'all flesh that was upon the dry land'.[10] They also perished. These became as though they had never been, because they did their own pleasure and kept not the commandments of their Maker. In the end His anger was kindled against them.

In the same way, too, the sons of Noah went astray,[11] and thereby they and their families were cut off.

Abraham, however, did not walk in this way. Therefore, because he kept the commandments of God and did not prefer the desires of his own spirit, he was accounted the Friend of God[12] and transmitted this status in turn to Isaac and Jacob. They too kept the commandments, and they too were recorded as Friends of God and as partners in His everlasting Covenant.

But the sons of Jacob strayed in that way and they were punished for their aberration.

Their sons, too, when they were in Egypt, walked in the stubbornness of their hearts, plotting against the commandments of God and doing each what was right in his own eyes. Because they ate blood all their males were cut off in the wilderness. God said to them at Kadesh: 'Go up and possess the land' [Deut. 9.23], [but they followed the desire of] their own spirits and hearkened not to the voice of their Maker neither to the orders of their leader, but kept murmuring in their tents. So the anger of God was kindled against their horde.[13]

Their sons too perished by such conduct. Their kings were cut off through it, and their heroes perished through it, and their land was laid waste through it.

Thus, whenever in ancient times those who had entered the Covenant became guilty on this account, forsaking that Covenant of God, preferring their own pleasure and going astray after the stubbornness of their hearts, doing each man as he pleased, they were invariably delivered to the sword.

Of the righteous remnant   (iii, 12–iv, 6)

Howbeit, with the rest of them—that is, with those that held fast to His commandments—God ever made good His everlasting Covenant with Israel, revealing to them the hidden things concerning which Israel in general had gone astray—even His holy sabbaths and His glorious festivals, His righteous ordinances, the ways of His truth and the purposes of His will, 'the which, if a man do, he shall live'

[Lev. 18.5]. He opened for them a well with water abounding,[14] which they might dig. But them that spurned those waters He did not permit to live. And though they kept sullying themselves with human transgression and with filthy ways, and kept saying, ' 'Tis our own concern,' yet did God with His mysterious power shrive their iniquity and forgive their transgression and build for them in Israel a firmly established House the like of which has not existed from ancient times until this day.

They that hold fast unto Him are destined for life eternal, and theirs is all mortal glory, even as God has sworn unto them by the hand of the prophet Ezekiel, saying: 'The priests and the levites and the sons of Zadok that kept the charge of My sanctuary when the children of Israel went astray from Me, these it is that shall offer unto Me the fat and the blood' [Ez. 44.15]. By 'priests' is meant those in Israel that repented and departed from the land of Judah. [By 'levites'] is meant those that associated themselves[15] with them. By 'sons of Zadok' is meant those elect of Israel that have been designated by name and that shall go on functioning in the last days. Behold, their names have been specified, the families into which they are to be born, the epochs in which they are to function, the full tale of their tribulations, the length of their sojourn in exile, and the precise nature of their deeds.

Of the reward of the faithful (iv, 6–12)

These were the 'holy men'[16] of former times—the men whose sins God pardoned, who knew right for right and wrong for wrong. But all who up to the present time have succeeded them in carrying out explicitly the Law from which those ancients drew their lessons, them too will God forgive, in accordance with the Covenant which He made with those ancients to forgive their iniquities. And when the present era is completed, there will be no more express affiliation with the house of Judah; every man will 'mount guard' for himself. 'The fence will be rebuilt, and the bounds be far-flung' [cf. Micah 7.11].[17]

Of the works of Belial   (iv, 12–v, 17)

Meanwhile, however, Belial will be rampant in Israel,
even as God has said through the prophet Isaiah, the son
of Amoz: 'Terror and the pit and the trap shall be upon
thee, O inhabitant of the land!' [Isa. 24.17]. The reference is to those three snares, viz. (a) whoredom, (b) lucre,
and (c) desecration, concerning which Levi the son of
Jacob said[18] that by making them look like three kinds of
righteousness Belial ensnares Israel in them. He who
escapes the one gets caught in the other, and he who
escapes the other gets caught in the third.

Such men may be described as 'builders of a rickety
wall' [Ez. 13.10], or as persons that have 'walked after
filth' [Hos. 5.11]. The 'filth' in question is the babbling
preacher of whom God said, 'Babble-babble shall they
preach' [Micah 2.6]; while the fact that *two* words [viz.
'pit' and 'trap'] are used to describe the net in which they
will be caught alludes to the whorish practice of taking *two*
wives at the same time, the true basis of nature being the
pairing of one male with one female, even as it is said (of
Adam and Eve), 'A male and a female created He them'
[Gen. 1.27], and of those that went into the ark, 'In pairs
they entered' [Gen. 7.9]. Similarly, too, it is said concerning a prince: 'He shall not take more than one wife' [Deut.
17.17].* [19]

Such persons commit [desecration] inasmuch as they lie
with women in their periods and do not put them aside, as
enjoined in the Law.[20] Moreover, they marry the daughters

---

* David, however, had never read the Book of Law, for it was
sealed up in the ark and remained unopened in Israel from the
day when Eleazar and Joshua and the Elders were gathered to
their rest. The people worshiped Ashtoreth, while the ark remained hidden and unopened until indeed a Zadokite entered
into office [in the person of Hilkiah the priest]. Accordingly,
David's actions were not punished, save the spilling of the blood
of Uriah, but God remitted the penalty for them.

*This is part of the original text, but is here relegated to a foot-
note, as it would have been in a modern work, in order not to
interrupt the sequence of thought.*

of their brothers and sisters, whereas Moses has said: 'Thou shalt not enter into intimate relations with the sister of thy mother; she is thy mother's kin' [cf. Lev. 18.13]. (The laws of forbidden degrees are written, to be sure, with reference to males, but they hold good equally for females. A niece, for instance, who indulges in carnal intercourse with her paternal uncle is equally to be regarded as his kin.)

Furthermore, such men have desecrated the holy spirit within them, and with mocking tongue have opened their mouths against the statutes of God's Covenant, declaring, 'They have no foundation'. They have spoken disgracefully about them.

All such men may be described as persons that 'kindle a fire and set firebrands alight' [Isa. 50.11]. Of them it may be said that 'their webs are spiders' webs and their eggs basilisks' eggs' [Isa. 59.5]. None that have contact with them shall go unscathed; the more one does so, the more guilty he becomes—unless, of course, he does so under compulsion.

Throughout antiquity, however, God has always taken note of the deeds of such men, and His anger has always been kindled against their acts. Always, in fact, they have proved to be 'a witless folk' [Isa. 27.11], a nation void of sense [Deut. 32.28] in that they lacked discernment.

Of the Remnant   (v, 17–vi, 11)

When, in antiquity, Israel was first delivered, Moses and Aaron still continued in their charge, through the help of the Angel of Lights,* even though Belial in his cunning had set up Jannes and his brother in opposition to them.[21]

Similarly, at the time when the land was destroyed, men arose who removed the ancient landmarks and led Israel astray; and it was, indeed, because they uttered sedition against the commandments of God which He had given through Moses and through His holy anointed priest Aaron, and because they gave forth false prophecies in order to subvert Israel from God, that the land was laid ut-

* Heb. *Urim*. See *Manual of Discipline*, iii.20.

terly waste. Nevertheless, God still remembered the Covenant which He had made with their forbears and raised
from the priesthood men of discernment and from the laity
men of wisdom, and He made them hearken to Him. And
these men 'dug the well'—that well whereof it is written,
'Princes digged it, nobles of the people delved it, with the
aid of a *mehôqeq* [Num. 21.18]. The 'well' in question is
the Law. They that 'digged' are those of Israel who repented and departed from the land of Judah to sojourn in
'the land of Damascus'.* God called them all 'princes' because they went in search of Him and because their glory
was never gainsaid (?) by any man's mouth.[22] The term
mehôqeq [which can mean 'lawgiver' as well as 'stave']
refers to the man who expounds the Law. Isaiah has employed an analogous piece of imagery when in allusion to
the Law he has spoken of God's 'producing a tool for His
work' [cf. Isa. 54.16]. As for the 'nobles of the people',
these are the men that come, in every era of wickedness,
to delve the well, using as their staves [Heb. *me-hôq-eq*]
the statutes [Heb. *huq-îm*] which the Lawgiver prescribed
[Heb. *haqaq ha-mehôqeq*] for them to walk in. Without
such 'implements', they would, indeed, never achieve their
goal until such time as the true Expositor arises at the end
of days.

Of the obligation   (vi, 11–vii, 6a)
of the Covenant

All that enter the covenant with no intention of going
into the sanctuary to keep the flame alive on the altar do
so in vain. They have as good as shut the door. Of them
God has said: 'Who is there among you that would shut
the door, and who of you would not keep alive the flame
upon Mine altar?' In vain [Mal. 1.10] [are all their deeds]
if, in an era of wickedness, they do not take heed
to act in accordance with the explicit injunctions of the
Law;
to keep away from men of ill-repute;
to hold themselves aloof from ill-gotten gain;

* Scarcely to be taken literally. See Introduction, pp. 4, 24.

not to defile themselves by laying hands on that which has been vowed or devoted to God or on the property of the sanctuary;

not to rob the poor of God's people;

not to make widows their prey or murder the fatherless;

to distinguish between unclean and clean and to recognize holy from profane;

to keep the sabbath in its every detail, and the festivals and fasts in accordance with the practice laid down originally by the men who entered the covenant in 'the land of Damascus';[23]

to pay their required dues in conformity with the detailed rules thereof;

to love each man his neighbor like himself;

to grasp the hand of the poor, the needy and the stranger;

to seek each man the welfare of his fellow;

to cheat not his own kin;

to abstain from whoredom, as is meet;

to bring no charge against his neighbor except by due process, and not to nurse grudges from day to day;

to keep away from all unclean things, in accordance with what has been prescribed in each case and with the distinctions which God Himself has drawn for them;

not to sully any man the holy spirit within him.[24]

Howbeit, for all that perform these rules in holiness unimpaired, according to all the instruction that has been given them—for them will God's Covenant be made good, that they shall be preserved for a thousand generations, even as it is written: 'He keepeth Covenant and loyalty with them that love Him and keep His commandments, even unto a thousand generations' [Deut. 7.9].

Of family life   (vii, 6a–9)

If members of the community happen to be living in encampments,[25] in accordance with a usage which obtains in this country, and if they marry and beget children,[26] they are [in such matters] to follow the precepts of the Law [Torah] and the disciplinary regulations therein prescribed for the relationship of husband to wife and of father to child.*

Of the future requital   (vii, 9–viii, 21)
of the disobedient

All that reject these things shall be doomed to extinction when God visits the world to requite the wicked—that is, when that ensues which is described by the prophet Isaiah the son of Amoz in the words: 'There shall come upon thee and upon thy kindred and upon thy father's house days the like of which have not come since the time that Ephraim departed from Judah' [Isa. 7.17]. In other words, the same situation will then obtain as obtained at the time of the great schism between the two houses of Israel, when Ephraim departed from Judah. At that time all who turned back were delivered to the sword, whereas all who stood fast were vouchsafed escape to 'the land of the north'.[27]

It is to this that allusion is also made in the statement: 'I will exile Sikkuth your king and Kiyyun your image, the star of your God . . . beyond Damascus' [cf. Amos 5.26].

The expression 'Sikkuth your king' refers to the Books of the Law, [for the word 'Sikkuth' is to be explained from the like-sounding *sukkah*, 'tabernacle']† as in the passage of Scripture which says: 'I will raise up the fallen *sukkah* [tabernacle] of David' [Amos 9.11].

The expression 'king' denotes the congregation;[28] and the expression 'Kiyyun your image' refers to the books of the prophets[29] whose words the House of Israel has despised.[30]

As for the 'star', that refers to every such interpreter of the Law as indeed repairs to 'Damascus',[31] even as it is written: 'There shall step forth a star out of Jacob, and a sceptre shall rise out of Israel' [Num. 24.17].[32] The

---

* Heb. even as God has said: 'Between a man and his wife and between a father and his son'—a loose quotation from Numbers 30.17.

† These words have here been inserted in order to bring out the word-play in the Hebrew original.

'sceptre', it may be added, is the leader of the community, for in the exercise of his office he shall 'batter all the sons of pride',[33] as the Scripture says.

In the former visitation, these faithful men escaped, while those that turned back were delivered to the sword. Such will be the fate also of those who in the latter days will have entered God's Covenant but not held fast to these things. Them will God punish unto extinction by the hand of Belial.

The day on which God will carry out the punishment will be that to which the prophet alluded when he said: 'The princes of Judah have become like them that remove landmarks; I will pour out My wrath upon them like water' [Hos. 5.10]. They shall hope for healing, but the blemish shall cling to them. They are all of them apostates in that they have not turned from the way of the treacherous but have sullied themselves with wantonness and with wicked lucre and with the nursing of grudges against their fellows and with hatred of their neighbors. They have cheated their own kin and have had contact with lewdness and have been overbearing by virtue of wealth and possession and have done every man of them what was right in his own eyes, and have preferred the stubbornness of their own hearts, and have not kept aloof from the rabble, but have behaved lawlessly and high-handedly, walking in the way of the wicked.

Concerning them has God said: 'Their wine shall prove the poison of serpents and the cruel venom of asps' [Deut. 32.33]. The 'wine' in question is their conduct; the 'serpents' are the kings of the nations; and the 'venom [Heb. *rô'sh*] of asps' is the chief [Heb. *rô'sh*] of the Grecian kings who will come to wreak vengeance upon them.

Those that have been 'builders of the rickety wall' and 'daubers of veneer upon it'[34] have never considered all this, because the man who walks in wind, who raises whirlwinds, who spouts lies—the kind of man against all of whose ilk God's wrath has always been kindled—has kept spouting at them.

Howbeit, what Moses said of old, 'Not for thy righteousness nor for the uprightness of thy heart art thou going in to possess these nations but because of His love wherewith He loved thy forefathers and because He would keep the oath' [cf. Deut. 9.5],[35] applies equally to those in Israel who in those latter days show repentance and eschew the way of the rabble. The same love which God showed to the men of old who pledged themselves to follow Him will He show also to their successors. The ancestral Covenant shall stand good for them.

But inasmuch as He hates and abominates all that 'build a rickety wall', His anger has been kindled against them; and all who reject His commandments and forsake them and go on walking in the stubbornness of their own hearts will be visited with such judgment as has been described. It is to this that Jeremiah was referring when he spoke to Baruch the son of Neriah,[36] and Elisha when he spoke to his servant Gehazi.[37]

All those that entered into the new covenant in 'the land of Damascus' but subsequently relapsed and played false and turned away from the well of living waters shall not be reckoned as of the communion of the people nor inscribed in the roster of it throughout the period from the time the teacher of the community is gathered to his rest until that in which the lay and the priestly Messiah [anointed] assume their office.[38]

The same applies also to all that entered the company of the 'specially holy and blameless'[39] but were loath to carry out the rules imposed upon the upright. Every such man is, as it were, like 'one molten in the furnace' [Ez. 22.22]. When his deeds come clearly to light, he shall be cast out of that company as being one who has no share among the disciples of God. Men of knowledge shall reprove him according to his perfidy until he repent and thereby resume his place among the specially holy and blameless—that is, until it become clear that his actions are again in accordance with the interpretation of the Law adopted by the specially holy and blameless. Meanwhile, no man shall have commerce with him in matters either of property or of employment, for he has been cursed by all the holy ones of God on high.

The same applies again—in the future as it did in the

past—to all who commit their hearts to idolatry and walk in the stubbornness of their hearts. All such have no portion in the household of the Law [*Torah*].

The same applies, once again, to all of their fellows that relapse in the company of scoffers. These too shall be judged; for they will have spoken error against the righteous ordinances and have rejected the Covenant of God and the pledge which they swore in 'the land of Damascus' —that is, the new covenant.[40] Neither they nor their families shall have a portion in the household of the Law [*Torah*].

About forty years will elapse from the death of the teacher of the community until all the men who take up arms and relapse in the company of the Man of Falsehood are brought to an end.[41] At that time, the wrath of God will be kindled against Israel, and that will ensue which is described by the prophet when he says: 'No king shall there be nor priest nor judge nor any that reproves aright' [cf. Hos. 3.4].

But they of Jacob that have repented, that have kept the Covenant of God, shall then speak each to his neighbor to bring him to righteousness, to direct his steps upon the way. And God will pay heed to their words and hearken, and He will draw up a record of those that fear Him and esteem His name,[42] to the end that salvation shall be revealed for all God-fearing men. Then ye shall again distinguish the righteous from the wicked, him that serves God from him that serves Him not. And God will 'show mercy unto thousands, unto them that love Him and keep His commandments'—yea, even unto a thousand generations.

The divisive elements[43] that, in the era of Israel's perfidy, when it defiled the sanctuary, indeed went out from the holy city and placed their reliance on God and returned to God, but through whose wrangles the people were thrown into discord*—these shall be subjected to judgment

* The writing is here obliterated, and the meaning therefore uncertain. I have translated what I believe I can see in the faint traces.

at the hands of the sacred council,[44] each according to
his attitude.

Those, however, who had entered the covenant but subsequently broke through the bounds of the Law—all of
those shall be 'cut off from the midst of the camp' at the
time when God's glory is made manifest to Israel. And
along with them shall go those that sought to turn Judah
to wickedness in the days when it was being put to the
test.

Of the future reward   (B. xx, 27–34)
of the faithful

Howbeit, all that hold fast to these enactments, going
and coming in accordance with the Law; that hearken to
the voice of the Teacher; that make confession before
God, saying: Just and truthful are Thy judgments against
us, for we have done wickedly, both we and our fathers,
in that we have gone contrary to the statutes of the Covenant; all who raise not their hands against His holy statutes
or His righteous judgments or His truthful ordinances; all
who learn the lessons of the former judgments wherewith
the men of the community were adjudged in time past; all
who give ear to him who imparts the true interpretation
of the Law and who do not controvert the right ordinances
when they hear them—all of these shall rejoice and their
hearts shall be strong, and they shall prevail over all that
dwell in the world. And God will accept their atonement,
and because they took refuge in His holy name they shall
indeed see salvation at His hand.

II. CODE FOR URBAN COMMUNITIES

Of capital punishment   (ix, 1)

As regards the law that no man who has been condemned on a capital charge is to be ransomed [Lev.
27.29], this is to be taken to imply that all sentences of
death are to be carried out by the Gentile authorities.[45]

Of grudges (ix, 2–8)

And as to the law which says, 'Thou shalt not take vengeance nor bear any grudge against the children of thy people' [Lev. 19.18]—if any of those that have entered the covenant bring charges against his neighbor without proving them by witnesses; or if he bring such charges merely through temper, or if he tell tales to his superiors simply to bring his neighbor into contempt, he ranks as one who takes vengeance and bears a grudge. Scripture says of God Himself that it is only upon His adversaries that He takes vengeance, and only against His enemies that He bears a grudge [Nah. 1.2]. Accordingly, if a man keep silent from day to day and then bring a charge against his neighbor in the heat of anger, it is as if he were laying capital charges against him, for he has not carried out the commandment of God Who said to him, 'Thou shalt surely reprove thy neighbor lest thou incur sin on his account' [Lev. 19.17].

Of involuntary oaths (ix, 8–10)

Now regarding oaths. The principle that 'thou art not to take the law into thine own hands'[46] implies that a man who compels another to take an oath in the open field and not in the presence of judges or at their order has taken the law into his own hands.

Of lost property (ix, 10–15)

In the case of a loss, if it is not known who stole the particular article from the property of the camp in which the theft occurs, the owner is to be required to make a solemn deposition on oath. Anyone who hears it, knows the culprit and does not tell, is then to be considered culpable.

If a man makes restitution for expropriated property and brings the required guilt-offering, but there are no claimants to that property, he is to make his confession to the priest, and everything except the actual ram of the sin-offering is to go to the latter.

Lost property that is found but unclaimed is to be entrusted to the priests, because the man who retrieved it may not know the law about it. If the owners cannot be discovered [at the time], the priests are to take it into custody.

Of testimony (ix, 16–x, 3)

In the case of offenses against the Torah, if a man sees such an offense committed but is alone at the time, and if the matter be one of a capital nature, he is to disclose it to the overseer by bringing a charge in the presence of the alleged culprit. The overseer is then to make a record of it. If the man repeat the offense, this time also in the presence of one man only, and if the latter come in turn and inform the overseer—in that case, i.e., if the offender do it again and be again caught by only one person—the case against him is to be regarded as complete.

However, if there be two witnesses, and they concur in their statements, the culprit is to be excluded from his customary degree of purity only if those witnesses are trustworthy and if they lay information before the overseer on the very day when they saw the man [committing the offense].

In cases involving property, *two* trustworthy witnesses are required.[47] In those, however, that involve [no question of restitution but simply of] exclusion from the degree of purity, one alone is sufficient.

No man who has not yet completed his probationary period with the community and has not yet passed the statutory examination as a truly God-fearing person[48] is to be permitted as a witness before its judges in a capital case.

No man who has flagrantly transgressed the commandment is to be deemed a trustworthy witness against his neighbor until he has succeeded in winning re-acceptance into the community.

Of judges (x, 4–10)

This is the rule concerning the judges of the community. Periodically, a complement of ten men shall be selected from the community. Four of them shall belong to the tribe of Levi and Aaron, and six shall be laymen.[49] They shall be men versed in the Book of Study[50] and in the fundamentals of the Covenant. Their minimum age shall be twenty-five, and their maximum sixty. No man over sixty shall occupy judicial office in the community; for through the perfidy of man the potential span of human life has been reduced, and in the heat of His anger against the inhabitants of the earth, God decreed of old that their mental powers should recede before they complete their days.

Of ritual ablutions (x, 10–13)

Now concerning purification by water. No one is to bathe in dirty water or in water which is too scant to produce a ripple (?).[51]

No man is to purify himself with water drawn in a vessel or in a rock-pool where there is insufficient to produce a ripple (?). If an unclean person come in contact with such water, he merely renders it unclean; and the same is true of water drawn in a vessel.

Of the Sabbath (x, 14–xi, 18)

Now concerning the proper observance of the Sabbath. No one is to do any work on Friday from the moment that the sun's disk stands distant from the gate by the length of its own diameter; for this is what Scripture implies when it says explicitly, Observe the Sabbath day to keep it holy.[52]

On the Sabbath day, no one is to indulge in ribald or empty talk. No one is to claim repayment of debts. No one is to engage in lawsuits concerning property and gain. No one is to talk about labor or work to be done the next day. No one is to go out into the field while it is still Sabbath with the intention of resuming his work immediately the Sabbath ends. No one is to walk more than a thousand cubits outside his city.[53] No one is to eat on the Sabbath day anything that has not been prepared in advance. He is not to eat anything that happens to be lying about in the field, neither is he to drink of anything that was not [previously] in the camp. If, however, he is travelling, he may go down to bathe and may drink wherever he happens to be.

No one is to commission a Gentile to transact business for him on the Sabbath day. No one is to wear soiled clothes or clothes that have been put in storage unless they first be laundered and rubbed with frankincense. No one is to observe a voluntary fast on the Sabbath. No one is to follow his beast to pasture for more than a distance of two thousand cubits from his city. No one is to raise his hand to strike it with his fist. If the beast be stubborn, he is not to take it outdoors. No one is to take anything out of his house, or bring anything in from outside. If he is [lodging] in a booth, he is likewise to take nothing out nor bring anything in. No one is to break open a pitch-sealed vessel on the Sabbath. No one is to carry ointments upon his person or walk around with them* on the Sabbath. No one is to pick up rock or dust in a dwelling place. Nurses are not to carry babies around on the Sabbath. No one is to put pressure on his male or female servant or on his hired help on the Sabbath. No one is to foal a beast on the Sabbath day. Even if it drop its young into a cistern or a pit, he is not to lift it out on the Sabbath.

No one is to stop for the Sabbath in a place near the heathen. No one is to desecrate the Sabbath for the sake of wealth or gain.

If a human being falls into a place of water or into a dark place, one is to bring him up by means of a ladder or a rope or some other instrument.[54]

No one is to present any offering upon the altar on the Sabbath except the statutory Sabbath burnt-offering—as the

* Literally, 'go or come'.

Scripture puts it, 'your Sabbath-offerings exclusively' [Lev. 23.38].[55]

Of the defilement (xi,18–xii, 2)
of holy places

No one is to send to the altar either burnt-offering or meal-offering or frankincense or wood by the hand of one suffering from any of the proscribed impurities, thus permitting him to render the altar impure; for Scripture says, 'The sacrifice of the wicked is an abomination, but the mere prayer of the righteous is like an acceptable offering' [Prov. 15.8].

As for those who come to the house of worship, no one is to come in a state of uncleanness requiring ablution. Such a man is either to anticipate the sounding of the trumpets of assembly or else to stay behind, so that [the rest] will not have to stop the entire service.

[   ]; it is holy.

No one is to lie with a woman in the city of the sanctuary, thereby defiling the city of the sanctuary with their impurity.

Of demoniacal possession (xii, 2–6)

Any man who is dominated by demonic spirits to the extent that he gives voice to apostasy is to be subject to the judgment upon sorcerers and wizards. If, however, a man desecrate the Sabbath or the festivals through [mental] aberration, he is not to be put to death. In that case, it is the duty of men to keep him under observation. If he recovers, they are to watch him for seven years, and only thereafter may he be readmitted to public assemblies.

Of relations with the heathen (xii, 6–11)

No one is to put forth his hand to shed the blood of a heathen for the sake of wealth or gain. Moreover, to prevent the levelling of defamatory charges, no one is to expropriate any of their goods except by the decision of an Israelite court.

No one is to sell clean beasts or fowl to the heathen, lest they use them for sacrifices. No one is to sell them any of the produce of his threshing-floor or winepress or any of his possessions. Nor is he to sell to them any of his male or female servants that may have joined him in the Covenant of Abraham.[56]

Of food   (xii, 11–15)

No one is to defile his person by eating any unclean animal or reptile. This rule includes the larvae of bees and any living entity that creeps in water.

Fish are not to be eaten unless they are ripped open while still alive and their blood poured out.[57]

As for the various kinds of locust, these are to be put in fire or water while they are still alive; for that is what their nature demands.

Of contagious impurity   (xii, 15–18)

When wood, stone or dust is contaminated by human uncleanness, the degree of the contamination is to be determined by the rules governing that particular form of uncleanness; and it is by this standard that all contact with them is to be gauged.

When a dead body lies in a house, every utensil—even a nail or a peg in the wall—is to be regarded as defiled, just as much as implements of work.

Epilogue   (xii, 19–22)

The foregoing is the rule concerning the various regulations for distinguishing clean from unclean and for recognizing holy from profane, such as it is to obtain in the urban communities of Israel. It is by these ordinances that the enlightened man may correctly determine his human relations on this or that particular occasion; and it is in this manner that the progeny of Israel is to conduct itself in order to avoid damnation.[58]

III. CODE FOR CAMP-COMMUNITIES

Prologue   (xii, 22–xiii, 7)

Here, however, is the rule for such camp-communities as
may come into existence throughout the Era of Wickedness—that is, until the priestly and the lay 'messiah' again
assume office.[59] The people who follow these rules must
consist in any given instance of a minimum of ten,[60] and
beyond that must be grouped by thousands, hundreds,
fifties and tens.

In any place where there are ten, a priest versed in the
Book of Study is not to be absent; 'by his word shall they
all be ruled' [Gen. 41.40]. If, however, he is not experi-
enced in all these matters, the members of the camp may
elect by vote one of the levites, 'by whose orders they may
come and go'.[61] Nevertheless, whenever a decision has to
be rendered involving the law of bodily blemishes, the
priest is to come and officiate in the camp, the overseer
instructing him in the detailed interpretation of the Law.
Moreover, if the priest be feeble-minded, that official must
simply keep him under lock and key at all other times;
for it is nonetheless by the priests that the decision in such
matters must be rendered.[62]

Of the overseer[63]   (xiii, 7–19)

This is the rule for the overseer of the camp.

It is his duty to enlighten the masses about the works
of God, and to make them understand His wondrous
powers. He is to tell them in detail the story of things
that happened in the past. He is to show them the same
compassion as a father shows for his children. He is to
bring back all of them that stray, as does a shepherd his
flock.[64] He is to loose all the bonds that constrain them, so
that there be no one in his community who is oppressed or
crushed.

He is also to examine every new adherent to his community regarding his conduct, intelligence, strength, valor and wealth, and to register him in his due status, according to his stake in the portion of Truth. No member of the camp is to have authority to introduce anyone into the community in defiance of the camp's overseer.

No one who has entered the Covenant is to have any traffic with the 'men of corruption' [i.e., outsiders] except in spot cash transactions. No one is to enter into any sort of commercial partnership without informing the camp's overseer. Moreover, if he has made an agreement, but does not. . . . [*Four fragmentary lines.*]

Epilogue   (xiii, 20–xiv, 2)

Such, then, is to be the disposition of the camps throughout the Era of Wickedness. Those who do not adhere to these things shall not succeed in reoccupying their native soil [   ]. These, in fact, are the regulations for the social conduct of the 'enlightened' until God eventually visits the earth, even as He has said: 'There shall come upon thee and upon thy people and upon thy kinsfolk days the like of which have not been since Ephraim departed from Judah' [Isa. 7.17]. With those that follow them God's covenant will be confirmed; they will be delivered from all the snares of corruption. The foolish, however, will [   ] and be punished.

IV. A SUPPLEMENTARY CODE

Of rank and precedence   (xiv, 3–12)

This is the rule for the disposition of all camp-settlements.

Everyone is to be registered by name in a census; first, the priests; second, the levites; third, the laymen; and fourth, the proselytes. Each individual is to be registered by name, one after another; first, the priests; second, the levites; third, the laymen; and fourth, the proselytes. It is in this order that they are to be seated at public sessions, and in this order that their opinions are to be invited on all matters.

The priest who holds office over the masses is to be from thirty to sixty years old, versed in the Book of Study and in all the regulations of the Torah, so as to be able to declare them on each appropriate occasion.

As for the overseer of all the camps, he is to be from thirty to fifty years old, adept in human relations and in all the varied languages of men.[65] It is as he determines that those who enter the community are to be admitted, each in his assigned order. Anything that any one has to say in a matter of dispute or litigation, he is to say to the overseer.

Of the communal economy   (xiv, 12–18)

This is the rule for regulating public needs.

Their wages for at least two days per month are to be handed over to the overseer. The judges are then to take thereof and give it away for the benefit of orphans. They are also to support therefrom the poor and needy, the aged who are dying, the [   ] persons captured by foreign peoples, unprotected girls, unmarriageable virgins, general communal officials [   ].

This, in specific form, is the way [   ] is to be disposed [   ] [com]munally.

Of personal morality   (xiv, 18–22)

And these, in specific form, are the regulations which they are to follow throughout the Era of Wickedness, until the priestly and lay 'messiahs' enter upon their office and expiate their iniquities.

No one is to practice conscious falsehood in matters of money [   ]; he is to be mulcted [of his rations] for six days.

If a man utter [   ], [or harbor an] unjustified [grudge against his neighbor, he is to be mulcted for one] year [   ].

Of oaths   (xv, 1–xvi, 20)

No one is to take the oath by EL—* or by AD—,† but
only by a formula of assent which invokes the curses prescribed in the Covenant [cf. Lev. 26.14–45]. Nor is he
to make mention in this connection of the Law of Moses,
for (the name of God is spelled out in that Law); so that
if he swears by it and then transgresses, he commits profanation of the Holy Name; whereas if he swears before
the judges by the curses of the Covenant—then, if he
transgresses, he becomes liable only for a guilt-offering,
confession and restitution, but does not have to pay the
penalty of death.[66]

It is to be a perpetual ordinance for the whole of Israel
that whoever enters into the covenant is to impose the oath
of the covenant also upon his sons when they reach the
age for the preliminary examination.

Similarly, it is to be the rule throughout the Epoch of
Wickedness that anyone who repents his corrupt conduct
is to be enrolled, on the day when he speaks of it to the
general overseer, with an oath binding him to the covenant
which Moses made with Israel—that is, with a covenanted
obligation that [in all] the varied activities of his life he
will return to the Law of Moses with all his heart and
soul. No one, however, is to acquaint him with the regulations of the community prior to his actually standing in
the presence of the overseer, lest, when the latter examines
him, he turn out to be a dolt. But once the overseer has
sworn him by oath to return to the Law of Moses with all
his heart and soul, he is to be liable to punishment for any
breach of faith. If he fail to understand anything in the
Law which is patently revealed to the normal mind, the
overseer is to [   ] and then issue an order concerning him that he be kept in confinement for a full year on
the grounds of its having been ascertained that he is feeble-
minded and deranged.

In the case of one who is a chronic imbecile or is in-

* The initial letters of *ELohim,* the Hebrew word for 'God'.
† The initial letters of *ADonai,* the Hebrew word for 'Lord'.

sane, the judge is to come and [   ]. Such a man is
not to appear in public. . . . [*The next two lines are fragmentary, and four more have been lost.*]

There is an ancient text which says: 'It was by the Law
of Moses that God made the covenant with you and with
all Israel'.[67] It is for this reason that the man [who enters
the covenant] must pledge himself 'to return to the Law
of Moses'. Therein is everything explicitly spelled out,
while an exact specification of the time when Israel will
be blind to all these things is spelled out with equal exact-
ness in the Book of the Divisions of the Times into their
Jubilees and Weeks.[68]

On the day that a man pledges himself to return to the
Law of Moses, the Angel of Obstruction[69] will start reced-
ing from him—that is, if he keep his word. It is in line with
this that Abraham underwent circumcision on the day that
he attained true knowledge.

In all cases where a man pledges himself by a binding
oath to perform any precept of the Law, he is not to free
himself therefrom even at the price of death. For this is
what Scripture means when it says, 'That which is gone
out of thy lips thou shalt observe', i.e., 'to make good'
[Deut. 23.23]. On the other hand, in all cases where a man
pledges himself by a binding oath to depart from the Law,
he is not to confirm it even at the price of death.

Now, concerning a woman's oath. Scripture says that it
is her husband's duty in certain cases to void her oath
[cf. Num. 30.14]. He is not to do so, however, if he does
not know whether it is one that ought to be made good or
voided. If it involves transgression of the Covenant, he is
to void it and not make it good. The same rule applies
also to her father.

Now, concerning the rules for free-will offerings. No one
is to vow for the altar anything acquired by violence; nor,
indeed, are the priests to accept from a layman anything
so acquired. No one is to offer polluted food for sacred
purposes. That is what Scripture means when it says, 'They
trap each man his neighbor in respect to the consecrated
thing' [Mic. 7.2]. . . . [*Five fragmentary lines.*]

Our God and God of our fathers,

bless us with the threefold blessing in the Law,
written by the hand of Thy servant Moses,
spoken by the mouth of Aaron and his sons,
the priests, Thy holy people:

'The Lord bless thee, and keep thee;
The Lord make His face to shine upon thee
and be gracious unto thee;
The Lord lift up His countenance upon thee,
and give thee peace'.

Ancient Jewish Prayer; based on NUM. 6.24–26

A Formulary of Blessings

A. For blessing laymen

Form of blessing (greeting) to be used by the
'enlightened' in blessing (greeting) those who
fear [God, do] His will, keep His commandments, hold fast to His holy Covenant and
walk blamelessly [in all the ways of] His truth
—that is, such men as He has chosen to be
partners in an eternal Covenant [which shall]
stand for ever.

THE LORD BLESS THEE [from His holy habitation] and
open for thee from heaven the perpetual spring un[fail-
ing].[1]

[   ] in/at thy hand, and FAVOR THEE with all
manner of blessing, and make thee [privy] to that knowledge which is possessed by the Holy Beings.[2]

[Verily, with Him is] a perpetual spring, and He
[withholds] not [living waters from] such as thirst (for
them). So mayest thou too [drink therefrom].[3]

[THE LORD KEEP THEE from all evil and] deliver thee
from all [domination by Belial],[4] and may the frenzy
thereof be (destroyed) without re[mnant].

[THE LORD KEEP THEE and deliver thee] from every
satanic spirit* [and from every corrupting spirit].[5]

* Heb. 'satan', i.e., adversary.

[There follow three broken lines, in two of which there is specific mention of 'holiness' (or of something holy) and the third of which refers to 'holy teaching.'

This is followed in turn by three more broken lines, the first and last of which contain specific reference to 'eternity' (or to something eternal), and the second of which alludes to 'all appointed times'.]

THE LORD KEEP [unto thee the covenant sworn to] thy fathers.[6]

[There follow five broken lines containing various elaborations of the formula, THE LORD LIFT UP HIS COUNTENANCE UNTO THEE.]

THE LORD FAVOR THEE with [His salvation] [   ] and cause thee to delight in peace [abounding].[7]

THE LORD FAVOR THEE also with [   ].

THE LORD FAVOR THEE with the holy spirit, with lovingkindness [   ].

THE LORD FAVOR THEE also with [His] eternal covenant and [   ] thee [   ].

THE LORD FAVOR THEE by visiting upon thee just judgment, [that] thy [foot may not] stumble [upon thy way].[8]

THE LORD FAVOR THEE also in all thy works [and in all that] thy [hand undertaketh] and in all the [   ].[9]

[THE LORD FAVOR THEE also with insight into] eternal truth.

[THE LORD GIVE PEACE unto thee and] unto all thine offspring [   ].

B. For blessing the high priest

[Introductory words missing.]

THE LORD LIFT UP HIS COUNTENANCE UNTO THEE and [accept] the sweet savor of [thy sacrifices][10] and choose as His own all them that abide in [thy] priestly care, and take note of all thy sacred acts[11] and be pleased with all thy seas[onal offices,[12] and increase] thy seed.

THE LORD LIFT UP HIS COUNTENANCE unto all thy congregation.

THE LORD LIFT UP upon thy head [a crown of honor],[13] and may thy [   ] [abide] in glory [eternal], and may He hallow thy seed with glory everlasting.

THE LORD LIFT UP [HIS COUNTENANCE UNTO THEE] and grant thee grace [and peace everlast]ing, and [an inheritance in] the kingdom of [heaven].[14]

[THE LORD LIFT UP thy soul and raise thy spirit] out of the flesh[15] and [set it] amid the holy angels.[16]

[THE LORD LIFT UP His banner[17] and] do battle for thee [at the head of] thy thousands [against this] iniquitous generation.

[*Three fragmentary lines.*]

[THE LORD LIFT UP His sword for thee][18] to humble many peoples before thee [   ], and mayest thou not [rely] upon worldly wealth, to become estranged from the perpetual spring, [but find it when] thou seekest it.

Verily, God stayeth the foundations of the earth. [So may He stay thy steps.]

[Verily, He stablisheth the world upon its basis. So] may He stablish thy wellbeing[19] for ever.

C. For blessing the priests

Formula of blessing to be used by the 'enlightened' in blessing the sons of Zadok—that is, the priests whom God has chosen to keep His covenant firm for ever, to act as the testers of all matters involving the performance of His rules among His people and to teach them according to that which He hath commanded, to the end that they may confirm His covenant in truth and supervise correctly [the performance] of all His ordinances and walk in the way which He hath chosen:

THE LORD BLESS THEE from His holy habitation and set thee crowned in majesty[20] in the midst of the Holy Beings, and renew unto thee the covenant of priesthood everlasting, and give thee place in the holy habitation.[21]

By thine offices may all princes be judged, and all the [lords] of the peoples by thine unstained lips.

May He give thee as thine inheritance the firstfruits of all delights,[22] and at thy hand may He bless all mortal designs.

May He be pleased with [all] the steps of thy feet, and make thee acceptable in the eyes of men and of the Holy Beings.

May He apportion unto thee[23] [   ] and mayest thou immerse thyself therein. And all mortal [   ] and delights [   ].

May He set eternal blessings as a crown upon thy head, and fill thine hands with holiness and [   ].

[*Line missing.*]

May He cause thee to do rightly in all thy ministrations. For thee hath He chosen [to perform the office] and to carry out the charge at the head of them that be sacred, and to give His blessing unto thy people, and thee [hath He appointed] that the men of the company of God may be [rendered pure?] at thy hand and not at the hand of any monarch or [potentate; and with thee He speaketh] as a man unto his neighbor; and thou art as a ministering angel in the holy habitation. [Mayest thou serve ever] unto the glory of the God of Hosts, and mayest thou be about Him as one that ministereth in a royal palace. And mayest thou share the lot of the ministering angels* and be one in the company of [the Holy Beings] for all time and for all the epochs of eternity. [For He hath entrusted thee with] His judgments, and hath made thee an holy thing among His people, to be as a light [   ] to [illumine] the world with knowledge and to enlighten the faces of men far and wide.

May He set upon thine head a diadem to proclaim thee holy of holies,[24] for [it is thou that evincest His] holiness and showest forth the glory of His name.

And may His Holy Beings [wait upon thee].

* Heb. 'angel(s) of the Presence'.

D. For blessing the king

[Introductory words missing.]

Thou hast been set apart from [all other men] [   ] them that see thee [   ].

May He renew unto thee [   ].

[Line missing.]

[   ] who hath commissioned thee [   ] for all time and for all the seasons of eternity. And may He not gi[ve] thy glory [unto another].

May God [set] the fear of thee upon all that hear tell of thee, and be thy majesty [upon all that] [   ].

E. For blessing the president of the community

Formula of blessing to be used by the 'en-lightened' in blessing (greeting) the president of the community—that is, the man whom God hath chosen to represent His power and through whom He renews the covenant con-tracted with the community, to the end that He may maintain the sovereignty of His people for ever, and [whom He has appointed to judge the needy in righteousness] and to re-prove in equi[ty the me]ek of the earth,[25] and to walk blamelessly in all the ways of [His truth], and to confirm His holy covenant when distress befalls them that seek Him:

THE LORD LIFT thee up unto the summit of the world, like a strong tower on a lofty wall.[26]

Mayest thou [smite nations] with the vehemence of thy mouth. With thy rod mayest thou dry up the [fountain-heads] of the earth, and with the breath of thy lips mayest thou slay the wicked.[27]

[THE LORD FAVOR THEE with a spirit of sound counsel] and with perpetual strength and with a spirit of knowl-edge and with the fear of God.[28]

May righteousness be the girding [of thy loins and faith-fulness] that of thy thighs.[29]

May God make thy horns of iron and thy hoofs of brass;[30] and mayest thou gore the [iniquitous] like a steer [and trample nations] like mire in the streets.[31]

For God hath appointed thee to be the scourge of rulers.[32] They shall [come] before thee [and make obeisance unto thee, and all peoples] shall serve thee. By His holy Name may He give thee power that thou be as a lion [which raveneth and as a wolf which smi]teth the prey, with none to retrieve it. And may thy chargers ride abroad[33] over [all the broad places of the earth].

NOTES*

The Manual of Discipline

1. Jer. 3.17.

2. Cp. Num. 15.39; Ez. 6.9.

3. Luke 16.8; John 12.36; Eph. 5.8. Cp. also Luke 1.79; Rom. 2.19.

4. So too among the Essenes: Josephus, *War*, II, viii, 3; Philo, quoted by Eusebius, *Praep. Ev.*, viii, 11; Porphyry, *On Abstention from Animal Food*, p. 381 (ed. Leyden, 1620). Likewise among the early Christians: Lucian, *De morte Peregrini*, c.13.

5. Variant calculations of the calendar were a regular bone of contention among normative Jews and dissident sects, as also between Jews and Samaritans.

6. The word 'truth' is often used in the Scrolls in the specific sense of the Mosaic Law (*Torah*). So, too, the Samaritans commonly refer to it as 'the Verity' (*Qushtâ*).

7. Cp. Mishnah, *Berachoth*, V, 4.

8. Cp. *Jubilees*, 1.20; *Testament of Reuben*, ii; *of Levi*, iii; *of Zebulun*, ix; *of Naphtali*, ii; *of Benjamin*, vi. Cp. also *Didache*, xxi.3.

* The Dead Sea Scriptures are cited according to the columns and lines of the original texts. Old Testament references follow the numeration of the *Hebrew* text, which sometimes differs by a verse or two from the English version. Where the discrepancy is likely to be troublesome, the English numbering is indicated in parentheses.

9. 'Amen' (or 'Amen, amen') was the standard response to an oath: Num. 5.22; Deut. 27, *passim;* Mishnah, *Shebu'oth,* V, 2.

10. Ps. 106.6. This is the regular formula of confession on the Day of Atonement.

11. Cp. the development of this idea in Eph. 1.11; Rom. 8.17; Gal. 3.29, etc., and cp. G. Dalman, *The Words of Jesus* (1902), pp. 125ff.

12. An expansion of the Priestly Benediction, Num. 6.22–27.

13. Cp. Mat. 18.9; Mark 9.43; Dalman, *Words,* p. 161.

14. The Hebrew is obscure, and various interpretations have been proposed.

15. By a scribal error, the word for 'every one that hath come' has been transferred in the original text to follow 'enter' rather than 'cursed be'.

16. Ez. 7.19; 14.3, 7.

17. Deut. 29.19. The same passage is quoted in the same sense in the Syriac *Teachings of the Apostles,* ii 23.

18. The Heb. term *gillulim,* commonly rendered 'idols', was understood by early Jewish commentators on the Bible to mean 'filthiness'. Our author evidently had the same tradition.

19. This was the regular order of precedence among Jews; cp. Mishnah, *Horayoth,* III, 8.

20. The Brotherhood regarded itself as part of the ideal, sempiternal congregation of God—the Church Invisible.

21. Cp. II Corinthians 5.1.

22. This is one of the most puzzling phrases in the entire document, and the translation is therefore uncertain. The Hebrew says: 'in the *se'ôn* of wickedness is his plowing'. The word *se'ôn* occurs only in Isa. 9.4 (5), where it means 'sandal, boot'—a meaning which does not fit here. The medieval Jewish commentators, however, tended to equate it with the like-sounding Aramaic *seyan,* 'mud', and it is in this sense, I suggest, that our author likewise understood it. Furthermore, the

notion of 'plowing wickedness' was clearly influenced by the occurrence of a similar expression in Hos. 10.13.

23. Cp. Mat. 3.11; Mark 1.8; Luke 3.16; John 1.33; Acts 1.5, etc.

24. The Hebrew word is that rendered 'teachers' in Dan. 11.33, 35; 12.3, 10. The FORMULARY OF BLESSINGS bears the same heading. Both texts were probably designed as 'assists' for the teachers of the Brotherhood, this one being a kind of sermon—possibly delivered as an exposition of the Scriptural Lesson, Deut. 30.15ff.: 'See, I have set before thee this day life and good, and death and evil', etc.

25. Cp. I Sam. 2.3.

26. Cp. Didache; Testament of Levi, 5.30; Mat. 7.13f.; Barnabas, xiv.3ff. The same doctrine occurs in the pseudepigraphic Testament of Asher, 1.3–9, and in the Testament of Judah, 20.1. It developed into the Jewish concept of the yezer tob (good inclination) and yezer ra' (evil inclination) in every man. On the background of the concept, see A. Dupont-Sommer, The Jewish Sect of Qumran and the Essenes (1954), pp. 118–30.

27. Mentioned again in the Zadokite Document, V.18. Possibly, this is the real meaning of II Cor. 11.14, 'Satan himself is transformed into an angel of light', i.e., Satan disguises himself as the Angel of Light and then misleads.

28. In Testament of Levi, xix and in Testament of Joseph, vii, xx, Belial is called 'the spirit of darkness'.

29. The term used in the Hebrew (viz. mastemah) is related to the word 'Satan'. It is personified in Jubilees 11.5; 17.16; 18.9.

30. The angel in question is probably Gabriel, for not only is Gabriel the revealer of God's truth—he revealed the basic Koran to Mohammed—but he is also the champion of the faithful in the final battle against the powers of darkness; cp. War of the Sons of Light, etc.

31. Josephus (War, II, viii, 7) says that the Essenes were sworn not to divulge their doctrines to outsiders.

32. The text reads: 'These are the foundations of the spirit for the children of the truth of the world'. It is obvious that the scribe has erroneously altered the true order of the words; see above, n. 15.

33. Cp. I Peter 5.4. The Mandaeans attach great importance to the 'lustrous crown' (*Kelilâ de-zivâ*).

34. Cp. Rev. 6.11; 7.9. 'All God's chillun got robes'.

35. Cp. the lists of vices in Gal. 5.19ff.; Rom. 1.29ff.; I Cor. 6. 9ff.; Col. 3.5, 8. Rendel Harris (*Teaching of the Apostles* [1887], pp. 82ff.) derives these lists from the catalogue of sins recited in the confessions on the Day of Atonement. Others claim that they were borrowed from the Stoics, and cite similar texts in A. Dieterich, *Nekyia*, pp. 163ff.

36. Cp. Jer. Talmud, Sheb., vi. 37a. Cp. also Slavonic Enoch, 53.3; 56.1.

37. Cp. Isa. 44.3; Joel 2.28–29; Acts 2.17; 10.45; Titus 3.5–6.

38. This idea was common in the Graeco-Roman world; see F. Cumont, *After Life in Roman Paganism* (1923), p. 121.

39. Cp. John 12.43.

40. Cp. Isa. 65.17, and especially Mat. 19.28. Cp. also Dalman, *Words*, pp. 177ff.; Cumont, *op. cit.*, p. 13.

41. See General Introduction, p. 4.

42. Evidently, non-Jewish proselytes are meant.

43. Josephus tells us (*War*, II, viii, 6) that the Essenes avoided taking oaths. The only exception was the oath of allegiance on being admitted to the Brotherhood. Jesus counselled his disciples in the same sense (Mat. 5.33–37). It is interesting to observe that this rule obtained also among the Waldensians.

44. I.e., the curses prescribed in Deut. 28–29, known in Jewish tradition as 'the Commination' (Heb. *tôchechah*). When the passage is read in the Synagogue, it is customary among the Ashkenazim (German-Polish Jews) to 'call to the Law' the humblest member of the congregation—usually, the beadle or

sexton. The Sephardim (Spanish-Portuguese Jews), however, insist that the rabbi (*haham*) must be 'called', to show that the Law is no respecter of persons!

45. This is not a protest against baptism, as has been supposed, but rather against the idea that the act of immersion can *by itself* absolve sins.

46. The Scriptural text refers specifically to *falsehood*.

47. The Scriptural text was evidently taken to mean 'whose spirit lies only in his breath', i.e. not in his 'soul'.

48. Philo (*Quod Omnis Probus Liber*, §13) commends the Essenes for their 'cheerfulness of temper'. So, too, Josephus (*War*, II, viii, 6) says that 'they are just dispensers of their anger, curbers of their passions . . . ministers of peace'.

49. The text says, 'the small is to obey the great'; but this evidently refers to rank, not age. However, Philo says of the Essenes that in synagogue the younger sat below the elder (*Quod Omnis Probus Liber*, §12).

50. So too among the Essenes: Philo, *loc. cit.*; Josephus, *War*, II, viii, 5.

51. Ten persons is the minimum required in Jewish law to form a congregation. So too, apparently, among the Essenes: Josephus, *War*, II, viii, 9.

52. So too among the Essenes: Josephus, *War*, II, viii, 5. In early Christian usage, the first act at an *agape* (lovefeast) was to bless the cup. The duty devolved on the bishop, if present; see Dom Conolly, *Didascalia Apostolorum* (1929), pp. lii,ff.

53. On such exposition, cf. Mishnah, *Yôma*, vii, 6; I Cor. 14.28. The *Didascalia Apostolorum* prescribes that the bishop is to be the 'interpreter'.

54. For the conjunction of 'studying' and 'worshipping' (lit. 'blessing'), cp. Mishnah, *Yôma*, VII, 7.

55. Josephus (*War*, II, viii, 5) says of the Essenes that 'no noise or uproar ever desecrates their house. Rather do

they let everyone take part in the conversation in turn'.

56. Josephus (*War*, II, viii, 9) says of the Essenes that 'when ten of them [i.e., the minimal quorum] sit together, no one will speak if the other nine do not agree to it'.

57. The Hebrew word is the exact equivalent of the Greek *episkopos*, 'bishop'. We thus see the original form of this office, which later assumed sacerdotal functions. Comparable also is the 'steward' or 'overseer' of the Essenes, mentioned by Philo (in Eusebius, *Praep. Ev.*, viii, 11) and Josephus (*War*, II, viii, 3).

58. Josephus (*War*, II, viii, 10) mentions four categories among the Essenes, and tells us also (*ib.*, 7), that a postulant was not admitted to 'the holier water of purification' until after a year's probation. The 'common or general purity' (literally, 'the purity of the many') was evidently the lowest degree. The system was a special development of the four degrees of purity recognized in Jewish law and specified in the Babylonian Talmud, *Hagigah* 18b.

59. So too among the Essenes, according to Josephus (*loc. cit.*).

60. The *Didascalia* (54.26) likewise excludes initiants from the common meal. So too among the Essenes (Josephus, *loc. cit.*).

61. Josephus (*loc. cit.*) says that those who wished to join the Essenes had to spend a trial year 'outside' and two full years (in varied degrees of probation) 'inside' before they were eligible for admission. There is no real discrepancy between his statement and our author's, for the latter starts, as it were, from the moment the postulant has entered 'within'.

62. Deut. 28.58. Cp. James 2.7.

63. For the terms employed in the Hebrew, cp. Mishnah, *Yôma*, vii, 7. For the office involved, cp. Mishnah, *Berachôth*, V, 5; *Rôsh Ha-Shanah*, IV, 9.

64. The point is that the left hand is used in the Near East for all unclean purposes.

65. According to Josephus (*War*, II, viii, 8), expulsion was the penalty among the Essenes for heinous offenses.

66. This recalls the three 'pillars' of the Church (Gal. 2.9f.) and the Twelve Apostles. Cp. *Didascalia* 45.23; Ignatius, *Trall.*, 2.2f.; *Magnes.*, 6.1; *Philad.*, 5.1.

67. Cp. Isa. 65.9; Ps. 105.43; II John 1; I Peter 2.9; Rev. 17.14, etc. The Mandaeans likewise call themselves 'the elect' (Lidzbarski, *Mandäische Liturgien*, pp. 75, 106f.; id., *Johannesbuch*, ii, pp. 69, 102, 221). So too the Manichaeans styled themselves (*vičidagan*).

68. Quoted in the same sense in I Peter 2.6.

69. Philo tells us (*Quod Omnis Probus Liber*, §12) that when the Scriptures were read publicly among the Essenes, on the sabbath, the 'expert' who expounded them 'passed over that which is not generally known,' i.e., within the grasp of the rank and file.

70. The same quotation is used in the same sense by John the Baptist; Mat. 3.3; John 1.23.

71. Literally, 'the Messiahs (i.e., anointed) of Aaron and Israel'. See General Introduction, p. 5.

72. The expression derives from Deut. 32.35, according to the text found in the Samaritan Recension, the Greek (Septuagint) Version, and a fragment discovered at Qumran itself. It recurs at Isa. 34.8, 61.2, and 63.4, and is the standard term for Doomsday among the Samaritans.

The Zadokite Document

1. Based on Ezekiel 4.5, 'For I have appointed the years of their iniquity to be unto thee a number of days, even three hundred and ninety days'. It is perhaps worthy of note that in the 'Chain of High Priests' supplied by the Samaritans to Rev. John Mills and published by him in his *The Modern Samaritans* (1864),

pp. 333f., 'the kingdom of Nebuchadnezzar' is said
to have lasted 390 years, viz. from 3488 until 3877
A.M. This must represent an independent tradition,
for the Samaritans do not accept any Scripture other
than the Five Books of Moses.

2. As Isaac Rabinowitz has pointed out (*Journal of Biblical Literature*, 73 [1954], 11), the reference is to the
events narrated in Nehemiah 1.1ff., 'Now it came to
pass in the twentieth year [after the restoration from
the Babylonian Captivity]'. I should prefer, however,
to see in the 'right-teacher' Ezra rather than Nehemiah.
First, as explained in the Introduction, it seems to me
that the 'right-teacher' was in all epochs necessarily a
priest—and that Ezra was. Second, it was indeed Ezra
who expounded the Law (Neh. 8.2ff.).

3. Here we have the term usually rendered 'Teacher of
Righteousness'.

4. The reference is obscure. Possibly it is to Sanballat
(Neh. 4.1ff.), though it is not recorded that he and
his followers were annihilated. However, our text may
be a general polemic against the Samaritans.

5. An ancient Jewish morning-prayer, ascribed by some
to the Essenes, speaks of 'Knowledge and Discernment' as encompassing God like attendants.

6. Common figures of rabbinic lore; cf. also Enoch 56.1.

7. I.e., the anointed priests, custodians and teachers of
the Law, which is here called 'the Truth', as regularly
among the Samaritans and Mandaeans.

8. The reference is to the widespread post-Biblical legend
of the rebel angels (headed by 'Lucifer') who were
cast out of heaven. The legend is fully discussed in
B. Bamberger's excellent work, *Fallen Angels* (New
York, 1954). The name 'Watchers' is taken from Dan.
4.13, 17, 23.

9. The allusion is to Gen. 6.1–4. The Hebrew word usually rendered 'mighty men' was interpreted in antiquity
as 'giants'.

10. The reference is to the generation of the Flood. Compare especially Gen. 6.17.

11. Gen. 9.20–28.

12. Note that the same example is cited, with the same point, in James 2.23.

13. Ps. 106. 18.

14. Cp. Jer. 2.13; 17.13; *Odes of Solomon*, 6.7; 30.1–2.

15. The point depends on a play on words: the Hebrew for 'associate oneself' is *l-v-h*, which at once suggests Levi.

16. I.e., the prototypes of the 'men of special holiness' mentioned in the *Manual*.

17. The Hebrew word for 'boundary' also means 'statute', and is used especially of the statutes, or provisions, of the Covenant.

18. The source of this quotation is unknown. It does *not* occur in the pseudepigraphical *Testament of Levi*, as one might expect.

19. RV. 'Neither shall he multiply wives unto himself'.

20. Lev. 15.19.

21. Cp. II Tim. 3.8. For the legend in Jewish sources, cp. L. Ginzberg, *The Legends of the Jews*, vi, 144.

22. The Hebrew word for prince is *sar*. The point obviously depends upon some fanciful interpretation of this term, that now eludes us. Possibly it was connected on the one hand with the word *shur*, 'to look around for something', and on the other with a root appearing in the Assyro-Babylonian *shâru*, 'to belie, traduce'.

23. This passage has been taken to indicate that the Covenanters later betook themselves to Damascus, and it has been assumed that our present document emanates from that settlement. I agree entirely, however, with the view of I. Rabinowitz (*Journal of Biblical Literature*, 73 [1954], 11–35) that the language is purely figurative, being based on Amos 5.27. See Introduction, pp. 4, 24.

24. See *Manual*, vols. iii–iv.

25. Josephus tells us clearly that not all of the Essenes lived in the desert (*War*, II, viii, 4), and the present

document subsequently lays down rules for urban communities and for 'camps' respectively. Obviously, then, this literature did not emanate from, nor was it exclusive to, the particular group at Qumran.

26. Josephus tells us that while some Essenic groups discountenanced marriage, others did not (*War*, II, viii, 13). The Qumran group apparently fell in the latter category, for skeletons of women have been disinterred from its cemetery.

27. Comp. Zech. 6.8.

28. The text is defective, and it is therefore not quite clear how the author actually interpreted the Scriptural passage. C. Rabin makes the attractive suggestion that we should read: 'The King is the [prince of all the congregation; the image(s) are the instructors of the] congregation'. The point, he says, depends on a play on words, whereby the Hebrew *zelem*, 'image' is fancifully interpreted (by metathesis) as *meliz*, 'interpreter'. An alternative suggestion is, however, that the author was playing on the words of Deut. 33.4–5, 'Moses commanded us a law as an inheritance, O congregation of Jacob. And there was a King in Jeshurun, when the heads of the people were gathered, all the tribes of Israel together'.

29. Possibly, the writer was fancifully interpreting the word *Kiyyun* (really the name of the planet Saturn) as containing the initial letters of the Hebrew expression, *Kitbê Nebi'îm*, 'writings of the prophets'. An exactly parallel mode of interpretation appears in the Commentary on Habakkuk, xiii, 2 (on 2.20).

30. The writer is playing on the words of Ps. 73.20, 'Their image wilt Thou despise'.

31. See above, n. 23.

32. The pseudepigraphic *Testaments of Levi* (18.3) and *Judah* (24.1) likewise refer this to the Messiah. Rev. 22.16 refers it to Jesus.

33. The writer interprets the Hebrew word *sheth* of the Biblical quotation—really, the name of a nomadic people called the Shûtu—as equivalent to *se'eth*, 'pride'.

The same interpretation obtains among the Samaritans. Jeremiah (48.45) took the words somewhat similarly.

34. Ez. 13.10.

35. The writer manipulates the Biblical text to suit his purpose and does not quote it accurately.

36. Cp. Jer. 45.1, 4–5: The word that Jeremiah the prophet spoke unto Baruch, the son of Neriah . . . 'that which I have built will I break down, and that which I have planted will I pluck up; the same is the whole land . . . for, behold, I will bring evil on all flesh'.

37. Cp. II Kings 5.26–27, where Elisha curses Gehazi for disobedience.

38. The reference is to the future (prophetic) teacher who will precede the eventual restoration of the priesthood and sovereignty; see Introduction, pp. 5, 26.

39. See *Manual*, viii, 1–19.

40. This is *not* a 'New Testament' in the Christian sense. It refers simply to the future reaffirmation of the old covenant. See Introduction, p. 4.

41. Rabbinic tradition likewise assigns a period of forty years for the 'ministry' of the Messiah before the final restoration of Israel. The identity of the Man of Falsehood is unknown, and this is one of the major points of controversy among students of the Scrolls. I believe, however, that the reference is purely general, and refers to 'Belial' or 'Antichrist'—a regular figure of Jewish and Christian eschatology from about the second century B.C. onwards.

42. This idea recurs in the *Book of Hymns*, xvi, 10. Cp. also *Odes of Solomon*, 9.12.

43. Heb. 'the house of Peleg' (cf. Gen. 10.25)—a fanciful designation based on the fact that the Hebrew word *p-l-g* means 'divide'. The reference is to men who were originally schismatics but joined up with the faithful in the hour of crisis, without offering long-winded explanations.

44. See *Manual*, vi, 8–13.

45. I adopt the interpretation of C. Rabin (*The Zadokite*

Documents [1954], p. 54, n.8), who reminds us that the Sanhedrin likewise handed over to the gentiles persons condemned to death.

46. Not in the Bible.

47. Cf. Mishnah, *Makkôth*, I.7.

48. This may also mean: no man who has not yet reached the age when he is eligible for enrollment in the Brotherhood, i.e., no one under twenty; cf. xv,6.

49. Cf. Mishnah, *Sanhedrin*, I.3, which implies a court of ten.

50. Heb. 'Book of Hagu', which has been the subject of considerable speculation. The fact is, however, that the word *hagu* actually occurs in the *Hymns* (xi, 2, 21) in the sense of 'meditation', and the cognate word denotes 'study' in late Hebrew. There is thus no difficulty about the term.

51. The meaning is uncertain. The Hebrew word is *marʿil*, which I connect with the root *rʿl*, 'quiver, shake, be agitated'.

52. I.e., the emphasis is on the word 'day', which was reckoned from sunset to sunset. The moment indicated would thus imply the imminence of the sabbath day, Friday's sun being now about to set.

53. For the regular Jewish rule (2000 cubits), see Mishnah, *Sotah*, V.3.

54. The text seems to say: 'If a human being falls into a place of water or into a place of . . . let no man bring him up by a ladder or a rope or by any other implement'. But this would be against the universal Jewish rule that sabbath laws may be broken in cases of life and death. Hence some scholars have assumed that a word has dropped out by haplography and read: 'If a human being fall . . . whence he cannot come up, one is to bring him up by means of a ladder', etc. But this involves bad grammar. I therefore adopt R. Leszinsky's emendation (*afel* for *al*); cf. Babylonian Talmud, *Yôma*, 84b.

55. The Scripture says, 'apart from your Sabbath offering';

but our author took the word rendered 'apart from' as an adverb meaning 'exclusively'.

56. I.e., accepted Judaism. Cf. Bab. Talmud, *Yebamot*, 48b. The expression is a trifle odd, because it refers properly to circumcision.

57. Ritual slaughtering of fish is discussed in Bab. Talmud, *Ḥullin*, 27b.

58. I.e., in order to avoid the curses specified in Deut. 28–29.

59. See Introduction, pp. 5, 26.

60. See *Manual of Discipline*, note 51.

61. Num. 27.21. The *Didache* likewise provides for a junior substitute, if the bishop is incapacitated or incompetent.

62. Lev. 13.2ff. Cf. Mishnah, *Negaʿim*, III, 1.

63. Cf. *Manual of Discipline*, note 57.

64. So too in the *Apostolic Constitutions*, ii, 6, 7, in defining the duties of a bishop ('pastor').

65. Literally, 'In all communion with men and in every language according to their several families'. This scarcely means that he is to be a polyglot, but simply —as we should say—that he is to be adept at 'talking the other fellow's language'.

66. Swearing by AD . . . and by YH (the initial letters of YHVH, the Ineffable Name of God) is mentioned in Mishnah, *Shebuʿoth*, IV, 13.

66a. Blasphemy was punishable by death: Lev. 24.10–23. Cf. Mishnah, *Sanhedrin*, VII, 5.

67. The quotation is not from the Bible.

68. I.e., the Book of Jubilees.

69. Heb. *Mastemah*, mentioned again in Jubilees 11.5; 17.16; 18.9. Cf. *Manual of Discipline*, note 29.

A Formulary of Blessings

1. Based on Deut. 28.12. The same passage is quoted in connection with the Priestly Benediction in *Sifrê*, §43.

2. Cp. *Sifrê*, §41.

3. Based on Ps. 36.9, 'For with Thee is the wellspring of life; in Thy light do we see light'. The passage naturally came to mind in connection with the Priestly Benediction's 'May He cause His face to *shine upon* (literally, *give light to*) thee'. Cp. also Jer 2.13; 17.13.

4. Cp. *Manual of Discipline,* col. iii.

5. Cp. the Palestinian Targum's paraphrase of Num. 6.24: 'The Lord . . . keep thee from liliths and things that cause terror and from demons of noonday (cf. Ps. 91.5–6) and of morning, and from malign spirits and phantoms' (tr. Etheridge). Similarly, *Sifrê*, §40.

6. Based on Deut. 7.12, the passage being suggested by the expression 'and *keep* thee' in the Priestly Benediction. Similarly, *Sifrê*, §40.

7. Suggested by the expression, 'and give thee *peace*'. Cp. *Sifrê*, §42: 'Rabbi Eleazar ha-Kappar (2nd cent.) saith, Great is peace, for every blessing is sealed with it, as it is said, The Lord bless thee . . . and grant thee peace'.

8. Based on I Sam. 2.9, 'He *keepeth* the feet of His devoted servants'. Similarly, *Sifrê*, §40.

9. Cp. Deut. 28.8.

10. Cp. Lev. 26.31. This shows clearly that the passage is addressed to a *priest*.

11. I.e., the sacred offerings of the priests.

12. Cp. Neh. 10.34.

13. A reference to the crown of the high priest; cp. Ex. 29.6; Lev. 8.9.

14. Perhaps suggested by reference to the *crown*.

15. Cp. *Hymns*, iii, 20; xi, 12; xviii, 28–29. This suggests at once a play on the words 'lift up'.

16. A play on the fact that the high priest officiates on earth in the midst of 'holy ones', i.e., the other priests.

17. The allusion to leading troops into battle suggests yet another play on the expression 'lift up', viz. *lift up a banner;* cp. Isa. 5.26; 11.12; 18.3; Jer. 4.6; 50.2, etc.

18. The restoration is based on the assumption that there is once again a play on the expression 'lift up'—this time in the sense of *lift up a sword;* cp. Isa. 2.4; Mic. 4.3. Cf. also Deut. 9.3; Ps. 81.15; I Chron. 17.10.

19. Or, 'thy peace'.

20. Cp. Ez. 16.14.

21. Service in the earthly sanctuary is to be but a prelude to similar office in the heavenly sanctuary. The latter, in which the angel Michael officiates as high priest, is mentioned in Talmud, *Hagigah*, 12b.

22. A reference to the fact that the priest received the first-fruits or the prime part of certain offerings; cp. Num. 18.12; Deut. 18.4; Ez. 44.30.

23. A reference to the priestly 'portion' of offerings; cp. Lev. 7.33; II Chron. 31.4.

24. A reference to the priestly diadem; cp. Ex. 29.6; 39.30; Lev. 8.9.

25. Cp. Isa. 11.4.

26. Cp. Isa. 30.13.

27. Cp. Isa. 11.4.

28. Cp. Isa. 11.2.

29. Cp. Isa. 11.5.

30. Cp. Mic. 4.13.

31. Cp. Mic. 7.10; Zech. 9.3; 10.5; Ps. 18.43, etc.

32. Cp. Isa. 14.5.

33. The word rendered 'chargers' is used in *The War of the Sons of Light and the Sons of Darkness* to denote 'light-armed troops' (the Roman *velites*). The suggestion is, therefore: 'May thy troops spread far and wide'.

THE PRAISE
OF GOD

Hymns and Psalms

My soul thirsteth for Thee; my flesh longeth for Thee, in a dry and weary land, where no water is.

PSALM 63.1

INTRODUCTION The chanting of psalms was one of the basic elements of worship in the Second Temple, and continued as a main feature of public devotions in the synagogue and church. In course of time, however, the Biblical repertoire was supplemented by more 'modern' compositions in the same style.

The Brotherhood possessed its own *Book of Hymns* written in this vein. It is contained in one of the scrolls discovered by the Bedouin boys in 1947 and extends to eighteen columns plus a large number of fragments too disjointed to translate. The end of each hymn was marked carefully by a blank space, but since the lower portion of each column has been eaten away, this indication must often have occurred in places where it is no longer evident. Hence, we cannot tell how many compositions even the main portion of the scroll originally contained, nor is it always possible to distinguish any one of them from the next. This is especially the case in the latter part of the manuscript, where the best that can be done in a translation is simply to indicate where a new column begins.

In cases where their beginnings can still be recognized, the hymns often open with the words, 'I give thanks unto Thee, O Lord'. For this reason they have come to be known as the *Psalms* (or *Hymns*) *of Thanksgiving*—a title which is all the more appropriate when it is remembered that in the early synagogue and church, 'thanksgiving' was a technical term for a clearly defined type of liturgical composition. Some of the pieces, however, begin with the alternative formula, 'Blessed art Thou', and this is equally significant in view of the fact that 'blessing' seems likewise to have denoted in antiquity not only a formula of benediction but also a specific type of hymn. Accordingly, the joint title, *Blessings and Thanksgivings* (Hebrew, *Berachôth we-Hodayôth*) would appear to be the most adequate.

The hymns represent the most original literary creation in the Dead Sea Scriptures. It is true that they are, in the main, mosaics of Biblical quotations and that they often exhibit all the learned and tortured exploitation of Scripture that we find later in the medieval poetasters (*payyetanim*) of the synagogue. This, however, is merely the trammel of literary convention, and it should no more dull our ears to the underlying passion and authenticity of feeling than do the mannered conceits of a Donne or a Herbert or a Vaughan.

Especially noteworthy is the prevalence in these hymns of the vocabulary which Evelyn Underhill and others have recognized as the standard and characteristic idiom of mystical experience. There is the same harping on the wilderness of isolation; the same reference to the 'ascent' to God and to 'the height of eternal things'; the same metaphor (particularly in Hymn No. 5) of the New Birth and the 'travail of the world'; the same intensive apprehension of Divine providence, communion and 'enlightenment'; and the same sense of nursing a precious secret against the day of revelation. Apprehension of these notes is of the essence in understanding the spirit of the hymns in particular and of the Brotherhood in general.

It has been suggested that some of the hymns, which speak of deliverance from froward assailants ('the company of Belial' or 'the men of corruption'), were designed for the use of soldiers who had escaped their adversaries or defeated them. To the present writer, such a view seems singularly and unperceptively overliteral; it confuses the 'slings and arrows of outrageous fortune' with concrete bazookas and guided missiles. Similarly, there seems no good reason for assuming, as has been done, that Hymn No. 8 must necessarily have been written by 'the teacher of Righteousness' simply because it speaks of one who sought to impart God's law to his brethren but was constantly thwarted and abused by 'preachers of lies' and 'prophets of deceit'. What the text is describing is the normal and typical frustration of the mystic—the experience of *every* man who believes that he has seen God and that he is burning a small candle in the darkness of a world unredeemed.

To the main body of hymns we have here prefixed another, which the ancient librarians of Qumran attached to a copy of the *Manual of Discipline*. If one reads it carefully, one will find that it repeats almost verbatim the list of obligations and the basic oath of allegiance laid down in that document for new members of the Brotherhood. It may therefore be regarded as a hymn chanted by initiants when they were formally received into the community; and this would in turn explain why the ancient librarians considered it an appropriate liturgical 'appendix' to the *Manual*. On this hypothesis we have called it *The Hymn of the Initiants*. The Scrolls themselves, it may be added, bear no titles; those assigned by modern scholars are therefore in any case quite arbitrary.

The Hymn of the Initiants

[*Manual of Discipline*, cols. x–xi]

[Day and night will I offer my praise]
and at all the appointed times which God has prescribed.

When daylight begins its rule,
   when it reaches its turning-point,[1]
   and when it again withdraws to its appointed abode;

When the watches of darkness begin,
   when God opens the storehouse thereof,[2]
   when He sets that darkness against the light,[3]
   when it reaches its turning-point,[4]
   and when it again withdraws in face of the light;

When sun and moon shine forth from the holy Height,
and when they again withdraw to the glorious Abode;[5]

When the formal seasons come on the days of new moon,[6]
   when they reach their turning-points,[7]
   and when they yield place to one another,
   as each comes round anew;*

When the natural seasons come, at whatever time may be;
when, too, the months begin;
   on their feasts and on holy days,
   as they come in order due,
   each as a memorial in its season[8]—

---

* The text includes a series of esoteric glosses which have been
omitted from the translation.

I shall hold it as one of the laws
engraven of old on the tablets[9]
to render to God as my tribute
  —the blessings of my lips.[10]

When the (natural) years begin;
  at the turning-points of their seasons,
  and when each completes its term
  on its natural day,
  yielding each to each—
  reaping-time to summer,
  sowing-time to verdure;

In the (formal) years of weeks,
  in the several seasons thereof,
  and when, at the jubilee,
  the series of weeks begins[11]—

I shall hold it as one of the laws
engraven of old on the tablets
to offer to God as my fruits—
  the praises of my tongue,
and to cull for Him as my tithe
  —the skilled music of my lips.[12]

With the coming of day and night
  I shall come ever anew
  into God's covenant;
and when evening and morning depart,
  shall observe how He sets their bounds.[13]

Only where God sets bounds
  —the unchangeable bounds of His Law—
will I too set my domain.[14]

I shall hold it as one of the laws
engraven of old on the tablets
to face my sin and transgression
and avouch the justice of God.

I shall say unto God:
'Thou, for me, art the Right!'
and unto the Most High:
'For me Thou art cause of all good!'

Fountain of all knowledge,
Spring of holiness,
Zenith of all glory,
Might omnipotent,
Beauty that never fades,
   I will choose the path He shows me,
   and be content with His judgments.

Whenever I first put forth my hand or foot,
I will bless His name;[15]
when first I go or come,
when I sit and when I rise,[16]
when I lie down on my couch,
I will sing unto Him.
   At the common board,
or ever I raise my hand
to enjoy the rich fruits of the earth,
with that which flows from my lips
   I will bless Him as with an oblation.[17]

At the onset of fear and alarm,
or when trouble and stress are at hand,
I will bless him with special thanksgiving
and muse upon His power,
and rely on His mercies alway,
and come thereby to know
that in His hand lies the judgment of all living,
and that all His works are truth.[18]

Whenever distress breaks out,
   I still will praise Him;
and when His salvation comes,
   join the chorus of praise.[19]

I will heap no evil on any,
but pursue all men with good,[20]
knowing that only with God
lies the judgment of all living,
and He it is will award
each man his deserts.

I will not be envious
of the profit of wickedness;
    for wealth unrighteously gotten my soul shall not lust.[21]

I will not engage in strife
with reprobate men,[22]
    forestalling the Day of Requital.[23]

I will not turn back my wrath
from froward men,
    nor rest content until justice be affirmed.

I will harbor no angry grudge
against those that indeed repent,[24]
but neither will I show compassion
    to any that turn from the way.

I will not console the smitten
until they amend their course.

I will cherish no baseness in my heart,
nor shall there be heard in my mouth
coarseness[25] or wanton deceit;
neither shall there be found upon my lips
    deception and lies.[26]
The fruit of holiness shall be on my tongue,
and no heathen filth be found thereon.
    I will open my mouth with thanksgiving,
and my tongue shall ever relate
the bounteousness of God
and the perfidy of men
until men's transgressions be ended.

Empty words will I banish from my lips;
filth and perverseness from my mind.

I will shelter knowledge with sound counsel,
and protect [it] with shrewdness of mind.

I will [set] a sober limit
to all defending of faith
and exacting of justice by force.
  I will bound God's righteousness
by the measuring-line of occasion.
  [I will temper] justice [with mercy],
will show kindness to men downtrodden,
bring firmness to fearful hearts,
discernment to spirits that stray,
enlighten the bowed with sound doctrine,
reply to the proud with meekness,
with humility answer the base
—men rich in worldly goods,
who point the finger of scorn
and utter iniquitous thoughts.

To God I commit my cause.
It is His to perfect my way,
His to make straight my heart.
He, in His charity,
  will wipe away my transgression.

For He from the Wellspring of Knowledge
has made His light to burst forth,
and mine eye has gazed on His wonders;
and the light that is in my heart
has pierced the deep things of existence.

  He is ever the stay of my right hand.[27]
The path beneath my feet
is set on a mighty rock[28]
unshaken before all things.

For that rock beneath my feet
is the truth of God,
and His power is the stay of my right hand;
from the fount of His charity
my vindication goes forth.

Through His mysterious wonder
light is come into my heart;
mine eye has set its gaze
on everlasting things.
A virtue hidden from man,
a knowledge and subtle lore
concealed from human kind;
a fount of righteousness,
a reservoir of strength,
a wellspring of all glory
wherewith no flesh has converse—
these has God bestowed
on them that He has chosen,
to possess them for ever.
He has given them an inheritance
in the lot of the Holy Beings,
and joined them in communion with the Sons of Heaven,[29]
to form one congregation,
one single communion,
a fabric of holiness,
a plant evergreen,[30]
    for all time to come.

But I— I belong to wicked mankind,
to the communion of sinful flesh.
    My transgressions, my iniquities and sins,
and the waywardness of my heart
condemn me to communion with the worm
and with all that walk in darkness.
    For a mortal's way is [not] of himself,
neither can a man direct his own steps.
The judgment lies with God,
and 'tis His to perfect man's way.

Only through His knowledge
have all things come to be,
and all that is, is ordained by His thought;
and apart from Him is nothing wrought.[31]

Behold, if I should totter,
God's mercies will be my salvation.
If I stumble in the error of the flesh,
I shall be set aright
through God's righteousness ever-enduring.
If distress break out,
He will snatch my soul from perdition,
and set my foot on the path.
    For He, in His compassion,
has drawn me near unto Him,[32]
and His judgment upon me shall be rendered in His mercy.
    In his bounteous truth He has judged me,
and in His abundant goodness
will shrive my iniquities,
and in His righteousness cleanse me
from all the pollution of man
and the sin of human kind,
that I may acknowledge unto God His righteousness,
and unto the Most High His majestic splendor.

    Blessed art Thou, O my God,
Who hast opened the heart of Thy servant unto knowledge.
Direct all his works in righteousness,
and vouchsafe unto the son of Thine handmaid
the favor which Thou hast assured to all the mortal elect,
to stand in Thy presence for ever.
    For apart from Thee no man's way can be perfect,
and without Thy will is nothing wrought.

Thou it is that hath taught all knowledge,
and all things exist by Thy will;
and there is none beside Thee
to controvert Thy plan;
none to understand all Thy holy thought,

none to gaze into the depths of Thy secrets,
none to perceive all Thy wonders and the might of Thy
    power.

Who can compass the sum of Thy glory?
And what is mere mortal man
amid Thy wondrous works?
And what the child of woman
to sit in Thy presence?
For, behold, he is kneaded of dust,
and his [   ] is the food of worms.
He is but a molded shape,[33]
a thing nipped out of the clay,[34]
whose attachment is but to the dust.
    What can such clay reply,
      or that which is molded by hand?
    What thought can it comprehend?

The Book of Hymns

or

Psalms of Thanksgiving

[Thou art the source of all might]
and the wellspring of all power;
[yet art Thou also rich in wisdom]
[and] great in counsel.²
    Thy fury [is vented] in the presence of [   ];
[yet are Thy mercies] beyond number.
    [Thou are a God that visits wrongdoing;]
[yet also a God] longsuffering in judgment.³
    In whatsoever Thou doest,
    Thou hast ever done justly.

    In Thy wisdom didst [Thou call into being]
[spirits] immortal,
and ere Thou didst create them,
didst determine their works for all time.
    [Apart from Thee] can naught be done,
    and naught apprehended save by Thy will.⁴
Thou it is formed every spirit,
[and set due rule] and role for all their works.

    When Thou didst stretch out the heavens for Thy glory,
and [command] all [their host] to do Thy will,⁵

Thou didst also make potent spirits
to keep them in bounds.

Or ever spirits immortal
took on the form of ho[ly] angels,[6]
Thou didst assign them to bear rule
over divers domains:
over the sun and moon,
to govern their hidden powers;
over the stars,
to hold them to their courses;
over [rain and snow,]
to make them fulfill their functions;
over meteors and lightnings,
to make them discharge their tasks;[8]
over the treasures of the deeps,[9]
to make them serve their ends;
[over fire and water,]
to control their hidden force.

When, too, Thou didst create in Thy power
earth and seas and deeps,
in Thy wisdom didst Thou set [in] their [depths]
[spirits immortal,][10]
and thereby dispose to Thy will
all that therein is.

[So too hast Thou done]
touching the spirit of man
which Thou hast created[11] in the world
for all the days of time
and for ages infinite,
to be[ar rule over all his works.]

Thou hast assigned the tasks of men's spirits
duly, moment by moment,[12]
throughout their generations;
and Thou hast determined the mode
in which they shall wield their sway,
season by season;
yea, [Thou hast prescribed] their [works,]
age after age—

alike when they shall be visited with peace
and when they shall suffer affliction.[13]

    Thou hast [man's spirit]
and duly assigned its role
for all his offspring
throughout the generations of time;
and [Thou hast   ] it
for all years of eternity.
And in Thy knowing wisdom
Thou hast ordained its fate,
or ever it came into being.

    By [Thy will all things exi]st,
and without Thee is nothing wrought.[14]

    Shapen of clay and kneaded with water,
a bedrock of shame and a source of pollution,
a cauldron of iniquity and a fabric of sin,
a spirit errant and wayward,[15]
distraught by every just judgment—
what can I say that hath not been foreknown,
or what disclose that hath not been foretold?
All things are inscribed before Thee
in a recording script,[16]
for every moment of time,
for the infinite cycles of years,
in their several appointed times.
No single thing is hidden,
naught missing from Thy presence.

    How can man say aught
to account for his sins?
How argue in excuse of his misdeeds?
How can he enter reply
to any just sentence upon him?
    Thine, O God of all knowledge,[17]
are all works of righteousness
and the secret of truth;
while man's is but thralldom to wrongdoing,
and works of deceit.
    The spirit that lies in man's speech,

Thou didst create.
Thou hast known all the words of man's tongue
and determined the fruit of his lips,[18]
ere those lips themselves had being.
It is Thou that disposeth all words in due sequence[19]
and giveth to the spirit of the lips
ordered mode of expression;[20]
that bringeth forth their secrets
in measured utterances,[21]
and granteth unto spirits
means to express their thoughts,
that Thy glory may be made known,
and Thy wonders told forth
in all Thine unerring works,
and that Thy righteousness [may be proclaimed,]
and Thy name be praised in the mouth of all things,
and that all creatures may know Thee,
each to the meed of his insight,
and bless Thee alway.

But Thou in Thy mercy and Thy great lovingkindness
hast strengthened the spirit of man
to face [his] afflictions,
and hast cleansed it of the taint
of multifarious wrongdoing,
to the end that Thy wonders may be shown forth
in the sight of all Thy works.

So, for mine own part,
[I am braced against] all the afflictions
whereto I am condemned;
and [will tell] unto men all Thy wonders
wherein, through me, Thou hast shown Thy power.

    Hearken, O ye wise,
ye, too, that are witless[22] and rash,
and be of sober mind.
Ye [,] sharpen your wits![23]
Ye righteous, have done with wrongdoing!
And all ye that are blameless of conduct,
hold fast to the [   ] of the meek!

Be slow to anger and spurn not [   ]!
For men that are foolish at heart
cannot understand these things, [   ]
and men of unbridled temper
can but gnash their teeth.[24]

.   .   .   .

[I give thanks unto Thee, O Lord,]
for Thou art my strength and [my stronghold,[1]]
and Thou hast delivered my soul
from all works of unrighteousness.
 [For Thou hast] put [truth in my heart]
and righteousness [in my spirit,]
along with all gifts of Thy wisd[om;]
and hast crushed the loins [of them]
[that have risen up against me.[2]]

 Thou bringest me cheer, O Lord,[3]
amid the sorrow of mourning,
words of peace amid havoc,
stoutness of heart when I faint,
fortitude in the face of affliction.

 Thou hast given free flow of speech
to my stammering lips;
stayed my drooping spirit
with vigor and strength;
made my feet to stand firm
when they stood where wickedness reigns.[4]

Albeit unto transgressors
I am but a symbol of weakness,[5]
yet unto them that repent
I am a source of healing;
prudence to the unwary,
temperance to the rash.
    Thou hast made me a reproach and a derision
to them that live by deceit,
but a symbol of truth and understanding
to all whose way is straight.

    A laughing-stock I am
in the eyes of the wicked,
a slander on the lips of the unbridled;[6]
scoffers gnash their teeth.
    A song am I unto transgressors,[7]
and the hordes of the wicked rage against me;[8]
like ocean gales they storm
which, when their billows rage,
cast up mire and dirt.[9]

    Yet, Thou hast set me as a banner
in the vanguard[10] of Righteousness,
as one who interprets with knowledge
deep, mysterious things;
as a touchstone for them that seek the truth,
a standard for them that love correction.[11]

To them that preach misguidance
I am but a man of strife;[12]
but to them that see straight,[13]
[a very symbol of pe]ace.
    To them that pursue delusion
I am but a gust of zeal;[14]
men that live by deceit
roar against me like the roar of many waters.

Naught is there in their thoughts
save mischievous designs.

When, opening the fount of knowledge
to all that have understanding,
Thou hast set a man's life to rights
by the words of my mouth,
and hast taught unto him Thy lesson,
and put understanding in his heart
—they thrust him back into the pit.
    In place of these Thy gifts
they offer a witless folk—[15]
stammering lips and barbarous tongue,[16]
that, wandering astray,
they rush headlong to their doom.[17]

I give thanks unto Thee, O Lord,
for Thou hast put my soul in the bundle of life[1]
and hedged me[2] against all the snares of corruption.

Because I clung to Thy covenant,
fierce men sought after my life.[3]
But they—a league of Falsehood, a congregation of Belial—
they knew not that through Thee I would stand.
For Thou in Thy mercy dost save my life;
for by Thee are my footsteps guided.

Of Thy doing it was that they assailed me,
to the end that by Thy judgment on the wicked
Thy glory might stand revealed,
and that Thou mightest show forth through me
Thy power against mankind;
for by Thy mercy I have stood.

Mighty men, I said, have pitched their camp against
me,
their weapons have compassed me,
their shafts have been loosed unceasing;
the flash of their spears is like fire devouring timber

and the roar of their voices like the roar of many waters.
Like a floodburst bringing ruin far and wide,[4]
all weak things and frail
they crush in a pounding cascade.[5]

Yet, while my heart was dissolving like water,
my soul held firm to Thy covenant,
and they—their own foot was caught
in the net they had spread for me;
in the traps they had hidden for my soul
themselves they fell.[6]

'Now that my foot on level ground doth rest,
Where men foregather, I will call Thee blest'.[7]

   I give thanks unto Thee, O Lord,
for Thine eye is ever awake,
watching over my soul.
   Thou hast delivered me
from envy of them that preach falsehood,
and hast freed this hapless soul[1]
from the congregation of them
that seek smooth things
—men who sought to destroy me
and spill my blood in Thy service.

   Little did they know
that my steps were ordered of Thee,
when they made me a mock and a reproach
in the mouths of all men of deceit.
   But ever, O my God,
hast Thou holpen the needy and weak
and snatched him from the grasp
of him that was stronger than he.[2]
   So hast Thou freed my soul
from the grasp of mighty men,
nor suffered me so to be crushed by their taunts
that for fear of the mischief which the wicked might wreak

I should forsake Thy service,
or change for wild delusion
the sound spirit which Thou hast vouchsafed me.

.   .   .   .

III, 3-18

[I give thanks unto Thee, O Lord,]
for Thou hast illumined [my face]
[with the vision of Thy truth;]
wherefore I yet shall walk in glory everlasting
along with all [the holy that hear the words of] Thy mouth;
  and Thou wilt deliver me from [the pit and the slough.]

Howbeit, at this hour
my soul is [sore dism]ayed.
Men deem me a [worthless shard]
and render my life like a ship stormtossed on the deep,
or like a bastion city[1] beleaguered by the [foe.]

Yea, I am in distress
as a woman in travail
bringing forth her firstborn,[2]
when, as her time draws near,
the pangs come swiftly upon her[3]
and all the grievous throes[4]
that rack those heavy with child.

For now, amid throes of death,
new life is coming to birth,[5]

and the pangs of travail set in,
as at last there enters the world
the man-child long conceived.

Now, amid throes of death,
that man-child long foretold
is about to be brought forth.[6]

Now, amid pangs of hell,[7]
there will burst forth from the womb
that marvel of mind and might,[8]
and that man-child will spring from the throes![9]

Delivery comes apace
for him that now lies in the womb;
as the hour of his birth draws near,
the pangs begin!

Come too the grievous throes,
the racking birth-pains come
upon all that bear in the womb
the seeds of the new life!

Yet, likewise unto them
that carry in their womb
the seeds of worthless things[10]
are come the grievous throes,
the pangs of hell and the torment.

For lo, the wall shall rock
unto its prime foundation,
even as rocks a ship
stormtossed on the waters.

The heavens shall thunder loud,
and they that now do dwell
on the crumbling dust of the earth
be as sailors on the seas,
aghast at the roaring of the waters;
and all the wise men thereof
be as mariners on the deep
when all their skill is confounded[11]
by the roaring of the seas,
the seething of the depths,[12]
the swirling of the tides.[13]

High shall the billows [surge,]
loud the breakers roar;
and, even as they surge,
the gates of Hell shall be opened,[14]
Perdition's shafts be loosed.[15]

Down shall they go screaming to the abyss,
and the gates of [Hell] shall open
upon all worthless things,*
and the doors of Perdition shall close
on all the iniquity
which they would yet bring forth;
and the bars of eternity[16]
on all unworthy intent.†

* Heb. 'acts'.
† Heb. 'on all spirits of worthlessness'.

I give thanks unto Thee, O Lord,
for Thou hast freed my soul from the pit[1]
and drawn me up from the slough of hell[2]
to the crest of the world.

So walk I on uplands unbounded
and know that there is hope[3]
for that which Thou didst mold out of dust
to have consort with things eternal.

For lo, Thou hast taken a spirit
distorted by sin,[4]
and purged it of the taint of much transgression,[5]
and given it a place
in the host of the holy beings,
and brought it into communion
with the sons of heaven.
Thou hast made a mere man to share
the lot of the Spirits of Knowledge,[6]
to praise Thy name in their chorus[7]
and rehearse Thy wondrous deeds
before all Thy works.[8]

I, that am molded of clay,
what am I?

I, that am kneaded with water,
what is my worth?
   I, that have taken my stand
where wickedness reigns,[9]
that have cast my lot with the froward;
whose soul has lodged like a beggar
in a place of wild unrest;[10]
I, whose every step
has been amid ruin and rout[11]—
on what strength of mine own may I count
   when Corruption's snares are laid,
and the nets of Wickedness spread,
when far and wide on the waters
Frowardness sets her drags,[12]
when the shafts of Corruption fly[13]
with none to turn them back,
when they are hurled amain
with no hope of escape;
   when the hour of judgment strikes,*
when the lot of God's anger is cast
upon the abandoned,
when His fury is poured forth[14] upon dissemblers,[15]
when the final doom of His rage
falls on all worthless things;
   when the torrents of Death do swirl,[16]
and there is none escape;
when the rivers of Belial[17]
burst their high banks
—rivers that are like fire
devouring all that draw their waters,
rivers whose runnels destroy
green tree and dry tree alike,[18]
rivers that are like fire
which sweeps with flaming sparks
devouring all that drink their waters
—a fire which consumes
all foundations of clay,
every solid bedrock;

* Heb. 'When the line falls upon judgment'; cf. Isa. 28.27.

when the foundations of the mountains
become a raging blaze,[19]
when granite roots are turned
to streams of pitch,[20]
when the flame devours
down to the great abyss,[21]
when the floods of Belial burst forth
unto hell itself;
    when the depths of the abyss are in turmoil,
cast up mire in abundance,[22]
when the earth cries out in anguish
for the havoc wrought in the world,
when all its depths are aquake,
and all that is on it quails
and quivers in [mighty] havoc;
    when with His mighty roar
God thunders forth,[23]
and His holy welkin[24] trembles
through dread* of His glory,
and the hosts of heaven give forth their voice,
and the world's foundations rock and reel;
    when warfare waged by the soldiers of heaven
sweeps through the world[25]
and turns not back until final doom[26]
—warfare the like of which
has never been?

* The text reads, 'through the *truth* of His glory', but the Hebrew word rendered 'truth' is probably a scribal error for a very similar word meaning 'dread' (viz. *be-emeth* for *be-êmath*).

[Fragment]

   I give thanks unto Thee, O Lord,
for Thou hast been unto me a strong wall[1]
against all that would destroy me
and all that would [traduce me.]
   Thou dost shelter me from the disasters
of a turbulent time,
[   ] that it come not [   ]

.   .   .   .

   [Thou hast set] my foot upon a rock[2]

.   .   .   .

   [I will walk] the age-old way
and the paths which Thou hast chosen.

.   .   .   .

I give thanks unto Thee, O Lord,
for Thou hast illumined my face
with the light of Thy covenant.
　[Day by day] I seek Thee,
and ever Thou shinest upon me
bright as the perfect dawn.[1]

　But as for *them*—
they have [dealt treacherously] with Thee,
have made smooth their words.[2]
Garblers of truth are [they all,]
witlessly stumbling along.[3]
They [have turned] all their deeds to folly;
they have become abhorrent unto themselves.
　Though Thou show Thy power through me,
they regard me not,
but thrust me forth from my land
like a sparrow from its nest;
all my friends and familiars
are thrust away from me,
and deem me a broken pot.[4]

　Preachers of lies are they,
prophets of deceit.

They have plotted mischief against me,
to make Thy people exchange for smooth words
Thy teaching which Thou hast engraven on my heart.
They have kept the draught of knowledge
from them that are athirst,
and given them in their thirst
vinegar to drink,[5]
making them turn their gaze
unto the errors they teach,[6]
revel in their feasts,
be caught in their snares.

But Thou, O God, wilt spurn
all mischievous designs.
Thy counsel it is will prevail,[7]
and the thought of Thy heart endure for ever.

Crafty men are they;[8]
they think base thoughts,
seek Thee with heart divided,
stand not firm in Thy truth.
In their every thought is a root
which blossoms to wormwood and gall.[9]
In the stubbornness of their hearts
they wander astray
and go seeking Thee through idols.
They make their iniquity
a stumbling-block before them,[10]
and come to inquire of Thee
from the mouths of lying prophets,
men by error seduced.
Then, with stammering tongue
and with barbarous lips[11]
they speak unto Thy people,
seeking guilefully
to turn their deeds to delusion.
They have [paid no heed to] Thy teaching,
nor given ear to Thy word,
but have said of the vision of knowledge,
'It is not sure',

and of the way Thou desirest,
'There is no such thing'.

But Thou, O God, wilt give them their answer,
judging them in Thy power
for all their idolatrous acts
and their manifold transgressions,
to the end that they shall be caught
in their own designs[12]
who have turned away from Thy covenant.
Thou wilt sentence all men of deceit
to be cut off,[13]
and all the prophets of error
will be found no more.
For in all Thou doest there is no delusion,
and in all Thou thinkest no deceit.
And they that are pleasing to Thee
shall stand in Thy presence for ever,
and they that walk in the way Thou desirest
rest firm for all time.

So, for mine own part,
because I have clung unto Thee,
I shall yet arise and stand upright[14]
against them that revile me;
and my hand shall yet be upon all
that hold me in contempt.
Though Thou show Thy power through me,
they regard me not.
Howbeit, Thou in Thy might
hast shed upon me the Perfect Light,
and bedaubed not their faces with shame[15]
that have let themselves be found
when that I sought them out,
who, in a common accord,
have pledged themselves to Thee.
They that walked in the way Thou desirest
have hearkened unto me
and rallied to Thy cause
in the legion of the saints.[16]

And Thou wilt vindicate them
and plainly show forth the truth;[17]
and suffer them not to stray
at the hand of froward men,
what time these plot against them.

 Thou wilt yet cause Thy people
to stand in awe of them.
But for them that transgress Thy word
Thou shalt ordain dispersal
among all the peoples on earth,
passing sentence on them
that they be cut off.

 Through me hast Thou illumined
the faces of full many,
and countless be the times
Thou hast shown Thy power through me.
For Thou hast made known unto me
Thy deep, mysterious things,
hast shared Thy secret with me
and so shown forth Thy power;
and before the eyes of full many
this wonder stands revealed,
that Thy glory may be shown forth,
and all living know of Thy power.

 Yet, never could flesh alone
attain unto this,
nor that which is molded of clay
do wonders so great
—steeped in sin from the womb
and in guilt of perfidy unto old age.
 Verily I know
that righteousness lies not with man,
nor perfection of conduct with mortals.
Only with God On High
are all works of righteousness;
and ne'er can the way of man
be stablished save by the spirit
which God has fashioned for him,

to bring unto perfection
the life of mortal man;
that all His works may know
how mighty is His power,
how plenteous His love
to all who do His will.

When I called to mind
all my guilty deeds
and the perfidy of my sires
—when wicked men
opposed Thy covenant,
and froward men Thy word—
trembling seized hold on me and quaking,
all my bones were a-quiver;
my heart became like wax
melting before a fire,
my knees were like to water[18]
pouring over a steep;[19]
  and I said: 'Because of my transgressions
I have been abandoned,
that Thy covenant holds not with me'.

But then, when I remembered
the strength of Thy hand
and Thy multitudinous mercies,
I rose again and stood upright,
and my spirit was fortified
to stand against affliction;
for I was stayed by Thy grace
and by Thine abundant love.
  For Thou wilt wipe out all sin,[20]
and in Thy bounty it lies
to purify man from guilt.
Man alone cannot do
as Thou hast done;
for Thou it is didst create
both the righteous and the wicked.
  And I said: 'Through Thy covenant
I shall go strengthened for ever,

. . . . .

and on Thy grace be stayed.
For Thou Thyself art truth,
and all Thy works are righteousness'.[21]

.   .   .   .

I give thanks unto Thee, O Lord,
for Thou hast not forsaken me
though I dwell as a sojourner
among an alien people,[1]
[nor cast me forth from Thy sight,]
[nor] judged me according to my guilt,
nor abandoned me to my lusts;
    but hast rescued my life from the pit.

Though Thou hast set [my soul] amid lions[2]
prompt to spring on the guilty
—fearful lions that break men's bones,
mighty lions that drink their blood—
and though Thou hast placed me full oft
in ready reach of their haul
who spread their nets for the froward
like fishers upon the waters,
or seek, like hunters, to trap them,[3]
    yet, when Thou hast placed me there,
    Thou hast dealt justly with me.[4]

For Thou hast set firm in my heart
Thy deep, deep truth;

and to them that seek after that truth
Thou bindest Thyself in pledge.
　So hast Thou put a lock
upon the mouths of those lions,
whose teeth are like a sword,[5]
whose fangs like a sharp spear,[6]
<whose breath> is the venom of serpents.[7]
　Though ever they seek to raven,
and though ever they lie in wait,
　　they have closed not their jaws upon me.

　Thou hast sheltered me, O God,
in the face of all mankind,
and hidden Thy teaching [within me],
until it be shown unto me
that the hour of Thy triumph is come.[8]

　In all the distress of my soul
Thou hast not abandoned me.
　In the bitterness of my spirit
Thou hast heard my cry,
and in my sighing discerned
the song of my pain.

　When I have found myself
in a very den of lions,[9]
whetting their tongues like a sword,[10]
Thou hast rescued me in my plight.
Yea, O my God, Thou hast locked their teeth
lest they rend a hapless man apart;
and Thou hast drawn back their tongue
like a sword into its sheath,[11]
lest it [do hurt] to Thy servant.

　Moreover, to show forth Thy power
in the sight of all men,
Thou hast singled me out, a hapless wretch,
and worked a wonder in me,
passing me [like gold] through a furn[ace,]
even through the action of fire,

and like silver that is refined
in the crucible of the smith,
to come forth sevenfold pure.[12]

The wicked rush wildly upon me
to [grasp] me in their vice,
and they crush my spirit all day,
  but Thou, O my God, dost turn the storm to a calm.[13]

From the jaws of very lions
Thou hast snatched a poor lost soul,
[when it was nigh] to be rent.

Blessed art Thou, O Lord,
for Thou hast never abandoned the orphan
neither despised the poor.
  [Unbounded is] Thy power,
and Thy glory hath no measure.

Angels of wondrous strength
minister unto Thee,
and [they walk] at the side of the meek
and of them that are fearful of right-doing,[1]
and of all the lost and lorn
that stand in need of mercy,
lifting them out of the slough[2]
when that their feet are mired.[3]

So, for mine own part,
to them that were my [familiars]
I had become [a thing of contention;]
a symbol of strife and discord[4]
unto my friends;
an occasion of fury and anger
unto my fellows;
of murmuring and complaint
to all mine acquaintances.

[All] that ate of my bread[5]
lifted their heels against me;[6]
all that shared my board
mouthed distortions about me;[7]
and they with whom I [consorted]
turned their backs upon me
and defamed me up and down.

By reason of the secret
which Thou hast hidden within me
they went spreading slander against me
to men that were bent on mischief.

Because they hem[med in my w]ay,[8]
and because of their infamy,
the fount of understanding was hidden
and the secret of truth,
while they—they went on contriving
the mischief of their hearts,
opening their shameless [mouths,]
unleashing their lying tongues
which were like the venom of adders[9]
fitfully spurting forth;[10]
like reptiles they shot forth their his[sing]
—vipers that could not be charmed.[11]

It was as a constant pain,[12]
a fretting wound[13]
in the body of Thy servant,
causing his spirit to droop,
wearing down his strength,[14]
until he could not withstand.

They overtook me between the straits,[15]
where there was no escape.

.   .   .   .

They thundered abuse of me
to the tune of the harp,
and in jingles chorused their jeers.

Confusion and panic beset me,[16]
horrendous anguish[17] and pain,
like to the throes of travail.
My heart was distraught within me;

I clothed me in mourning garb;[18]
my tongue cleaved to the roof of my mouth.[19]
In their hearts they rev[iled me,]
and openly vented their spleen.
The light of my face turned to darkness.
my radiance to gloom.

    Thou, O my God,
hadst enlarged my heart,
but ever they sought to constrict it.
They hedged me about with thick darkness.
I ate my bread amid sighs,
and my drink was mingled with tears[20]
which had none end.
Mine eyes were dimmed with anguish,[21]
and with all that beclouds the daylight[22]
my soul was over[cast.]
Sorrow was all about me,
and the pall of shame o'er my face.
The very bre[ad] that I ate
seemed to be quarreling with me,
the very drink that I drank
to be at odds with me.

    They purposed to trammel my spirit,
to wear down all my strength
with blasphemous mystic lore,
converting the works of God
into that which they guiltily imagined.

    I was bound with unbreakable cords,
with fetters that could not be sundered.
A strong wall [was upreared against me;]
bars of iron [restrained me]
and doors of brass.[23]

. . . .

Over my soul swirled the torrents of hell.[24]

. . . .

My heart [was sore distraught]
because of their obloquy
which they did heap upon me.

. . . .

[Ruin encompassed me,]
disaster which knew no bound,
destruction which had no [end.]

.   .   .   .

1

¶But Thou, O my God,
didst open mine ear,[25]
didst vindicate my cause
against [all them that traduced me.]
[Yea, Thou didst deliver me]
from the company of the vain,
from fellowship with crime,
and bring me into communion
[with all the holy and pure,]
[purging my soul of] guilt.

So am I come to know
that in [Thy] loving [kindness]
lies hope for them that repent
and for them that abandon sin,
[and confidence for him]
who walks in the way of Thy heart
without perversity.
Therefore, though peoples roar,
though kingdoms rage,[26]
I shall go comforted.
When that they gather together,
I shall [not] be dismayed,
knowing that in a space
Thou wilt raise a reviving for Thy people
and grant to Thine inheritance a remnant,[27]
and refine them, to purge them of guilt.
Whenas in all their deeds
they have done as Thy truth* enjoined,
Thou wilt judge them with lovingkindness,
with plenteous compassion
and abundance of forgiveness,
guiding them according to Thy word,

* I.e., the Scriptures.

stablishing them by Thy counsel,*
by Thine unswerving truth.

¶Thou hast acted for Thyself and for Thy glory,
that the Law may come to [fruition,]
and has [sent] among mankind
men that be schooled in Thy counsel
to tell forth Thy wonders through the ages,
world without end,
to rehearse Thy deeds of power
without surcease,
that all nations may know Thy truth,
and all peoples Thy glory.

    All these men hast Thou brought
into [com]munion with Thee,
and hast given them common estate
with the Angels of Thy Presence.[28]
There stands no intermediary among them
to appr[oach Thee in their behalf]
and bring them back Thy word[29]
filtered through their mind (?);[30]
for they themselves are answered
from out of Thy glorious mouth.
They are Thy courtiers,†
sharing the high estate
of [all the heavenly beings.]

¶[The seed which these men sow]
shall yield a flower unfading,
the twig shall put forth thick leaves,
become an evergreen,
give shade to all things;
[the branches shall tower] to hea[ven,]
the roots sink down to the abyss.[31]
All the rivers of Eden
[shall water] its boughs;[32]
it shall thrive beyond [all bounds,]

* Or, 'in Thy council'.
† Heb. 'princes'. The word is commonly used in post-Biblical
Hebrew to denote angels.

[burgeon beyond all] measure.
But the [plant of Beli]al shall fade,
that it be no more,
[and its roots shall sink down] into hell.

The Fountain of Light shall well forth,
a perpetual spring unfailing,
but in its [fiery] sparks all [infamous] men shall be burned;
it shall be as a flame devouring the guilty,
until they be destroyed.

They who were my familiars,
who shared the same fortune as I,
were all of them seduced
by garbl[ers of truth,]
[that they no longer wished] to do right.
Thou hadst given them commandments, O God,
that they might have profit of their lives
by walking Thy ho[ly way,]
whereon the uncircumcised and unclean
and profane may not pass.[33]
But they wavered from the way of Thy heart
and ensnared themselves in their lusts.
Mischief counselled their hearts[34]
and, through their wicked devisings,
they tainted themselves with guilt.
Wherefore on their account
I was as a sailor in a ship
when the seas do froth and foam.
All the breakers thereof
kept pounding against me,
and the whirlwind[35] blew about me,
[and there was no] moment of calm
wherein to catch my breath,
neither could I steer
a course upon the waters.
The deeps echoed my groaning,
and I [came near] to the gates of death.[36]

¶But now I am as one
that hath entered a stronghold,

taken refuge behind a high wall
until deliverance come.
For I have stayed myself on Thy truth, O my God,
knowing full well
that Thou foundest Thy structure on a rock,
that its rafters are truly poised
and its stones well laid,
that of tested stone[37] are its walls
and unbreakably strong its bars,
that all who repair unto it
shall never be moved,
for there shall no stranger invade it.
Its doors are a sheet of protection
which none may force,
and its bars are strong bars
which cannot be broken.
No armed band can storm it,
neither all the war hosts of wickedness together.

    For, should they so essay,
the sword of God will be swift
to wreak a final judgment,
and all who acknowledge His truth
will rouse themselves to [do battle]
[against the forces of] wickedness,
and all the sons of guilt
will be no more.

    The Warrior[38] will bend his bow,
and lift the siege for ever,
and open the gates everlasting
to bring forth His weapons of war;
and His legions shall go marching
from end to [end of the earth,]
[and there shall be no es]cape
for the guilty impulse of men.
They shall trample it to destruction,
that naught re[main thereof.]
There shall be no hope for it
in [weapons] never so many,
neither any escape
for all that fight in its cause.

For the [victory] shall belong
unto God on High,

.   .   .   .

and though they that lie in the dust
will have raised their flag,[39]
and though this worm which is man[40]
will have lifted up his banner
to do [battle against the truth,]
[yet shall they be] cut off
when battle is joined with the presumptious;
and he that sought to bring
the scourge of a flood overflowing[41]
will never reach that stronghold.

.   .   .   .

Lo, I am stricken dumb,
for naught comes out of men's mouths
but swearing and lying.
My arm is wrenched from its socket;[1]
my foot is sunken in mire;
mine eyes are dimmed[2] from looking on evil;
mine ears are deafened from hearing of bloodshed;
my heart is numbed with thinking on evil;
for wheresoever men show
the temper of their being,
there is the spirit of baseness.

The structure of my being
is rocked to its very foundation;
my bones are out of joint;[3]
mine inwards heave like a ship
when the searing eastwind soughs;[4]
my heart is sore distraught.

In the havoc of their transgression
a whirlwind swallows me up.

I give thanks unto Thee, O Lord,
for by Thine own strength hast Thou stayed me,
and hast wafted o'er me Thy holy spirit
that I cannot be moved.

Thou hast braced me for all the battles
that Wickedness wages against me,
and hast let not the havoc dismay me
to break faith with Thee.

Thou hast set me as in a strong tower
upon a lofty wall,[1]
founded upon a rock,[2]
reared on eternal foundations,
whose walls are a proven bulwark
that cannot be shaken
—a tower provided by Thee, O my God,
for all that would rise as on wings
to the heights of an holy resolve.[3]

[Thou hast brought me into] Thy covenant.
Words flow free on my tongue,
as it were trained by Thee,[4]
while the Spirit of Havoc stays speechless,
and the reprobate ope not their mouth.

Through me Thou hast kept Thy pledge:
'False lips shall be stricken dumb'.*
All them that challenge me
Thou makest to stand condemned,
distinguishing through me
the right from the wrong.

¶Thou knowest the impulse of every act,
and discernest the purpose of every speech,
yet, by Thy teaching and truth
Thou hast directed my heart
that I set my steps straight forward
upon right paths
and walk where Thy presence is
across the stretch [of life,]
finding upon my path
honor and peace unbo[unded,]
and ending all [waywardness] for ever.

Thou knowest also the nature
of this Thy servant,
how that I have not relied
[upon the things of the world,]
lifting [my heart] in pride,
vaunting my strength.
No refuge have I in flesh,
nor righteousness [in my soul,]
that I may be saved from the snare
except by Thy pardon.
On [Thy mercy alone] I rely,
and for Thy grace I hope,
to bring Thy triumph to flower,
to make the shoot to grow,
to find cause for vaunting strength,
for [lifting heart.]

¶And Thou, O God of mercy,
hast in Thy bounty given me place
* Psalm 31.18.

among those to whom Thou art pledged;[5]
and unto Thy truth will I cling.

Thou hast [chosen me] and set me
as a father to them Thou holdest dear,[6]
and as a nurse unto them
whom Thou hast made exemplars of men.[7]
They open their mouths for my words,
like sucklings [at the breast,]
and like as a babe that plays
on the bosom of its nurse.

Thou hast raised high my horn[8]
over all that revile me,
and all who wage battle against me
are rou[ted without remnant,]
and all that contend with me
are as chaff before the wind;[9]
and all impiety bows to my sway.

For Thou, O my God, hast holpen my soul
and raised high my horn.

I am lit with a light sevenfold,
with that same [lustre] of glory
which Thou didst create for Thyself.[10]
For Thou art unto me as a light eternal[11]
keeping my feet upon [the way.]

I give [thanks unto Thee, O Lord,]
for Thou hast given me insight into Thy truth
and knowledge of Thy wondrous secrets.

In lovingkindness to [lowly] man,
in abundance of mercy to wayward hearts,
who is like Thee among the gods, O Lord,[1]
and what truth is like Thine?

Who can prove righteous in Thy sight
when Thou bringest him unto judgment?
Not even a spirit can answer Thy charge,
and none can withstand Thy wrath.
Yet, all that are children of Thy truth
Thou bringest before Thee with forgiveness,
[clean]sing them of their transgressions
through Thine abundant goodness,
and, through Thy plenteous mercies,
causing them to stand in Thy presence for ever.
For Thou art a God everlasting,
and all Thy ways hold firm for all time;[2]
and there is none else beside Thee.
But what is man—vain, empty man,
that he should understand Thy wondrous works
or be [enlightened] therein?

[I give thanks] unto Thee, O Lord,
for Thou hast cast not my lot in the congregation of the
    false,
nor set my portion in the company of dissemblers.

Behold, in Thy mercy [I trust],
in Thy pardon [confide],
and on Thine abundant mercies [I lean],
when all [just] judgments are passed upon me.
[For Thou dost tend me as a mother tendeth] her babe,
and [like a child] on the bosom of [its nurse dost Thou
    sustain me].

.   .   .   .

Thy justice holdeth firm for ever,
for [Thou dost] not [abandon them that seek Thee].[1]

I give thanks unto Thee, O Lord,
for Thou hast placed me where rills burst forth in dry land,
where waters gush in thirsty soil,[1]
where an oasis blooms in the desert;
where, hidden 'mid all trees else
—all trees that live on mere water—
stand planted, for Thy glory alone,
the trees that never die,
the fir, the pine and the cypress,[2]
fed from a secret source,
putting forth branches unfading,[3]
striking firm root ere they flower,
spreading their roots to the stream.

[Thy Law, O God, is an evergreen][3a]
whose stem stands exposed to living waters
and whose [   ] to a perpetual fount.
Yet all the beasts of the woodland
are feeding upon its branches;
all that pass by the way
are trampling upon its stump;
every wingèd bird is perching on its boughs.[4]
All the trees that live on mere water
are vaunting themselves against it,[5]

for they spread far and wide in their plantations
though they send not their roots to the stream;
while the tree which was planted in truth
and was destined to bring to flower branches of holiness
keeps its secret hidden and sealed,
unesteemed and unnoticed.

Moreover, O God, Thou hast hedged in its fruit
by the secret power of stalwart angels,[6]
by holy spirits,
and by a flaming sword turning this way and that,[7]
so that [   ] not [   ] the fountain of life,
nor drink the waters of holiness
as do the eternal trees,
nor put forth its fruit through the [rains] of heaven,
because it saw but did not perceive,
thought but did not believe in the Wellspring of Life,
even though it was yielding [   ] everlasting.[8]

As for me,
I had become as the [   ] of rivers in flood,
for they poured forth their mire upon me.[9]

¶But Thou, O my God, hast set in my mouth, as it were,
rain at all seasons,
and a fountain of waters unfailing,[10]
opening the heavens without surcease,[11]
so that they are become as a stream in flood[12]
bursting over its banks,[13]
and as seas unfathomable
which, long hidden in secret,
suddenly burst forth [   ][14]
and quicken every tree,
green and dry alike,[15]
and serve as a pool for wild beasts.

[The trees of the wicked shall be felled][16]
and sink like lead in mighty waters;[17]
and a fire shall go forth, and they shall wither.
But the orchard which I have planted
shall bloom fair for ever,
a glorious richness, a flower of beauty.

At my hands hast Thou opened a wellspring for it,
yielding runnels of water,
that its roots may be firmly set
and its trees planted in line of the sun,[18]
in light [unfailing;]
that its [boughs] may yield glorious foliage.

When I apply my hand
to dig the furrows thereof,[19]
its roots strike even on granite,
its stocks are firm-grounded in the earth,[20]
and in the time of heat it secures protection.

But if I relax my hand,
it becomes like a [heath in the desert,][21]
and its stocks like nettles in a salt-marsh,
and out of its furrows grow thorns and thistles;[21a]
it turns to briars and brambles,[22]
and its [   ] are turned to stinking weeds;[22a]
its leaves fade before the heat;
it is not exposed to water.
It suffers mishap and disease
and becomes a [target] for all manner of blight.

¶I was as a man forsaken in [   ],
no refuge had I.
For that which I had planted
was turned into wormwood.
Grievous was my pain,[22b] and could not be stayed.
[My soul was overw]helmed,[22c]
like them that go down to Sheol,
and my spirit was sunken low amid the dead.[23]
My life had reached the Pit,[24]
and my soul waxed faint[24a] day and night without rest.
There burst forth, as it were, a blazing fire,
held in my [bones,][25]
the flame whereof devoured unto the nethermost seas
exhausting my strength every moment,
consuming my flesh every minute.
Disasters hovered about me,
and my soul was utterly bowed down.[25a]

For all my strength had ceased from my body,
and my heart was poured out like water,
and my flesh melted like wax,
and the strength of my loins was turned to confusion,
and my arm was wrenched from the shoulder.[26]
I [could not] move my hand,
and my [foot] was caught in a shackle,
and my knees were dissolved like water.
I could take neither pace nor step;
[heaviness] replaced my fleetness of foot;
[my steps] were trammeled.
My tongue was tied and protruded;[26a]
I could not lift my voice
in any articulate [speech,]
to revive the spirit of the stumbling,
or encourage the faint with a word.[27]
My lips were dumb altogether.

.   .   .   .

. . . .
Though [mine eye] sleep [not] at night,
[though God assail me] without mercy,
though in anger He stir up His fury[1]
[and pursue me] unto destruction;
though the breakers of death swirl around me,[2]
though Sheol[2] be upon my couch;
though my bed take up a lament,[3]
and [my couch] a cry of anguish;
though mine eye smart as through the smoke of an oven,[4]
though my tears flow like rivers;[5]
though mine eyes fail,[6] and I have no rest;
though [my strength] stand afar off,
and my life be put aside;
though I go from rout to ruin,[7]
from pain to plague,
from pangs to throes,

Yet will I muse on Thy wonders;
for Thou, in Thy lovingkindness,
hast at no time cast me off.
My soul will delight in the abundance of Thy mercies,
and I shall have wherewith to reply
to him that would confound me,

and to gainsay him that would abase me.
I shall refute his case,
and vindicate Thy judgment.

For I have come to know Thy truth;
I accept Thy judgments upon me,
and am content with my afflictions.
I have learned to put hope in Thy mercy;
for Thou hast placed in the mouth of Thy servant
the power to win Thy grace,[8]
and hast not mortally rebuked him,
neither renounced his wellbeing,
neither frustrated his hope.
Rather hast Thou braced his spirit
to withstand affliction.

Thou it is emplanted* my spirit,
and Thou knowest its every intent;
and so in my straitness
Thou hast given me reassurance.
I delight in the promise of pardon,
and repent my former transgression;
for in Thy mercy lies hope,
and confidence in Thine abundant power.

For none can prove himself righteous
when Thou bringest him unto judgment.
Though man may prove more righteous than man,
none can contend [with Thee.]
Though a human may prove wiser than [a beast,]
though flesh may rank higher than dumb [clay,]†
though one spirit may prove mightier than another,
yet naught can match [Thy power] in strength.
Thy glory hath no equal,
Thy wisdom no measure,
Thy tr[uth no bound;]
and all that have forfeited them
[are doomed to perdition.]

* Heb. 'founded'.
† Literally, 'than that which is molded out of clay'.

¶Behold, for my own part,
through Thee I have pr[ospered my way,]
[through Thee maintained] my stand;
for Thou hast not [abandoned me]
[unto them that] seek my hurt.
Whenever they plot against me,
Thou [savest me from their grasp,]
and if they are bent to disgrace me,
Thou in Thy mercy [dost confound] them.
If mine enemy vaunt himself against me,
it proves to his own undoing;*
and they that battle against me
[are overwhelmed] with disgrace,
and shame overtakes them that revile me.

For at [every] time, O my God,
Thou dost fight my fight.[9]
Though now, in Thine inscrutable wisdom, Thou rebuke
    me,
yet art Thou but hiding the truth until [its time]
and [Thy glory] until its season.
Then will Thy rebuking of me
be turned into gladness and joy;
my plague shall be turned to perpetual health,
the scorn of my foes to a diadem of glory,[10]
my halting steps to enduring strength.

Lo, through Thy Name and through Thy glory
light has shone forth upon me.
Thou hast brought me light out of darkness,
hast given me [health] in place of plague,[10a]
wondrous strength in place of stumbling,
and abiding enlargement for the straitness of my soul.

[Thou art] my refuge and my tower,
my rock of retreat and my stronghold;
in Thee do I take refuge from all that [pursue me,]
[and Thou art] mine escape evermore.

¶Or ever my father begat me,
Thou didst know me;

* Literally, 'stumbling'.

from the womb of my mother Thou didst shower me with
    Thy grace*
and from the breasts of her that conceived me
Thy mercies have been shed upon me.
On the bosom of my nurse [Thou didst sustain me,]
and from my youth up
Thou hast enlightened me with understanding of Thy
    judgments,
held me firm by Thy truth,
and caused me to delight in Thy holy spirit:
and even unto this day
Thou dost stay my goings.

Though Thy just rebuke be with my body,
yet will my soul be saved
by Thy watch over my wellbeing.
    With every step I take
Thine abundant forgiveness enfolds me,
and when Thou arraignest me,
Thy mercies overwhelm me.
    Even unto old age
Thou wilt yet sustain me.
For my father hath renounced me,
and my mother hath abandoned me to Thee;[11]
yet Thou art a father to all that [know] Thy truth,
and Thou wilt rejoice over them
like a mother who pitieth her babe,
and Thou wilt feed all Thy works
as a nurse feeds her charge at the bosom.[12]

¶[Who can fathom the des]igns of Thy heart?

.   .   .   .

Apart from Thee hath nothing existed,
and without Thy will will nothing be;
yet can none understand Thy [   ]
nor gaze upon Thy [.]

    What is man, mere earth,
kneaded out of [clay,]

* The Hebrew word can also mean 'Thou didst wean me'. There
is thus a *double-entendre*.

destined to return unto the dust,[13]
that Thou shouldst give him insight into Thy wonders
and make him privy to things divine?

  As for me,
I am but dust and ashes.
What can I devise except Thou hast desired it?
And what can I think apart from Thy will?
And how be strong except Thou hast stayed me,
or stumble except Thou hast constrained (?)[14] me?
How speak except Thou hast opened my mouth?
How reply except Thou hast given me sense?

  Lo, Thou art the Prince of the angels,
and the King of all that are in glory,
and the Lord of every spirit,
and the Ruler of every deed.
Without thee nothing is wrought,
and without Thy will can nothing be known.[15]
None there is beside Thee,
and none to share Thy power,
and none to match Thy glory,
and Thy power is beyond price.

  Which among all Thy great wondrous works
has power to stand before Thee?
How much less, then, can he who returns to his dust attain to [such power.]

  Only for Thine own glory hast Thou done all these things.

X, 14–XI, 2

Blessed art thou, O Lord,
Thou God of compassion and mercy,
for Thou hast given me knowledge of Thy truth
and insight to tell forth Thy wonders,
unhushed by day or night.

.   .   .   .

For Thy mercy I hope;
in Thy great goodness I trust,

.   .   .   .

for on Thy truth I have leaned.

.   .   .   .

Except Thou strengthen, there is no standing;
except Thou rebuke, no stumbling;
no affliction but Thou hast foreknown it,
no salvation but by Thy will.

So, for mine own part,
now that I know Thy truth,
now that I look on Thy glory,
I too will tell forth Thy wonders;
now that I understand them,
I will wait on Thy mercy
and upon Thine abundant compassion,
and for Thy pardon hope.

For Thou it is did shape my frame,
and Thou it is did determine my being
according to Thy will;
and Thou hast left me not to rely
upon worldly wealth,
or stay myself upon worldly gain.[1]
Thou hast made no creature of flesh
—no army of warriors—
to be my source of strength,
nor made me to rely
on riches of luxury
—of corn and wine and oil.

Yet, that which I possess
and that which I have gotten
is no mean thing withal.
For I am as a tree
green beside streams of water,[2]
bearing fruit, abounding in leaves;[3]
for Thou hast created plants
for the service of man,
and all things that spring from the earth
that he may be fed in abundance.[4]
And to them that acknowledge Thy truth
Thou hast also given insight
to divine Thy wondrous works
and to tell forth Thy glory
according to their knowledge,
learning each from each.

So hast Thou given abundance
to Thy servant, the son of Thine handmaid,
and hast richly endowed him
with knowledge of Thy truth;
and, to the meed of his knowledge,
he too will rehearse Thy glory.
Thy servant has learned to abhor
all worldly wealth and gain,
and in luxurious riches
his soul has no delight.

Nay, in Thy covenant
does my heart rejoice,
and in Thy truth my soul exults.
I bring my tongue to full flower,
and my heart is exposed to a spring unfailing,
and upon the strength of heaven
I place my reliance.
And I bear not blighted fruit
which withers while still in blossom
ere that it come to flower.*

Howbeit, when I hear
how Thou judgest even Thine angels
so mighty in strength,[5]
how that Thou arraignest
even the Holy Host,
my heart is sorely racked,
my loins are all a-quake,
my sighing reaches down
into the nethermost abyss
and penetrates withal
into the chambers of hell.[6]

.   .   .   .

For how much more upon man
will Thy sentence go forth?
And will not Thy judgment be wreaked
upon all Thy works?

.   .   .   .

I am stricken with dismay;

trouble and grief are not hid from mine eyes[7]

in the musing of my heart.

* Or, 'before the heat'.

I give thanks unto Thee, O Lord,
for Thou hast wrought a wonder with dust
and hast shown forth Thy power
in that which is molded of clay.
For Thou hast made me to know Thy deep, deep truth,
and to divine Thy wondrous works,
and hast put in my mouth the power to praise,
and psalmody on my tongue,
and hast given me lips unmarred[1]
and readiness of song,
that I may sing of Thy lovingkindness
and rehearse Thy might all the day
and continually bless Thy name.

I will show forth Thy glory
in the midst of the sons of men,
and in Thine abundant goodness
my soul will exult.
For I know that Thy mouth is truth,
and in Thy hand is bounty,
and in Thy thought all knowledge,
and in Thy power all might,
and that all glory is with Thee.

In Thine anger come all judgments of affliction,
but in Thy goodness pardon abounding;
and Thy mercies are shed upon all
who do Thy will.

For Thou hast made them to know Thy deep, deep
truth
and divine Thine inscrutable wonders;
and, for Thy glory's sake,
Thou hast granted it unto man
to be purged of transgression,
that he may hallow himself
and be free from all taint of filth
and all guilt of perfidy,
to be one with them that possess Thy truth
and to share the lot of Thy Holy Beings,
to the end that this worm which is man[2]
may be lifted out of the dust
to the height of eternal things,
and rise from a spirit perverse
to an holy understanding,
and stand in one company before Thee
with the host everlasting and the spirits of knowledge
and the choir invisible,[3]
to be for ever renewed
with all things that are.[4]

I give thanks unto Thee, O my God,
I extol Thee, O my Rock,[1]
and because Thou hast wrought wonders with me
[I bless Thy name.]

Thy wonders hast Thou revealed unto me,
and I have beholden [Thy truth]
[and witnessed Thy] deeds of lovingkindness.

So am I come to know
that though Thou art ever just,
yet in Thy lovingkindness
lies salvation for men,
and that without Thy mercy
theirs is but doom and perdition.

Lo, for mine own part,
when I marked the nature of man,
how he must return unto the dust,[2]
how his soul is surrendered
to sin and the anguish of guilt,
a fountain of bitter mourning
was opened for me;

[my tears flowed like rivers,][3]
and trouble was not hidden from mine eyes.[4]

    These things went to my heart
and touched me to the bone,[5]
that I raised a bitter lament
and made doleful moan and groan
and plied my harp in mournful dirge
and bitter lamentation,
crying that all perverseness might be brought to an end.

    But suddenly I perceived
that there was no more affliction
to rack me with pain.
    Then did I ply my harp
with music of salvation,
and my lyre to tune of joy;
yea, I plied the pipe and the flute
in praise without cease.

    Albeit none among all Thy works
can rehearse the full tale of Thy mercies,*
yet, in the mouths of them all
may Thy name be praised;
to the meed of their understanding
they yet may bless Thee for ever
and chorus their songs of triumph
all the day long.
    For sorrow and sighing are no more;[6]
Iniquity's mouth is stopped;[7]
Thou hast made Thy truth to shine forth
in glory everlasting
and peace for evermore.

* Or, 'wonders'.

XI, 27-XII, 35

Blessed art Thou, O Lord,
Who hast given unto man the insight of knowledge,
to understand Thy wonders,
[discern Thy truth,]
tell forth Thine abundant mercies.

Blessed art Thou, O God of compassion and grace,
for the greatness of [Thy] power,
the abundance of Thy truth,
the profusion of Thy mercies
over all Thy works.

Rejoice the soul of Thy servant in Thy truth,
and in Thy righteousness make me clean,
even as when [aforetime] I waited on Thy bounty
and hoped on Thy mercies,
and Thou, in Thy forgiveness, didst loose my bonds;[1]
and even as when I leaned on Thy compassion,
and Thou didst comfort me in my sorrow.

Blessed art Thou, O Lord,
for Thou it is hath wrought these things,
and placed in the mouth of Thy servant
[power to pray] and to win Thy grace,

and all readiness of tongue;
and hast prepared for me the guerdon of [righteousness]
[and the reward of devotion],
that I may attain to [stand in Thy presence].

[   ] my soul will exult[2]
[because it hath come to abide in Thy presence]
[and to dwell] secure in [Thy] ho[ly] abode,
in calm and quietude.
  [In] my tent [I will chant]
[songs of joy] and salvation,[3]
and in the midst of them that fear Thee
tell forth the praise of Thy name
to all ages to come;
pouring forth prayer and supplication[4]
always, at all times and seasons;[5]
when daylight comes forth from [its abode];
when, in its ordered course,
day reaches its turning-point,
in accordance with the rules of the sun;
and again at the turn of the evening,
when daylight departs,
as the rule of darkness begins;
and again in the season of night,
when it reaches its turning-point,
and when the morning breaks;
and when, in the presence of the daylight,
night withdraws to its abode;
when night departs and day comes in,
alway, at all the birthdays of time,
at the moments when seasons begin;[6]
when they reach their turning-points;
when they come in order due
according to their several signs,[7]
as these have dominion in due order assured,
[decreed] by the mouth of God
and by the laws of existence.

.   .   .   .

  Behold, for mine own part,
I have reached the inner vision,

and through the spirit Thou hast placed within me,
come to know Thee, my God.
   I have heard Thy wondrous secret,
nor heard it amiss.[8]
Through Thy holy spirit,
through Thy mystic insight,
Thou hast caused a spring of knowledge to well up within
      me,
a fountain of strength,
pouring forth waters unstinted,
a floodtide of lovingkindness and of all-consuming zeal.
Thou hast put an end to [my darkness],
and the splendor of Thy glory has become unto me as a
      light ev[erlasting].

   Wickedness hath been [consumed] altogether,
and deceit [existeth] no more.
[Perverseness is gone down] to perdition,
for [   ] existeth no more [   ]
insolent fury[9] is at an end,
for it [cannot withstand] thine anger.
   [The sins which I committed aforetime]
[I committed in] overhaste;
for [now am I come to know that] no man is righteous
      with Thee.
For there is none can understand all Thy hidden things,
nor answer Thy charge against him;
but all must needs wait upon Thy goodness,
for Thou, in [Thy] lovingkindness [wilt reveal to them Thy
      truth,]
that they may come to know Thee;
and when Thy glory bursts upon them, they shall rejoice.

   According to each man's knowledge,
and the meed of his understanding
hast Thou drawn them nigh [unto Thee,]
that they may serve Thee in their several domains,
as Thou hast assigned their roles,
[   ] transgressing not Thy word.

Behold, I was taken from dust,
nipped out of clay,
and I am become but a source of filth
and of shameful nakedness,
a heap of dust,
a thing kneaded with water,
a dwellingplace of darkness.

That which is molded of clay must needs return to dust
at the end of its [term,]
[and lie again] in the dust
whence it was taken.

How can mere dust and [clay] give answer to its
    [Maker,]
or how understand His works,
or how stand before its Accuser?

Even the holy [angels,]
the everlasting [spirits,]
the reservoirs of glory,
the wellsprings of knowledge and power,
—even they cannot tell forth all Thy glory,
nor stand against Thine anger,
nor answer Thy charge.
For Thou art ever righteous,
and none can gainsay Thee.
How much less, then, he who returns to his dust?

Lo, I am stricken dumb.
What can I say against this?
I have spoken but according to my knowledge
and only with such sense of right
as a creature of clay may possess.
But how can I speak except Thou open my mouth,
and how understand, if Thou give me not insight;
or how contend, save Thou open my heart;
or how walk straight save Thou gu[ide my feet?]
How can [my] fo[ot] stand,
how can I be strong in power,
how can I endure [save by Thy grace?]

.   .   .   .

(From this point it becomes impossible to distinguish the separate hymns.)

XIII, 1-21

When first the world began
Thou didst shed an holy spirit
on all Thou didst bring into being,
and make them all to attest
Thy wondrous mysteries.[1]

. . . .

Thou didst show Thy handiwork
in all that Thou didst make.
Thou didst reveal Thy glory
in all their varied shapes,
Thy truth in all their works.

. . . .

¶On all that keep Thy charge
Thou bestowest grace abounding
and mercies never failing;
but upon all things that defy Thee
Thou bringest perdition eternal.
So, if mortal men
keep faith with Thee,
behold, Thou crownest their heads
with glory everlasting[2]

and compassest their works
with perennial joy;
but [   ]
[   ] the wicked.

On those whom Thou hast honored
to show forth all Thy works
—on those, as on the host of Thy spirits,
  the congregation of Thy Holy Beings,
  the sky with all its array,
  the earth with all its produce,
  all things in lakes and seas
—on those, ere Thou didst create them,
Thou didst impose a task
and a perpetual charge.
For when first the world began
Thou didst so ordain them
and appoint the work of each
that they should tell forth Thy glory
throughout Thy dominion,
showing unto them
what none would else have seen,
how ancient things pass over
and new things are ever created,[3]
how the things established of old
become like pacts annulled,
yet the future is ever assured;[4]
  while Thou art a God everlasting,
  and Thou wilt endure for all time.

In Thine inscrutable wisdom
Thou hast assigned to all these
natures diverse and varied
that Thy glory may be made known.
  Yet, how can a spirit of flesh
understand all these things?
How can it conceive
Thy so great mystery?
How can the child of woman
fathom Thine awesome thoughts?

A fabric of dust is he,
a thing kneaded with water,
[a mass of filth,]
whose foundation is naked shame [   ],
and who is ruled by a spirit perverse.
Prone unto wrongdoing,*
he can serve but as a [thing of revulsion]
world without end,
a portent for all generations,[5]
an object of abhorrence to all flesh![6]
    Nay, it is only through Thy goodness
and through Thy mercies abundant
that Man can ever do right.
For it is with Thine own beauty
that Thou dost beautify him,
and only of Thy free bounty
dost Thou shower him with delights
and grant him peace enduring
and length of days.
    And, [Lord, when once Thou hast spoken,]
ne'er is Thy word revoked.[7]

¶So, for mine own part,
through the spirit Thou hast planted within me,
I, Thy servant, am come to know
that [all Thy judgments are truth,]
and righteousness all Thy works,
and ne'er is Thy word revoked.
None of the terms and times
which Thou hast foreordained
[shall fail to come to pass]
—all of them duly chosen
for their appointed ends.[8]
    Therefore I know full surely
[that yet the time will come]
[when Thou wilt reward the righteous,]
and the wicked be utterly [doomed.]

* Heb. 'If he do wrong'.

[I give thanks unto Thee, O Lord,
for Thou hast granted a remnant]
unto Thy people
and a re[vival]
[unto Thine inheritance.]¹

[Thou hast raised up among them]
men of truth
and sons [of light,]²

. . . .

men of abundant compassion,
men of stalwart [spirit,]
men of tempered [soul,]
men steeled to [sustain] Thy judgments.

[Through them hast Thou kept Thy covenant]
and confirmed Thy pledge,
to render us unto Thee
[a kingdom of priests and] an holy [nation]³
for all generations of time
and for all the [ages to come.]

[Verily, O Lord, Thou dost sustain]
them that have vision of Thee.

Blessed art Thou, O Lord,
Who puttest the sense of discernment

into the heart of Thy servants,[4]
[that they may walk blamelessly before Thee,]
and be steeled against all the devices of wickedness,
and that they may bless [Thy name,]
[loving] all that Thou lovest
and abhorring all that [Thou hatest,][5]
and that, through the spirit of reason within them,
but after the spirits eternal,
they may distinguish the good from the wicked
and keep all their deeds undefiled.

Behold, through that discernment
which is given by Thee,
I too have come to know
that only of Thy good pleasure
do I share in Thy holy spirit,
and only thus hast Thou brought me close
to an understanding of Thee.
The nearer I draw to Thee,[6]
the more am I filled with zeal
against all that do wickedness
and against all men of deceit.
For they that draw near to Thee
cannot see Thy commandments defied,
and they that have knowledge of Thee
can brook no change of Thy words,
seeing that Thou art the essence of right,
and all Thine elect are the proof of Thy truth.

Thou wilt bring eternal doom
on all frowardness and transgression,
and Thy righteousness will stand revealed
in the sight of all Thou hast made.

Lo, through Thy great goodness
I have come to know these things,
and committed myself by oath
never to sin against Thee
nor do aught that is evil in Thy sight;
and I have been granted admittance
to [this] community.

So, for mine own part,
I will admit no comrade
into fellowship with me
save by the measure of his understanding,
and only by the measure
of his share in this common lot
will I show friendship to him.
I will not countenance evil,
neither recognize fraud.
I will not barter Thy truth for wealth,
nor all Thy judgments for a bribe.
Only as Thou drawest a man unto Thee
will I draw him unto myself,
and as Thou keepest him afar,
so too will I abhor him;
and I will enter not into communion
with them that turn their back upon Thy covenant.[7]

Blessed art Thou, O Lord,
Who, in the greatness of Thy power,
in Thy manifold, infinite wonders
and in the greatness of Thy forbearance
forgivest them that repent their transgression,
but visitest the iniquity of the wicked.
Verily, on the righteous
Thou bestowest freely Thy love,
but perversity Thou hatest for ever.[8]
So hast Thou graced me, Thy servant,
with the spirit of knowledge and truth,[9]

.   .   .   .

and made me abominate
all ways of perversity.
So, for mine own part,
I in turn will love Thee freely[10]
and with all my heart
I will [   ] Thy [   ].
For by Thy hand has this thing been wrought,
and without [Thy will can naught be done].

.   .   .   .

[   ] they love Thee alway.

    So, for mine own part,
[I will] [   ]
and love Thee right freely
with all my heart and soul.[1]
    Yea, I have cleansed [my heart]
[to adhere to Thy] ho[ly Law]
[and not to] turn aside
from aught that Thou hast commanded;
and I have made Thy commandments
to take firm hold upon many
that they abandon not
any of Thy statutes.

    Moreover, through the discernment
which Thou hast bestowed upon me
I am come to know
that not by the hand of flesh
can a mortal order his way
neither can any man
direct his own steps.[2]
    I know that in Thy hand
is the shaping of each man's spirit,

and ere Thou didst create him
Thou didst ordain his works.[3]
And how can any man
change what Thou hast decreed?

    Thou alone it is
that hath created the righteous,
preparing him from the womb
for the time of Thy good pleasure,
to heed Thy covenant
and walk in Thy ways.
    Thou hast [lavished] upon him
the abundance of Thy mercies,
opening all the straitness of his soul
to everlasting salvation[4]
and perpetual peace unfailing.
    Thou hast raised his inner glory
    out of the flesh.

    The wicked also hast Thou created
for the time of Thy good pleasure,
reserving them from the womb
for the day of slaughter,
because they walk in the way of the bad
and spurn Thy covenant,
and their soul abhors Thy statutes
and they take no pleasure in all Thou hast commanded,
but choose that which Thou hatest.
    All them that hate Thee hast Thou prepared
to wreak great judgments upon them
in the sight of all Thy creatures,
to serve as a sign and a token for ever,
to make known to all men Thy glory and strength.

    How can flesh have reason,
or the earth-bound direct its steps,
except that Thou hadst created spirit*
and ordained the working thereof?

* Heb. 'Thou it is that created spirit, etc.'.

So am I come to know
that no wealth can equal Thy truth,
and Thy holiness has no match.
And I know that Thou hast chosen these things
above all else
to serve Thee alway.
    Thou wilt accept no bribe
and Thou wilt accept no ransom
for deeds of wickedness.
For Thou art a God of truth
and [hatest*] all wrongdoing;
and no iniquity
shall exist in Thy presence.
    And I am come also to know
that [righteousness] is Thine
[and a]ll [Thy works are truth.]

.   .   .   .

* Or, 'wilt destroy'.

[Thou hast shed] Thy holy spirit
on righteous and [wicked alike,]
[and Thou wilt judge all men]
[according to their deeds.]

Thy holy spirit can [pass] not [away.]
The fulness of heaven and earth [attests it,]
and the sum of all things
[stands witness to] Thy glory.[1]

I know that in Thy good pleasure
Thou hast bestowed upon man
[wisdom and discernment] in abundance
[and hast imparted to him]
communion with Thy truth
together with all [,]
and hast [entrusted] him
with maintenance of the right
in that Thou hast laid upon him
Thy charges [and ordinances]
[that he] stumble [not] in any of his deeds.

Because that all these things
are present in my mind,

I would put into words
my prayer and confession of sin,
my constant search for Thy spirit,
the inner strength which is mine
through the holy spirit,
my devotion to the truth of Thy covenant,
the truth and sincerity
in which I walk,
my love of Thy name:

> Blessed art thou, O Lord,
> creator of all things,
> mighty in deed,[2]
> by Whom all things are wrought.
> Behold, Thou hast granted mercy to Thy servant
> and shed upon him in Thy grace
> Thine ever-compassionate spirit
> and the splendor of Thy glory.

Thine, Thine alone, is righteousness,
for Thou it is made all things.

¶Moreover, because I know
that Thou dost keep a record
of every righteous spirit,[3]
therefore have I chosen
to keep my hands unstained,
according to Thy will;
and the soul of Thy servant has abhorred
all unrighteous deeds.

Nevertheless I know
that no man can be righteous
without Thy help.
Wherefore I entreat Thee,
through the spirit which Thou hast put [within me,]
to bring unto completion
the mercies Thou hast shown unto Thy servant,
cleansing him with Thy holy spirit,
drawing him to Thee in Thy good pleasure,
[   ] him in Thine abundant lovingkindness,
granting to him that place of favor
which Thou hast chosen for them that love Thee

and observe Thy commandments,
that they may stand in Thy presence for ever.

    [Suffer not Beli]al [to ari]se
and immerse himself in Thy servant's spirit,
neither let [a spirit] perverse
[rule over] any of his deeds.[4]
Let not affliction confront him
to make him to falter from the statutes of Thy covenant,
but [crown him] with glory and truth.

    [For Thou are a God gracious] and mericiful,
longsuffering and abounding in lovingkindness and truth,
forgiving transgression [   ]
and relenting of [evil]
[unto them that love Him] and keep His command-
[ments'][5]
—even unto them that return unto Thee
in faithfulness and wholeness of heart
to serve Thee [and do what is] good in Thy sight.

    So turn not away the face of Thy servant
neither [reject] the son of [Thine] handmaid;
[for to Thee, O Lord, belongeth forgiven]ess,
and by Thine own words have I call[ed upon Thee.][6]

.   .   .   .

XVII, 1-XVIII, 30

(Eleven lines too fragmentary to translate seem to describe the doom which awaits the wicked.)

[For divine forgiveness]

In Thine [abundant] mercy
Thou hast said by the hand of Moses
that Thou wouldst forgive all iniquity and sin
and shrive all guilt and treason.[1]
And verily, though the roots of the mountains have blazed
and though the fire [has devoured]
to nethermost hell,[2]
yet, whensoever Thou has wrought Thy judgments
them hast Thou ever [redeemed]
that were fa[ithful to Thee]
that they might serve Thee in constancy
and that their seed might be ever in Thy presence;[3]
and Thou hast ever confirmed unto them Thine o[ath]
[to pass over all transg]ression[4]
and to cast away all their iniquities,[5]
and to give them for their inheritance
every mortal glory
and abundance of days.

So, for mine own part,
by virtue of the spirits[6]
which Thou hast set within me,
I will give free rein to my tongue
to tell forth Thy bounteous acts
and Thy forbearance towards me
and the deeds of Thy strong right hand,
and to [confess] my former transgressions
and to make prayer and supplication[7] before Thee
concerning mine [evil] deeds
and the waywardness of [my heart.]
For I have stained myself with filth,
and [turned] from communion with Thee,
and I have not att[ach]ed myself
[unto Thy congregation.]

Thou—with Thee lies bounty,
and of Thy nature it is
ever to dower blessing.[8]
  [Proffer,] then, Thy bounty
and redeem [my soul,]
and let the wicked be brought to an end!

[*For spiritual strength*]

Moreover, I have come to understand
that Thou hast ever directed the course
of such as Thou hast chosen,
bestowing insight upon him
that he sin not against Thee,
repaying unto him
all his affliction of heart
in Thy chastisements and Thy trials.
Thou hast delivered Thy servants
from sinning against Thee
and from stumbling in doing Thy will.
  Strengthen, then, the stand of this Thy servant
against all spirits of perverseness,
that he walk in all the ways which Thou lovest,
reject all that Thou hatest,

and do what is good in Thy sight.
   Yea, [   ] within me,
for of flesh is the spirit of Thy servant.

[For inner enlightenment]

[I am come also to know]
Thou hast ever wafted Thy holy spirit
on him who is Thy servant,
i[llumi]ning for him
the [dark places] of his heart
[with light like the sun.]
But I—behold, I look
to all covenants made by man,
[and all are nothing worth;]⁹
[while they that seek after Thy truth]
do surely find it,
[for on them Thy light] shineth;
and they that love it [are illumined]
[and walk in the glow of] Thy light for ever,¹⁰
and Thou raisest their hearts out of the [darkness.]

.   .   .   .

  Let, then, Thy light [shine ever on Thy servant]

.   .   .   .

for with Thee is light everlasting.

[For divine protection]

[I am come also to know]
that once Thou didst [   ]
and open the ear of one
who was but dust
[that He might hear Thy teaching]
[and deliver Thy chosen people]
[from folly] and delusion
and from the uncleanness which [.]
And Thou didst [   ] Thy [   ],
and [the hands] of Thy servant were steadied by Thy
    tr[uth,]
and have remained so for ever,

that he might announce Thy wondrous tidings
and reveal them to all who would hear.
[Thou didst strengthen him] by Thy strong right hand to
      lead [   ]
and Thou didst [   ] [him] by Thy mighty strength,
[that he might achieve renown] for Thy name
and triumph in glory.[11]

Withdraw not now Thy hand [from Thy people,]
that now too there might be among* them
men† that hold firm to Thy covenant,
that stand blameless before Thee!

[For power of speech]

Moreover, in the mouth of Thy servant
Thou didst open, as it were, a fount
and duly set§ on his tongue
[the words of Thy Law,]
that he might proclaim to human mold
what its fabric is,
and serve as the interpreter of these things
to dust like myself.

That fount didst Thou open also
that he might reprove what is molded of clay
concerning its way
and that which is born of woman
concerning its guiltiness,
every man according to his deeds.

[Thanksgiving for divine grace]

But lo, that fount serves also
as a wellspring of Thy truth
for every man whose spirit
Thou hast stayed by Thine own strength,
that he may walk in Thy truth,

* Heb. 'unto.'

† Heb. sg., viz., 'a man' that holds firm, etc.

§ Or, 'engrave' (despite the mixed metaphor!).

a herald of Thy good tidings,[12]
bringing cheer to the humble
through Thine abundant compassion,
sating from that fount
them that are wounded in spirit,
bringing to them that mourn
everlasting joy.[13]

. . . .
. . . .

   [Were it not for Thy grace,]
I could not have seen this thing.
[For how can] I look on [Thy glory]
except Thou open mine eyes?
How hear [the words of Thy truth]
[except Thou open mine ears?]
   Behold, my heart was amazed
that thus the Word was revealed
to one with ears unattuned,
and that a [wayward] heart
[was suffered to grasp these things.]
But now have I come to know
that for Thyself, O my God,
hast Thou done these things.
For what is mortal flesh
[that Thou shouldst so exalt it]
and work such wonders with it?
   Howbeit, Thou wast minded*
to consummate all things
and ordain them into Thy glory,
and hast therefore called into being
a host endowed with knowledge
to tell forth Thy mighty acts
unto mortal flesh,
and Thy sure ordinances
to that which is born [of woman.]
And Thou hast brought [Thine elect]
into covenant with Thee
and opened their heart of dust

* Heb. 'it was in Thy thought'.

that, in the face of Thy compassion,
they may be guarded from [   ]
[and escape] the traps of judgment.

So, for mine own part,
molded [of clay] that I am,
with an heart of stone,[14]
lo, of what worth am I,
that I should attain unto this?
Yet, behold, Thou hast set [Thy word]
in this ear of dust,
and graven upon this heart
eternal verities;*
and Thou hast brought to an end
[all of my frowardness,]
to bring me into covenant with Thee,
that I may stand [before Thee]
evermore unshaken†
in the glow of the Perfect Light,[15]
till the end of time,
where [no] darkness is for ever,
and where all is peace unbounded
until the end of time.

.   .   .   .

* Heb. 'realities'.
† Heb. 'in an eternal station'.

NOTES

The Hymn of the Initiants

1. I.e., at noon.

2. 'Storehouses of darkness' are mentioned (metaphorically) in Isa. 45.3.

3. Literally, 'and sets against it (?)'; the text is somewhat obscure.

4. I.e., at midnight. The reference in these lines is to the three statutory times of daily prayer; cf. Mishnah, *Berachoth*, iv.1.

5. On the basis of such Biblical passages as Hab. 3.11; Deut. 26.15; Jer. 25.30 and II Chron. 30.27, the terms 'Height' (Heb. *Zebul*) and 'Abode' (Heb. *Ma'on*) came to be used in rabbinic literature as names of two of the seven heavens.

6. In the calendarical system underlying the pseudepigraphic books of *Jubilees* and *Enoch*, seasons formally begin at new moon.

7. I.e., at solstice and equinox.

8. Cf. Ex. 12.14; Lev. 23.24; Num. 10.10.

9. An allusion to the belief, still maintained by the Samaritans, that *all* the commandments given to Moses were engraven by God on tablets. Compare Ex. 32.16.

10. An allusion to the obligation of bringing tribute at seasonal festivals; cp. Num. 15.19–20. Jewish tradition declares that prayer now substitutes for offerings, and the statutory services are still named for those offerings. The Essenes, says Josephus (*War*, I, iii, 5) did

not make offerings but 'offered sacrifices within themselves'. This was also the attitude of the early Church. The *Didascalia Apostolorum* declare expressly that 'instead of sacrifices which then were, offer now prayers and petitions and thanksgivings' (p. 86, ed. Conolly).

11. Cf. Lev. 25.8ff.

12. The expression occurs also in the Psalms of Solomon, 15.3: 'The fruit of the lips with the well-tuned instrument of the tongue, the first fruits of the lips from a pious and righteous heart—he that offereth these shall never be shaken by evil'. There is a subtle play on words in the original, for the Hebrew word *azammerah* means at once 'cull' (strictly, 'trim vines'; cf. Lev. 25.3) and 'sing'. The concept of 'fruit of the lips' is derived from Isa. 57.19, and more especially from a variant reading of Hos. 14.3(2) preserved in the Greek (Septuagint) and Syriac (Peshitta) translation (and adopted by the Revised Standard Version).

13. Compare Jer. 31.35–36. The point is that the Hebrew word for 'bound' also means 'statute, ordinance'. In observing the fixed order of day and night, the psalmist will be inspired likewise to abide by God's rules.

14. Literally, 'and where they [i.e., God's bounds, statutes] are will I set my boundary'.

15. The pious Jew offers a blessing every morning as soon as he takes his first steps, viz. 'Blessed art Thou, O Lord, our God, King of the Universe, Who directest the steps of man'.

16. An adaptation of the words, 'when thou liest down and when thou risest up', in Deut. 6.7. The pious Jew recites the *Shema'* (Deut. 6.4–9, etc.) when he lies down to sleep and when he wakes up in the morning—in the former case, in a recumbent position, in the latter standing up; comp. Mishnah, *Berachoth*, i.3.

17. An allusion to the benediction pronounced before meals, viz. 'Blessed art Thou, O Lord our God, King of the Universe, Who bringest forth food (bread) from the earth'.

18. An allusion to the blessing offered by Jews on hearing bad news, viz. 'Blessed is He, the truthful Judge' (Mishnah, *Berachoth*, ix.2). Compare Mishnah, *Ber.* ix.5: 'Man is obliged to offer blessing for evil as well as for good'.

19. An allusion to the blessing offered by Jews on deliverance from danger, viz. 'Blessed art Thou, O Lord our God . . . Who bestowest good things on the guilty, and Who hast bestowed a good thing upon me'.

20. An adaptation of Ps. 23.6.

21. Comp. Manual, ix.22.

22. Comp. Manual, ix.16.

23. The expression is derived from Deut. 32.35, according to the reading found in the Samaritan recension and in the Greek (Septuagint) Version, viz. 'Is not this stored up with Me . . . against the Day of Requital?' This reading is actually found in a fragment of Deuteronomy discovered at Qumran. See also Isa. 34.8; 61.2. 'Day of Requital' is the technical term among the Samaritans for Doomsday.

24. Comp. Manual, vii.8.

25. Comp. Manual, vii.9.

26. Comp. Manual, vii.5ff.

27. Pss. 16.8; 121.5.

28. Ps. 40.3(2).

29. Cp. Ephesians 1.3; II Thess. 1.5. A similar expression occurs at the beginning of the *Apostolic Constitutions*.

30. Based on Isa. 60.21; 61.3. The *Apostolic Constitutions* speaks of 'God's planting and the holy vineyard, the church catholic, the elect', and so too does Epiphanius, *Haer.*, xiv.4.

31. Cf. John 1.3.

32. The word, I suggest, has a technical nuance, for Josephus (*War*, II, viii, 7) speaks of one who was admitted to the communion after the first year of probation as 'one who comes nearer'. I would therefore make a distinction between 'coming near' as indicating

the first stage, and 'coming nearer' as indicating the
second. The former is here intended, since the psalmist virtually repeats the *preliminary* oath described in
Manual, col.i.

33. The Hebrew text is doubtful. Others read, 'a draining
of spittle', but I find this meaningless, because spittle
is *ejected*, not *drained*.

34. Job 33.6.

The Book of Hymns

1

1. This is perhaps the most intricate psalm in the collec-
tion, and in order to bring out the nexus of thought I
have had to resort to a certain amount of expansion
and paraphrase. The central idea appears to be that
God has appointed sentient spirits to inform and govern the various elements of the universe. The functions
and operations of such spirits were determined even
before they were created. Man too is endowed with
such a spirit. Hence, God knows and determines all
that man will ever do, think or say. But since God's
power is matched by His benevolence, He also forti-
fies that spirit against the trials and afflictions of human existence; and when it gets tainted by worldly
corruption, He constantly cleanses it. Man can save
himself from error and profanation by adopting a sober
and temperate mode of life.

Back of the psalm lies the doctrine of predestina-
tion, and it is therefore of interest to recall that, according to Josephus (*Ant.*, XIII, 5.9), the Essenes
held that fate governs all things.

2. Cp. Jer. 32.19.

3. Cp. Ex. 34.6. The psalmist resorts to the common rabbinic device of constrasting, or juxtaposing, the various attributes of God.

4. Cp. John 1.3.

5. Restored from Isa. 45.12.

6. The rabbinic tradition was that angels were created only on the second or fifth day; cp. Genesis Rabbah, i,3.

7. The restoration is based both on the general sense and on the assumption that the poet has in mind the Scriptural passages, Jer. 10.13; 51.16; Ps. 135.7, which he interpreted to refer to the emergence of *spirits* (rather than *winds*) from God's treasuries. The latter he then identified as the treasuries of *rain* (cp. Deut. 28.12), of the *deeps* (cp. Ps. 33.7), and of *snow* (cp. Job 38.22).

8. The language is borrowed from Num. 4.27.

9. Cp. Ps. 33.7.

10. Note the contrast between the *power* and the *wisdom* of God, exemplifying the general statement made in the opening lines. The restoration is imposed by the basic theme of the psalm.

11. Cp. Zech. 12.1.

12. Literally, 'at their fixed times'.

13. Cp. *Manual of Discipline*, iii, 14–15.

14. Cp. John 1.3.

15. Cp. Isa. 29.24; Ps. 95.10; I John 4.6 ('the spirit of error').

16. Cp. *Hymns*, xvi.10. See also T. H. Gaster, *Thespis* (1950), p. 384.

17. Cp. I Sam. 2.3.

18. The phrase is based on Hos. 14.3, read as in the Greek (Septuagint) and Syriac (Peshitta) Versions.

19. Literally, 'settest words upon a line'.

20. Literally, 'and the expression of the spirit of the lips in due measure'.

21. Literally, 'and Thou producest lines for their secrets'.

22. Literally, 'ye of low intellect'.

23. Literally, 'increase prudence [subtlety]'.

24. Usually, this expression denotes a gesture of rage.

Here, however, it would seem to have the sense of 'bite their lips', i.e., in remorse.

2

1. Restored from Jer. 16.19.
2. Deut. 33.11.
3. Ps. 51.10.
4. Mal. 1.4.
5. Ostensibly, this line would mean, 'I was a trap unto transgressors', but in view of the contrasting 'source of healing', it is apparent that the poet (whose vernacular would have been Aramaic) identified the Hebrew word *pah*, which normally means 'trap', with an homonym preserved in Syriac and Arabic, signifying 'weakness, debility'.
6. Ez. 36.3.
7. Job 30.9; Lam. 3.14.
8. Cp. Isa. 17.12.
9. Isa. 57.20.
10. Literally, 'the elect of righteousness' or 'the rightfully chosen'. But there is a play on words, for 'elect' was the technical term in Hebrew (and already in the cuneiform documents from Mari, of the 18th cent., B.C.) for 'picked troops'. This explains the reference to the 'banner', which is understood in the sense of a military ensign.
11. Prov. 12.1.
12. Judges 12.2; Jer. 15.10.
13. Isa. 30.10. (RSV: 'Prophesy not unto us what is right'. But the word rendered 'prophesy' really means 'see, envision', and that rendered 'what is right' really means 'straight things'.)
14. Num. 5.14, 30. The poet gives his own interpretation of the words usually rendered 'spirit of jealousy' (or, 'zeal').

15. Isa. 27.11.
16. Isa. 28.11.
17. Cf. Hos. 4.14.

3

1. I Sam. 25.29. These famous words are usually rendered, 'The soul of my lord shall be bound up in the bundle of life [or, the living]', and it is in this sense that they are commonly inscribed on Jewish tombstones. But the word rendered 'bundle' can also mean 'pouch, wallet', and the poet evidently understood the sentence—as did several medieval Jewish commentators—to imply that God will keep the faithful, like a treasure in a wallet, safe from Death.

2. Job 1.10.

3. Pss. 54.5; 86.14.

4. Cf. Isa. 30.30.

5. A fanciful interpretation of the Hebrew text of Isa. 59.5 (American Jewish Version: 'And that which is crushed breaketh out into a viper'). By construing the words differently, the poet obtained the sense, 'By repeated crushings they split all trivial things'.

6. Pss. 9.16; 35.7–8.

7. Ps. 26.12.

4

1. Ps. 82.3.

2. Jer. 31.11.

5

1. I Sam. 6.18; II Kings 10.2; Jer. 1.18; Ps. 108.11.

2. Jer. 4.31.

3. I Sam. 4.19; Dan. 10.16.

4. A play on Micah 2.10, for the Hebrew words which in that context mean 'grievous destruction' can also be construed in the sense of 'grievous throes'.

5. A play on II Kings 19.3; Isa. 37.3, for the Hebrew words which in those contexts mean 'children are come to the birth' can also be taken to mean 'children have reached a moment of disaster'. Moreover, there is a further *double entendre,* for the word which means 'birth' or 'disaster' can in turn be taken (by a change of vowels) to mean 'breakers of the sea', so that the phrase 'lethal birth-pangs' or 'deathly disaster' can be understood at the same time in the sense of 'deathly billows'. The poet has all three meanings in mind.

6. Isa. 66.7.

7. II Sam. 22.6 (Ps. 18.6).

8. Literally, 'One who is wonderful in counsel, a hero divine', alluding to Isa. 9.5.

9. Cf. Job. 38.8.

10. The poet has in mind the words of Isa. 42.14, 'Like a woman in travail I will gasp', but he takes the Hebrew word for 'I will gasp', viz. *ef'eh,* in the sense of the very similar *ef'â,* 'nothingness, futility', in Isa. 41.24. The expression 'like a woman in travail with futility' then suggests to him the expression, 'They that carry in their wombs (Heb. sg.) the seeds of worthlessness'.

11. Ps. 107.27 (RSV: 'They are at their wits' end').

12. Job 41.23(31).

13. A play on Job 38.16, where (by changing the vowels) the Hebrew words for 'springs of the sea' can be interpreted to mean 'eddies of the sea'. This, it may be added, is the way in which the ancient Aramaic translation (Targum) understood them, and our poet had the same tradition.

14. In later times, it was a common Jewish superstition that demons were released from the netherworld during the week but confined there over the sabbath.

15. Disaster was often portrayed in antiquity as the loos-

ing of divine or demonic arrows; cf. Ps. 91.5; Job 6.4.
In the *Iliad* (i, 51), the plague which besets the
Greeks before Troy is attributed to the arrows of
Apollo, and in the Middle Ages, a man who was
diseased was said to be 'elf-shot'.

16. Cf. Jonah 2.6.

6

1. Isa. 38.17.

2. Prov. 15.11; 27.20. The term rendered 'Perdition' was
   sometimes used as a synonym for 'hell' (Ps. 88.12; Job
   26.6, etc.). It is the Hebrew Abbadon, which occurs in
   Revelation 9.11 as the name of the demon of the
   abyss.

3. Ezra 10.2.

4. The expression is based on Isa. 19.14 (RSV: 'spirit of
   confusion', literally, 'of distortions').

5. Ps. 19.14.

6. Cp. *Manual of Discipline* ii, 25; iv, 22; Ephes. 2.19.

7. Cf. Isa. 52.8; Ps. 98.9; Job 38.7—all of which passages
   show that the Hebrew words mean simply 'sing together, in chorus', not 'sing in the Community', as
   some scholars have mistakenly rendered.

   We may perhaps compare Plotinus, *Enneads*, vi, 9:
   'When we behold Him, we attain the end of our existence and our rest. Then we no longer sing out of tune,
   but form a truly divine chorus about Him'.

8. Pss. 9.2; 26.7; 75.2.

9. Mal. 1.4.

10. Amos 3.9.

11. This is simply an approximate rendering. The Hebrew
    word occurs only once in the Bible (Isa. 14.4)—and
    even there the reading is uncertain—and its meaning
    is not yet definitely determined (RSV: 'insolent fury';
    Moffatt: 'mad rage').

12. Based on Isa. 19.8.

13. See note 15 to Hymn No. 5.

14. Jer. 42.18; Nah. 1.6, etc.

15. The Hebrew word occurs only at Ps. 26.4. It is apparently derived from a verbal root meaning 'hide, conceal', and is therefore usually rendered 'dissemblers' (Moffatt: 'hypocrites'). However, it is quite common in the dialect of the Samaritans in the general sense of 'wrongdoers'.

16. Pss. 18.5; 116.3.

17. Ps. 18.5.

18. Ez. 21.3(20.47).

19. Cf. Deut. 32.22.

20. Cf. Isa. 34.9.

21. Suggested by Amos 7.4.

22. Isa. 57.20.

23. I Sam. 2.10; II Sam. 22.14; Ps. 18.14; Job 37.4.

24. Isa. 63.15. The archaic 'welkin' conveys the effect of the Hebrew word, which really means 'eminence, lofty structure', but came in post-Biblical Jewish literature to be the name of one of the seven heavens.

25. Cf. Zech., ch. 14. The idea is fully developed in the *War of the Sons of Light and the Sons of Darkness*. Armed soldiers of heaven are mentioned in Slavonic Enoch 17.1, and in rabbinic literature, the heavenly host are sometimes described as an 'army'.

26. Dan. 9.27.

7

1. Cf. Isa. 26.1.

2. Restored from Ps. 40.3.

8

1. Hos. 6.3 (which the poet construed in the light of a similar expression in Prov. 4.18).

2. Prov. 2.16; 7.5.

3. Hos. 4.14.

4. Ps. 31.13(12). Compare 'crackpot'.

5. Ps. 69.22.

6. The phrase is suggested by Hab. 2.15. The traditional ('Masoretic') text reads: 'Woe to him that plies his neighbor with drink . . . so as to gaze on his [Heb. 'their'] nakedness'. However, in the Dead Sea *Commentary on Habakkuk* the passage is read (with a change of but one letter in the Hebrew), '. . . so as to gaze on their festivals', and it is this reading that the poet clearly has in mind.

7. Prov. 19.21.

8. See note 15 to Hymn No. 6.

9. Deut. 29.17(18).

10. Ez. 14.3, 4, 7.

11. Isa. 28.11.

12. Ps. 10.2.

13. Extirpation from the community was the statutory punishment in Jewish law for blasphemy or idolatry; cf. Num. 15.30; Mishnah, *Kerithoth* ('Extirpations'), i, 1.

14. Ps. 20.9(8).

15. Cf. Isa. 44.18.

16. Heb. 'in the council of the holy beings' (cf. Ps. 89.7). Since the Hebrew word here rendered 'rallied' refers specifically to the marshaling of troops, and since the expression, 'have hearkened unto me' may very well allude to the Roman practice of reciting the military oath to new recruits, it seems permissible to recognize a military metaphor, and for that reason the term 'legion' has been used.

17. Hab. 1.4.

18. Ez. 7.17; 21.12(7).

19. Micah 1.4.

20. Ps. 65.4.

9

1. Ex. 21.8.

2. Ps. 57.5.

3. Literally, 'And Thou hast placed me in the drag [Heb. *magor*; cf. Hab. 1.15], with many fishermen spreading their nets on the face of the waters [cf. Isa. 19.8] and (with) huntsmen (hunting) after wrongdoers'.

4. An interpretation of Hab. 1.12.

5. Pss. 57.3; 59.8.

6. Ps. 57.5.

7. Deut. 32.33. A word has evidently fallen out of the Hebrew text.

8. Cf. Isa. 56.1.

9. Nah. 2.12.

10. Pss. 64.4; 120.4; 140.4.

11. Jer. 47.6.

12. Ps. 12.7.

13. Ps. 107.29.

10

1. An interpretation of a word which in Isa. 32.4 and 35.4 is usually rendered 'rash'. It comes from a root meaning 'be hasty', but the poet uses it here in the sense of 'timorous'.

2. An interpretation of Ps. 40.3(2) which is usually rendered, somewhat incongruously, 'He brought me up from the pit of tumult'. The poet understood the Hebrew word 'tumult', viz. *shaôn*, in the sense of the like-sounding Aramaic *seyan*, 'mud'—an interpretation which, it may be added, was proposed independently by the present writer many years ago.

3. Literally, 'in the mirings of [their] feet'. The poet em-

ploys a very rare term which occurs only in Isa. 14.23 and there means 'broom, besom'. However, ancient commentators and lexicographers connected it (perhaps correctly) with the like-sounding Hebrew word for 'mud'—the very word used in Ps. 40.3, which the poet has just quoted. It is evident that he had the same tradition.

4. Prov. 6.19; 10.12.

5. Obadiah 7; Ps. 41.10. Compare 'com-pani-on'.

6. Ps. 41.10(9).

7. Cp. Prov. 4.24, where similar Hebrew words are rendered 'devious speech'.

8. Restored after Lam. 3.9.

9. Deut. 32.33.

10. The Hebrew expression is a clever adaptation of Hab. 2.3 which the poet read according to the text preserved in the Greek Septuagint Version rather than in the traditional Jewish recension.

11. Ps. 58.6(5).

12. Isa. 17.11.

13. Lev. 13.51.

14. An adaptation of Lam. 1.14.

15. Lam. 1.3.

16. Zeph. 1.15; Job 30.3; 38.27. The words may also be rendered 'ruin and devastation'.

17. Ps. 11.6 (interpreted metaphorically).

18. Isa. 50.3.

19. Ps. 137.6; Job 29.10.

20. Ps. 102.10(9).

21. Pss. 6.8(7); 31.10(9).

22. Job 3.5. I read *bi-merîrê yôm* in place of *bi-merôdê yôm* of the *editio princeps*.

23. Isa. 45.2; Ps. 107.16.

24. Ps. 18.4.

25. I Sam. 9.15; 20.12–13; II Sam. 7.27, etc.

26. Cf. Isa. 13.4; Ps. 46.7.

27. Ezra 9.8–9.

28. A common expression in post-Biblical Hebrew for the ministering angels who stand before God.

29. The Hebrew text is here faint and fragmentary, so that the rendering is largely a guess. (For *banîm* of the transcription, which makes no sense, I have emended *bênam*, after Gen. 42.23.)

30. The Hebrew text is here virtually illegible.

31. Suggested by Ez. 31.3ff. and Dan. 4.8(11).

32. Inspired by Ez. 31.4, 7.

33. Cf. Isa. 52.1.

34. Adapted from Nah. 1.11.

35. Isa. 19.14 (where the term is used figuratively).

36. Ps. 107.18.

37. Isa. 28.16.

38. I.e., God; cf. Isa. 42.13; Zeph. 3.17.

39. Military ensigns were certainly used in Israelite warfare (cf. Isa. 5.26; Jer. 4.6), but perhaps the poet is thinking more specifically of the *Roman* technical expression, *signa tollere,* 'to lift the ensigns', in the sense of 'to set the army on the march'.

40. Cf. Job 25.6.

41. Isa. 28.15, 18.

10a

1. Job 31.22.

2. Isa. 6.10.

3. Ps. 22.15(14).

4. An interpretation of an obscure term in Jonah 4.8, usually rendered 'sultry wind'.

11

1. Isa. 26.6; 30.13; Ps. 139.6; Prov. 18.19.

2. For the sake of clarity, I have slightly altered the

structure of this sentence. In the original it reads: 'Thou hast set me as a strong tower on a high wall, and hast planted my structure firmly on a rock, and eternal foundations serve as my basis, and all my walls are a tested bastion that cannot be shaken'.

3. The Hebrew says literally: 'And Thou, O my God, hast provided (given) it for them that fly to the holy council (or, counsel)'. I am not at all sure what this means. But rather than suppose a corruption of the text—always the last shift of the desperate—I have assumed that the poet is combining two ideas, viz. (a) that of the high tower as a refuge for birds soaring heavenward, and (b) that of God's truth as a tower of refuge for spirits that aspire to communion with Him and that rise, as it were, on the wings of devotion. One may compare, perhaps, the great sentence in *The Mirror of Simple Souls* (Div. iv, c.1): 'This [soul] is the eagle that flies high, so right high and yet more high than doth any bird; for she is feathered with fine love'.

4. Cf. Isa. 50.4.

5. Literally, 'in Thy covenant'.

6. In the *Didascalia Apostolorum* (p. 45, ed. Achelis-Fleming), the bishop is called 'Father in God'.

7. Zech. 3.8.

8. Ps. 92.11, etc.

9. Isa. 17.13; Ps. 1.4; 35.5.

10. Comp. Isa. 60.19; Rev. 21.23, 25; 22.6. The Talmud says that the light of the Messianic sun will be sevenfold strong; TB Sanhedrin, 91b.

11. Isa. 60.20.

12

1. Ex. 15.11.

2. Prov. 4.26.

13

1. Restored on the basis of Ps. 9.11(10).

14

1. Isa. 35.7; 49.10.
2. Isa. 41.19.
3. Jer. 17.8.
3a. The restoration is dictated by the sense; cp. Prov. 3.18.
4. Cf. Dan. 4.9(12); Ez. 31.6.
5. Cf. Ez. 31.4.
6. Ps. 103.20.
7. Gen. 3.24.
8. The passage is obscure, and the rendering therefore provisional.
9. Isa. 57.20.
10. Isa. 58.11.
11. Cf. Deut. 28.12.
12. Jer. 47.2.
13. Cp. Isa. 8.7.
14. The reference is to the subterranean springs which suddenly burst forth at the foot of the hills to relieve the summer drought; see G. A. Smith, *Historical Geography of the Holy Land*, p. 77.
15. Ez. 21.3(20.47).
16. Something like this must obviously be supplied, to provide the requisite contrast.
17. Ex. 15.10.
18. For the Hebrew idiom, cp. Isa. 28.17.
19. Isa. 5.2.
20. Isa. 40.24.
21. Jer. 17.6; 48.6.

21a. Hos. 10.8.

22. Isa. 5.6.

22a. Isa. 5.2, 4 (commonly rendered 'wild grapes').

22b. Isa. 17.11.

22c. Ps. 42.6, 12(11); 43.5.

23. In the Hebrew, this is a combination of Ps. 77.7(6) and Ps. 88.6(5). In both passages, a word *ḥ-p-s* is employed. In the first, it actually means 'search out' (*ḥappes*); in the second, 'free, quit' (*ḥophshi*). But our author evidently equated it in both instances with a root akin to Arabic *ḥafatha*, 'be low, sordid'. In the Ras Shamra texts, of the fourteenth century B.C., the cognate term *ḥ-p-sh-t* denotes the 'charnel house' of the netherworld.

24. Ps. 88.4(3).

24a. Ps. 107.5; Jonah 2.8.

25. Jer. 20.9.

25a. Ps. 42.7(6); 43.5.

26. Job 31.22.

26a. Literally, 'Thou didst make my tongue dominate my mouth, without being drawn back'.

27. Isa. 50.4.

15

1. Cf. Isa. 42.13.

1a. II Sam. 22.5.

2. I.e., the netherworld.

3. Cf. Ps. 6.7(6).

4. There is a slight error in the text: for *k'sh* we must read *k'shn;* cf. Ex. 19.18.

5. Lam. 2.18.

6. Ps. 31.11; Lam. 2.11.

7. Cf. Zeph. 1.15; Job 30.3; 38.27.

8. Literally, 'supplication'; but the Hebrew word is connected with the idea of grace.

9. Jer. 50.34; 51.36.

10. Cp. *Manual of Discipline,* iv, 7; I Peter 5.4.

10a. I restore the Hebrew to read: *ve-[natatah le-ḥillu]ṣ makkati;* cf. Isa. 58.11.

11. Ps. 27.10.

12. Cf. Num. 11.12.

13. Job 34.15; Eccl. 3.20.

14. The Hebrew has: 'Except Thou hast formed me', which makes no sense. The word *yaṣartah,* 'Thou hast formed', is evidently an error for the very similar *haṣerotah* (or *'aṣartah?*), 'Thou hast constrained, hemmed in'.

15. John 1.3.

16

1. Philo (*Quod Omnis Probus Liber,* 12) says of the Essenes: 'They do not lay up treasures of gold and silver, nor acquire tracts of land out of a desire for revenues, but provide themselves only with the bare necessities of life'. Similarly, Josephus observes (*War,* II, viii, 2) that 'they despise riches', and Pliny (*Natural History,* V. 17) that 'they live without money'.

2. Jer. 17.8; Ps. 1.3.

3. Jer. 17.8.

4. Epiphanius (*Adv. Haer.,* I, ord. xix, p. 39) says that the Essenes eschewed meat. His statement, however, is held by many to be unreliable.

5. Ps. 103.20.

6. Cf. Prov. 7.27.

7. Job 3.10.

17

1. Literally, 'circumcision of lips'. The expression is modelled on the Biblical 'one of uncircumcised lips' ='stammerer' (Ex. 6.12, 30).

2. Isa. 41.14.

3. Literally, 'those versed in concerted song'. The Jewish Daily Morning Service speaks of the angelic choir as 'all of them opening their mouths in holiness and purity, in song and chant, blessing, praising, glorifying, and proclaiming both the awe and the holiness and the sovereignty of God . . . all of them giving accord to one another to praise their Creator in tranquillity of spirit and with holy chant; all of them taking up word as one and saying, Holy, holy, holy is the Lord of Hosts; the fullness of the whole earth is His glory'.

4. On regeneration as a mystical experience, see E. Underhill, *Mysticism* (ed. 1955), pp. 53f.

18

1. II Sam. 22.3, 47; Ps. 19.15(14); 28.1; 62.3, 7(2, 6); 144.1, etc.

2. Gen. 3.19; Job 34.15; Eccl. 12.7.

3. Lam. 2.18.

4. Job 3.10.

5. Literally, 'And reached [touched] my bones'.

6. Cf. Isa. 35.10; 51.11.

7. Restored from Ps. 107.42; Job 5.16.

19

1. I read *môserai*, after Ps. 116.16.

2. Cp. Ps. 138.3.

3. Restored from Ps. 118.15.

4. Cf. note 7 to *Column XVII.*

5–6. Cp. *Hymn of the Initiants*, 1–10.

7. I.e. their several governing constellations.

[From this point it becomes impossible to distinguish the separate hymns. The notes are therefore geared to the columns of the original text.]

Column XIII

1. The restoration is tentative, but it is obvious from the sequel that these lines must have recited the doctrine that all things have been endowed with spirit and intelligence wherewith to perceive the truth and reality of God. This is scarcely to be confused with the later more elaborate doctrine of the Gnostics.

2. Cf. *Manual of Discipline*, iv, 7; I Peter 5.4.

3. This chimes with the rabbinic doctrine of periodic renewal. An ancient prayer in the Jewish Daily Morning Service says of God that 'He reneweth every day continually the work of creation'. Not the least significant doctrine of the Brotherhood, from the religious point of view, was that of constant creation.

4. Literally, 'Annulling ancient pacts (the word means also 'established things') and [establi]shing the existences of the world' (or, 'of eternity', although this latter rendering involves a certain incongruity).

5. Modelled after the common rabbinic expression, 'portent of the age', usually applied to a prominent scholar.

6. Isa. 66.24. (Cp. also Dan. 12.2.)

7. Restored on the basis of Jos. 23.14.

8. Cp. Ps. 111.2 (which the author must have understood to mean 'sought out for their several purposes', rather than 'sought out [or, studied] by all who have pleasure in them', as usually rendered).

Column XIV

1. Restored on the basis of Ezra 9.8.
2. Another possible restoration is: 'men of truth and dis[cernment]'.
3. Restored from Ex. 19.6.
4. The fourth of the Eighteen Benedictions which form a staple element of all Jewish devotions ends: 'Blessed art Thou, O Lord, Who gracest man with knowledge'.
5. Cp. *Manual of Discipline*, i, 3–4.
6. Probably in the technical sense of admission to the Brotherhood; cf. *Hymn of the Initiants*, note 32.
7. Cp. *Manual*, ix, 20.
8. Cp. *Manual*, iv, 1.
9. See above, note 4.
10. Hos. 14.5.

Column XV

1. Hos. 14.5.
2. Ps. 37.23; Prov. 20.24.
3. Josephus (*Ant.*, XIII, 5.9) says of the Essenes that they believed all things were pre-ordained.
4. Isa. 45.17.

Column XVI

1. Isa. 6.3.
2. Jer. 32.19.
3. On this concept, cf. T. H. Gaster, *Thespis* (1950), p. 348f.
4. Cp. *Manual*, iii, 20ff.
5. Ex. 34.5, 7–9.

6. The reference is to Ex. 34.5ff., just quoted. According
   to the Talmud (*Rosh Ha-Shanah,* 17b), this formula
   was prescribed by God as that which Israel was to
   repeat when entreating forgiveness of sins. For that
   reason, it runs like a refrain through the Confessions
   on the Day of Atonement.

Columns XVII–XVIII

1. Ex. 34.5ff.
2. Deut. 32.22.
3. Cf. Ps. 102.29(28).
4. Ex. 34.6.
5. Cf. Micah 7.19, and see T. H. Gaster, *Festivals of the
   Jewish Year* (1953), pp. 121–23.
6. The reference is to the *two* spirits described in the
   Manual of Discipline, cols. iii–iv.
7. The terms employed in the Hebrew (viz. *tefillah* and
   tahanun) denote in Jewish usage statutory and spontaneous prayer.
8. An adaptation of Dan. 9.7, the Hebrew word *zeda-
   quah,* which there means 'righteousness', being taken
   in its later sense of 'charity, bounty'. Similarly, the
   common phrase, 'To Thy name pertains blessing', is
   taken to mean 'And of Thy nature it is to bestow
   blessing'.
9. The restoration is based on the obviously implied contrast between covenants made by men and those made
   by God.
10. Isa. 60.19–20.
11. The clue to this very difficult passage is to be found,
    I think, in the sequence of the phrases, 'The hands of
    Thy servant were steadied' and 'that he might triumph
    in glory'; for these expressions hark back to the inci-
    dent related in Ex. 17.8–13. During the battle against
    Amalek at Rephidim, 'when Moses held up his hand,
    Israel *triumphed;* and when he let down down his

hand, Amalek *triumphed*. But Moses' hands grew heavy . . . so Aaron and Hur stayed up his hands on either side; *and his hands were steady* until the going down of the sun'. The allusion, therefore, is to Moses, though the poet obviously uses the Biblical expressions in an extended sense.

12. Isa. 61.1. (The prototype of the term 'gospel'!)

13. Isa. 61.2–3.

14. Ez. 11.19; 36.26.

15. Heb. *Ôr-Tôm;* cf. Introduction, p. 21.

THE WORD
OF GOD

The Study of Scripture

The grass withereth, the flower fadeth; but the word of our God shall stand for ever.

ISAIAH 40.8.

INTRODUCTION Believing firmly that they stood on the threshold of the New Age, the members of the Brotherhood were especially interested in searching the Scriptures for intimations of current events. A form of interpretation thereby developed in which the words of the ancient prophets were deftly applied to the contemporary scene. Such interpretations were doubtless propounded not only in the course of general study but more especially when portions of the Law and the Prophets were read during the public devotions on the sabbath. Philo tells us distinctly concerning the Essenes that 'on the seventh day . . . they go to the sacred places called synagogues . . . and listen with becoming attention. Then one of them takes the Scriptures and reads, while another, selected from those most versed in the subject, comes forward and expounds it, passing over more recondite points. For they philosophize on most things by construing them symbolically [literally, by symbols], in accordance with ancient usage'. Similarly, in the Gospel of Luke we are told (4.16ff.) how Jesus once attended synagogue at Nazareth on the sabbath, read publicly the Lesson from the Prophets and then proceeded to expound it in terms of current events: 'Today hath this scripture been fulfilled in your hearing'.

The following texts represent this type of Scriptural exposition as it obtained among the Brotherhood. They may be regarded as coming from 'sermons' delivered by the various 'teachers of righteousness' or other instructors.

The *Commentary on Micah* (a mere fragment) scarcely deserves special comment, since it contains nothing of importance save the rather general polemic against the priests in Jerusalem.

The special interest of the *Commentary on Nahum* lies in the fact that it contains the only explicit historical allusion thus far found in the Scrolls—namely, a reference to an incident which occurred in 88 B.C. and which is related in detail by Josephus. This establishes beyond doubt the date before which it could not have been written; and if it really came from the library of the Qumran 'Monastery' and was cached at the approach of the Roman legions in 68 A.D., the time of its composition can thus be fixed within about one hundred and fifty years. It would be hazardous, however, to conclude that this necessarily settles the date of *all* the 'commentaries', though it clearly strengthens the hypothesis that they belong to the Roman rather than to an earlier period. Nor, further, should it be supposed that because the commentator illustrates a particular passage of Scripture by this reference to Demetrius Eucerus and Alexander Jannaeus, all other references to 'men of lies' and 'wicked priests' necessarily refer to the same persons. In other words, there is no warrant for the assumption that the *Commentary on Nahum* establishes a definitive frame of reference for the commentaries as a whole and hence a date for the Scrolls in general.

The *Commentary on Habakkuk* has aroused special interest for two reasons. The first is that an observation contained in it—namely, its comment on Hab. 2.15—has been taken by several scholars to imply that the Brotherhood believed in a Christ-like Teacher of Righteousness who suffered a martyr's death but subsequently 'reappeared in glory' to his disciples. The second is that the various allusions in this document to the 'teacher of righteous', the 'wicked priest', and the 'man of falsehood' have been thought to constitute a connected biographical narrative which, once the characters are identified, might provide a definitive clue to the antiquity of the text and thence possibly to that of the Scrolls as a whole. With the untenability of the former theory and with the precariousness of the latter we have already dealt in the General Introduction to this volume. Nothing further, therefore, need here be said on these matters.

On the other hand, there is a little detail in the *Commentary on Habakkuk* which appears to have been overlooked, but which may prove of considerable importance for the identification of the Brotherhood. Interpreting the prophet's words (2.17), 'The violence of Lebanon shall overwhelm thee', our author observes, 'Lebanon stands for the Communal Council'. The basis of this interpretation is, I suggest, that the name Lebanon really means 'white' (Heb. *laban*); and what the author had in mind was that the Communal Council was white-robed. His statement would then chime perfectly with Josephus' assertion (*War*, II, viii, 3) that 'the Essenes dressed in white'—a custom still observed by the Samaritans and Mandaeans. In other words, this comment might provide evidence that the Brotherhood were indeed Essenes.

The only noteworthy point in the *Commentary on Psalm Thirty-Seven* (again fragmentary) is the reference to the forty-year period of 'Messianic tribulation', harmonizing with what is said in the *War of the Sons of Light and the Sons of Darkness,* and with a well-known rabbinic tradition.

Of a different order is the work which Barthélemy and Milik have called *The Speeches of Moses.* Pieced together with phenomenal skill out of some forty-nine tiny fragments, this is a paraphrase of Moses' farewell address to Israel as recorded in the Book of Deuteronomy. The extant portion covers the exordium, the law about the Year of Release (Deut. 15.1ff.), and the ritual of the Day of Atonement. The author hews close to the Scriptural text, tricking it out from parallel passages in Leviticus. In one passage, however, he spices the narrative with the legend (apparently unknown to rabbinic sources) that the calendar date of the Day of Atonement coincides with that on which the Children of Israel ended their wanderings in the wilderness. This is a telltale addition, for it establishes clearly the *genre* of literature to which our document must be referred. Clearly no 'sermon'—for it contains no homiletical elaboration of the Scripture—it must be regarded as one of those popular 'expansions' of Holy Writ which are represented in antiquity by such works as the *Book of Jubilees*, the so-called *Biblical Antiquities of Philo*, and the several 'apocalypses' attached to old Testament characters; and in later ages, by the *Book of Jashar*, the *Chronicle of Yosippon*, the Samaritan *Stories [Asātir] of Moses*, the Byzantine *Palaea*, the *Historia Scholastica* of Petrus Comestor, and the celebrated *Bible Historiale*. Indeed, it is not without interest that a *Testament of Moses* (the nature of which has long been a matter of scholarly conjecture) is actually mentioned in the list of pseudepigraphic books appended to the chronography of Nicephorus, Patriarch of Constantinople in the early part of the ninth century, as well as in the so-called *Catalogue of the Sixty Books* sometimes tacked on to manuscripts of the *Quaestiones* of Anastasius of Sinai—a catalogue which may date from the sixth or seventh century.

The Oration of Moses

A PARAPHRASE OF THE LAW

Moses' farewell exhortation

¶And [God called] unto Moses in the [fortieth] year of the going out of the [children] of Israel [from the land of] Egypt, in the eleventh month, on the first day of the month, saying:

[Gather together] all the congregation, and go up unto [Mount Nebo] and stand there, thou and Eleazar, [the son of] Aaron.

Interpret [the Law] [unto the heads of the fam]ilies, unto the levites and all the [priests];

And enjoin upon the children of Israel the words of the Law which I commanded [thee] on Mount Sinai to enjoin upon [them].

Explain carefully in their hearing all that [I exact] of them; [and call] heaven and [earth to witness] concerning that which will befall them if they and their children [walk] not in the way which I have commanded [them throughout their lives] on earth.

[For] I declare that if they renounce Me and choose [the filthy ways of] the heathen and their abominations and their idols, and if they [worship] their godlings, these will prove but a trap and a snare.

And if they neglect [any] of the holy [convocations], or the sabbath which is itself a Covenant, [or the festivals] which I command them this day to observe, it shall redound to their being [smitten] with a great [smiting] in the midst of that land [for the possession of which] they are about to cross the Jordan.

For all the curses [of the Covenant] will come upon them and overtake them, to the end that they shall perish and be [destroyed]. Then shall they know [that] the truth has been evinced among them.

So Moses called Eleazar the son of [Aaron] and Joshua [the son of Nun and said unto] them: Rehearse [all the words of the Law] completely. . . .

¶[Give ear,] O Israel, and hearken! This [day art thou to become a people] unto GOD* [your God].

Thou shalt keep [My statutes] and Mine orders and My [commandments] which [I] command thee this day [to perform].

When thou crossest the [Jordan] to [possess thee] of great and goodly [cities], of houses filled with all [goodly things, of vineyards and olives] which thou didst not [plant], and of hewn wells which thou didst not hew; and when thou eatest and art satisfied,

[Beware] lest thy heart become haughty and thou [forget] that which I [command] thee this day. For it is [thy] life and the length of [thy] days.

¶Then Moses [summoned the children of] Israel and [said]:

This day it is forty [years] since we went out from the land of Egypt; and this [day] hath GOD our God [caused] all these words—[all] His judgments and commandments—[to issue] from His mouth.

How can [I myself alone bear] your cumbrance and your [burden and your strife? When I am done with imparting unto you] the Covenant and with enjoining the way in which ye are to walk, [take you wise men who] shall serve to explain [unto you] and your [children] all the words of the Law.

Take heed exceedingly unto your souls [that ye do them, lest] the wrath of [your God] be fanned into flame and

* A pious substitute for YHWH, the ineffable name.

blaze against you, and He shut up the heavens above that
they rain no rain upon you, and the [waters] below, that
[the earth] yield no [produce] for you.

And Moses [went on to rehearse] unto the children of
Israel all these commandments [which God] had commanded them to do. . . .

Of the Year of Release

¶[At the end of every seven] years [thou shalt observe] a
sabbatical rest [of the land. The produce of] the earth
[during that period of rest shall serve both thee and the
domestic beasts and the wild animals] of the field [for
food]; and what is left shall be for the [needy] among thy
brethren, who are [in the land].

No man shall [then] sow [his field] or prune his [vine-
yard, neither shall anyone glean the aftermath of the
harvest, nor] gather fruits for himself.

[Thou shalt observe] all these [words] of the Covenant,
[to perform them].

If thou [attend carefully] to the performance of [this
commandment], and if thou [truly] 'relax thy [hand]' in
that year, it shall mean also that anyone who is [a creditor
of another] and hath [a claim of any kind] upon him [in
respect of a loan] shall [likewise] 'relax [his hand'.] [It
shall be called the Release] ordained by GOD [your God.]

One may exact payment from an alien, but not from any
of one's own brethren. For in that year God will bless you,
and He [too] will absolve you—of your iniquities.

Of the Day of Atonement

¶[   ] on this day. . . .

For your [fathers] were wanderers [in the wilderness]
until the tenth day of the [seventh] month. . . .

On the tenth [day] of the month, [all work] shall be
forbidden; and on that tenth day, atonement shall be
made. . . .

[   ] [day] of the month [   ] shall take
[   ].

[   ] [On that day, judgment shall be passed] also
upon the congregation of the angels and upon the company of the Holy Beings. . . .

[   ] [on behalf of the children of] Israel and on
behalf of the land. He* shall [take of its blood] and pour
[it] upon the ground [   ]. And [atonement] shall
be made for them. (*The rest of the text is fragmentary. It
describes the ritual of the Day of Atonement.*)

* I.e., the high priest.

MICAH

1 THE word of the LORD that came to Micah the Morashtite in the days of Jotham, Ahaz, and Hezekiah, kings of Judah, which he saw concerning Samaria and Jerusalem.

2 Hear, ye peoples, all of you; hearken, O earth, and all that therein is: and let the Lord GOD be witness against you, the LORD from his holy

3 temple. For, behold, the LORD cometh forth out of his place, and will come down, and tread upon the high

4 places of the earth. And the mountains shall be molten under him, and the valleys shall be cleft, as wax before the fire, as waters that are poured down a steep place.

5 For the transgression of Jacob is all this, and for the sins of the house of Israel. What is the transgression of Jacob? is it not Samaria? and what are the high places of Judah? are they not Jerusa-

6 lem? Therefore I will make Samaria as an heap of the field, *and* as the plantings of a vineyard: and I will pour down the stones thereof into the valley, and I will discover the foundations there-

7 of. And all her graven images shall be beaten to pieces, and all her hires shall be burned with fire, and all her idols will I lay desolate: for of the hire of an harlot hath she gathered them, and unto the hire of an harlot shall

8 they return. For this will I wail and howl, I will go stripped and naked: I will make a wailing like the jackals, and a mourning like

9 the ostriches. For her wounds are incurable: for it is come even unto Judah; it reacheth unto the gate of my people, even to Jerusalem.

Commentary on the
Book of Micah

(5) *All this is because of the transgression of Jacob,
and the sins of the house of Israel. What is the transgression of Jacob? Surely, Samaria! . . . So I will turn Samaria into a heap in a field, a place for the planting of
a vineyard.* This refers to the preacher of falsehood, who
leads the simple-minded astray.[1]

*But what are the (true) 'high places' of Jewry? Surely,
Jerusalem!* This on the other hand refers to those who
expound the Law correctly to God's people and to all who
are willing to join His elect—that is, the doers of the Law
—when the latter meet together in the communal council.
These will be delivered from the Day of Judgment.[2]

(6) As to the words: *I will turn Samaria into a heap
in a field, a place for the planting of a vineyard; and I will
roll down her stones into the valley, and uncover her foundations* [   ], this refers to the Jerusalemitan priests
who are leading God's people astray. [God will thrust them
forth, to become sojourners in a foreign land; and He will
drive all] His enemies [into exile.][3]

*   *   *   *

(8) *I will go stripped and naked . . . for it is come unto
Judah; it reacheth unto the gate of my people, unto Jerusa-*

lem. [   ] [God] will wreak judgment on His enemies [   ] [them who sought] to betray Him.[4]

(9) As to the words: *It reacheth into the gate of my
people,* this means that God's glory will move (once
more) from Seir to Jerusalem. [   ] For God will come
forth from [   ].[5]

CHAPTER II

11 Where *is* the dwelling of the lions, and the feeding-place of the young lions, where the lion and lioness walked, *and* the lion's whelp, and none made *them* afraid?

12 The lion did tear in pieces enough for his whelps, and strangled for his lionesses, and filled his holes with prey, and his dens with ravin.

13 Behold, I *am* against thee, saith the LORD of hosts, and I will burn her chariots in the smoke, and the sword shall devour thy young lions: and I will cut off thy prey from the earth.

Commentary on
The Book of Nahum

(11) *Where is the abode of the lions, which was the feeding place of the young lions—* [This refers to Jerusalem which has become] an abode for the wicked men of the heathen.[1]

where the lion and lioness walked, and the lion's whelp, [and none made them afraid]? [This refers to Deme]trius, the king of Greece, who, at the instance of them 'that sought smooth things', sought to enter Jerusalem.[2] [Never] from the days of Antiochus[3] until the time when the rulers of the Kittians[4] arose, [has that city daun]ted the kings of Greece; and eventually it will be trodden under.

(12) *The lion rent the limbs[5] of his own whelps, and strangled his own lionesses* for prey. [This refers to] the Young Lion of Anger[6] who proceeded to smite his own great men and his own confederates.

and filled his caves with prey, and his abodes (dens) with torn flesh. [This refers to] the Young Lion who [wrought venge]ance on them 'that sought smooth things', in that he proceeded to hang them up alive.[7] [Such a thing had never] before [been done] in Israel, for the Scripture designates a man hung up alive as ['a reproach unto God'].[8]

(13) *Behold, I am against thee, saith the Lord of Hosts, and I will burn thy multitude[9] in smoke, and the sword shall devour thy young lions, and I will cut off thy prey*

from the earth. [This refers to   ]. 'Thy multitude'
means the great men of his army [and] his [confederates].
His 'young lions' are [   ], and his 'prey' is the property which [the priests of] Jerusalem amas[sed][10] (and)
which [   ]. [E]phraim [shall become]   ; Israel
shall be rendered [   ].[11]

HABAKKUK

CHAPTER ONE

1 The burden which Habakkuk the prophet did see.

2 O Lord, how long shall I cry, and thou wilt not hear? I cry out unto thee of violence, and thou wilt not

3 save. Why dost thou shew me iniquity, and look upon perverseness? for spoiling and violence are before me: and there is strife, and con-

4 tention riseth up. Therefore the law is slacked, and judgement doth never go forth: for the wicked doth compass about the righteous; therefore judgment

5 goeth forth perverted. Behold ye among the nations, and regard, and wonder marvellously: for I work a work in your days, which ye will not believe though it

6 be told you. For, lo, I raise up the Chaldeans, that bitter and hasty nation; which march through the breadth of the earth, to possess dwelling places that are not

7 theirs. They are terrible and dreadful: their judgement and their dignity proceed

8 from themselves. Their horses also are swifter than leopards, and are more fierce than the evening wolves; and their horsemen spread themselves: yea, their horsemen come from far; they fly as an eagle that

9 hasteth to devour. They come all of them for violence; their faces are set eagerly *as* the east wind; and they gather captives as

10 the sand. Yea, he scoffeth at kings, and princes are a derision unto him: he derideth every strong hold; for he heapeth up dust, and

11 taketh it. Then shall he sweep by *as* a wind, and shall pass over, and be guilty: *even* he whose

12 might is his god. Art not thou from everlasting, O Lord my God, mine Holy One? we shall not die. O Lord, thou hast ordained him for judgement; and thou, O Rock, hast established him

13 for correction. Thou that art of purer eyes than to behold evil, and that canst not look on perverseness, wherefore lookest thou upon them that deal treacherously, and holdest thy peace when the wicked swalloweth up the man that is more righteous than he;

14 and makest men as the fishes of the sea, as the creeping things, that have

15 no ruler over them? He taketh up all of them with the angle, he catcheth them in his net, and gathereth them in his drag: therefore he rejoiceth and is glad.

16 Therefore he sacrificeth unto his net, and burneth incense unto his drag; because by them his portion is

fat, and his meat plenteous.
17 Shall he therefore empty his net, and not spare to slay the nations continually?

CHAPTER TWO

1 I will stand upon my watch, and set me upon the tower, and will look forth to see what he will speak with me, and what I shall answer concerning my complaint.
2 And the LORD answered me, and said, Write the vision, and make it plain upon tables, that he may
3 run that readeth it. For the vision is yet for the appointed time, and it hasteth toward the end, and shall not lie: though it tarry, wait for it; because it will surely come, it will not de-
4 lay. Behold, his soul is puffed up, it is not upright in him: but the just shall
5 live by his faith. Yea, moreover, wine is a treacherous dealer, a haughty man, and that keepeth not at home; who enlargeth his desire as hell, and he is as death, and cannot be satisfied, but gathereth unto him all nations, and heapeth unto him
6 all peoples. Shall not all these take up a parable against him, and a taunting proverb against him, and say, Woe to him that increaseth that which is not his! how long? and that ladeth himself with pledges!
7 Shall they not rise up suddenly that shall bite thee, and awake that shall vex thee, and thou shalt be for

8 booties unto them? Because thou hast spoiled many nations, all the remnant of the peoples shall spoil thee; because of men's blood, and for the violence done to the land, to the city and to all that dwell therein.
9 Woe to him that getteth an evil gain for his house, that he may set his nest on high, that he may be delivered
10 from the hand of evil! Thou hast consulted shame to thy house, by cutting off many peoples, and hast sinned
11 against thy soul. For the stone shall cry out of the wall, and the beam out of the timber shall answer it.
12 Woe to him that buildeth a town with blood, and stablisheth a city by iniq-
13 uity! Behold, is it not of the LORD of hosts that the peoples labour for the fire, and the nations weary them-
14 selves for vanity? For the earth shall be filled with the knowledge of the glory of the LORD, as the waters cover the sea.
15 Woe unto him that giveth his neighbour drink, that addest thy venom *thereto*, and makest him drunken also, that thou mayest look
16 on their nakedness! Thou art filled with shame for glory: drink thou also, and be as one uncircumcised: the cup of the LORD's right hand shall be turned unto thee, and foul shame shall
17 be upon thy glory. For the violence done to Lebanon shall cover thee, and the destruction of the beasts, which made them afraid;

because of men's blood, and for the violence done to the land, to the city and to all that dwell therein.

18 What profiteth the graven image, that the maker thereof hath graven it; the molten image, and the teacher of lies, that the maker of his work trusteth therein, to make dumb 19 idols? Woe unto him that saith to the wood, Awake; to the dumb stone, Arise! Shall this teach? Behold, it is laid over with gold and silver, and there is no breath at all in the midst 20 of it. But the LORD is in his holy temple: let all the earth keep silence before him.

Commentary on
the Book of Habakkuk

CHAPTER ONE

(4) *Therefore the law is numbed.* This refers to the fact that they have rejected the *Torah*—that is, the Law—of God.

For the wicked besets the righteous . . . The reference (in the word 'righteous') is to the teacher who expounds the Law aright [   ].

Therefore justice goes forth perverted. (*The comment is lost.*)

(5) *Look, ye traitors,*[1] *and see: marvel and be astonished. For it is in your own days that the deed is being done. Ye do not believe when it is told.* This refers to the traitors who have aligned themselves with the man of lies. For they did not believe what he who expounded the Law aright told them on the authority* of God. It refers also to those who betrayed the new covenant,[2] for (the word rendered 'believe' also means 'keep faith' and therefore alludes to the fact that)[3] they have not kept faith with the Covenant of God, but have profaned His holy name. Again, it refers to future traitors—that is, to the lawless men who will betray the Covenant and not believe when they hear all the things that are to come upon the final age duly related by the priest whom God appoints to interpret in those days all the words of His servants the prophets by whom He has told of that impending disaster.

* Literally, 'from the mouth of'.

(6) *For lo, I raise up the Chaldeans, that wild and impetuous nation* This refers to the Kittaeans,[4] who are indeed swift and mighty in war, bent on destroying peoples far and wide and subduing them to their own domination. They dispossess [   ] but do not believe in the ordinances of God [   ]. Over lowland and plain they come to smite and pillage the cities of the land. This is what the Scripture means when it speaks of them as coming *to possess dwellings that are not their own.*

(7) *Dreadful and awful it is: out of itself proceed both its standard of justice and its (lust for) deception.*[5] This refers to the Kittaeans, the terror and dread of whom are upon all the nations. Moreover, when they meet in their council,[6] all their plans are directed to doing evil; and they behave towards all peoples with knavery and deceit.

(8, 9) *Swifter than leopards are its steeds, and keener than evening wolves. Their horsemen spread out and ride abroad: they come flying from afar like a vulture that hastes to devour. They all of them come for violence: the serried mass of their faces is a veritable eastwind*[7] This refers to the Kittaeans who thresh the earth with their horses and their beasts. Like a vulture they come from afar, from the isles of the sea, to devour all the nations; and they are insatiable. In the heat of fury, in searing rage, in scorching anger and with tempestuous mien[8] they speak with all the peoples; and this is what the Scripture means when it says, *the serried mass of their faces is a veritable eastwind, and they amass spoil like sand.*

(10) *At kings it scoffs, and lordlings are a derision unto it.* This refers to the fact that they scorn the great and mock the noble, make sport of kings and princes, and scoff at any numerous people.

It derides every stronghold: piles up an earthmound and takes it. This refers to the rulers of the Kittaeans who scorn the strongholds of the peoples and tauntingly deride them, surrounding them with a great host in order to capture them.[9] Through alarm and terror the latter are surrendered into their hands; and they overthrow them through the iniquity of those who dwell in them.

(11) *Then the wind sweeps by and passes: and an-*

other,[10] *whose might is his God, proceeds to wreak devastation*[11] This refers to the rulers of the Kittaeans. In their guilt-ridden Council House[12] they keep replacing those rulers one after another, and each comes in turn to destroy the earth.[13]

Another whose might is his God. This refers to [   ] all the peoples.

(12–13) *Him hast thou appointed, O Lord, to wreak the judgment: and him hast thou established, O Rock, to proffer the charge—him who has kept his vision pure, that it could not look upon perverseness*[14] This refers to the fact that God will not exterminate His people by the hand of the heathen, but will place the execution of judgment on all the heathen in the hands of His elect. Moreover, it is through charges proffered by the latter that the wicked among His own people will stand condemned—that is, the people who kept His commandments only when they were in trouble. This is what the Scripture means by the words, *him who has kept his vision pure that it could not look upon evil.* The reference is to the fact that [God's elect] did not go a-whoring after (the lust of) their eyes during the Era of Wickedness.

(13) *Why dost thou look (idly) upon traitors, and keep silent when the wicked confounds*[15] *him that is more righteous than he?* This refers to the 'house of Absalom'[16] and their cronies who kept silent when charges were levelled against the teacher who was expounding the Law aright, and who did not come to his aid against the man of lies when the latter rejected the *Torah* in the midst of their entire congregation.[17]

(14–16) *Thou hast made men like fishes of the sea, like crawling things, that he may have dominion over them.*[18] *He takes up all of them with the angle and hauls them in his net, and gathers them in his drag. Therefore he sacrifices to his net: therefore he rejoices and makes merry; therefore, too, he burns incense to his net: because thereby his portion is rich* . . . This again refers to the Kittaeans. What with all their plunder, they keep increasing their wealth like a shoal of fish. And as for the statement, *therefore he sacrifices to his net and burns incense to his drag,*

this refers to the fact that they offer sacrifice to their ensigns and that their weapons are objects of veneration to
them.[19]

For thereby is their portion fat and their food rich.
This refers to the fact that they apportion among all the
peoples annual assignments of forced labor* and tribute
designed to provide them with food, thereby devastating
many lands.[20]

(17) *Therefore does he bare his sword,*[21] *and never
spares to slay nations.* This refers to the Kittaeans who
destroy many by the sword—youths, adults (?)[22] and old
men, women and children alike—and have not pity even
on the fruit of the womb.

CHAPTER TWO

(1, 2) *I will take my stand on my watch and post myself on my tower, and scan the scene to see whereof He
will denounce me and what answer I might give when He
arraigns me. And the Lord took up word with me and said:
Write the vision, and make it plain upon tablets that he
who runs may read* God told Habakkuk to write down
the things that were to come upon the latter age, but He
did not inform him when that moment would come to ful-
filment. As to the phrase, *that he who runs may read,* this
refers to the teacher who expounds the Law aright, for
God has made him *au courant*[23] with all the deeper implications of the words of His servants the prophets.

(3) *For the vision is yet for the appointed time. Though
it lags*[24] *toward the moment, it will not be belied.* This
refers to the fact that the final moment may be protracted
beyond anything which the prophets have foretold, for
'God moves in a mysterious way His wonders to perform'.[25]

*Though it tarry, yet await it; for it will surely come, it
will not delay.* This is addressed† to the men of truth, the
men who carry out the Law [*Torah*], who do not relax
from serving the Truth even though the final moment be

* Literally, 'their yoke'.
† Literally, 'this refers'.

long drawn out. Assuredly, all the times appointed by God will come in due course, even as He has determined in His inscrutable wisdom.

(4) *Behold, his soul shall be swollen, not reduced therein** [26] This refers to the fact that they will pile up for themselves a double requital[27] for their sins, and shall not be quit of judgment for them.

But the righteous through his faithfulness shall live. This refers to all in Jewry[28] who carry out the Law [*Torah*]. On account of their labor and of their faith in him who expounded the Law aright, God will deliver them from the house of judgment.

(5, 6) *Moreover, because wealth*[29] *betrays, a man grows prurient*[30] *and behaves unseemly,*[31] *in that he grows greedy like Sheol*[32] *and insatiable as death. All the nations are gathered unto him, and all the peoples are amassed unto him. Shall not they all take up a parable against him and heap on him jesting satire and say: 'Woe unto him who amasses what is not his! How long shall it last! He is merely heaping pledges (which must someday be returned)!'*[33] This refers to the wicked priest who, when first he came to office, enjoyed a reputation for truth,[34] but who, when he came to rule in Israel, grew arrogant and abandoned God, betraying His statutes for the sake of wealth, plundering and amassing for himself the kind of wealth usually acquired by criminals who have rebelled against God. He also took public property, thereby merely heaping upon himself the penalty of guilt. Furthermore, he practiced abomination, involving every kind of impurity and filth.[35]

(7, 8) *Will not they suddenly rise who will 'put their bite'*[36] *on thee, and will they not (suddenly) 'sting'*[37] *who shall rudely disturb thee? Because thou hast plundered nations aplenty, all the rest of the peoples (will) plunder thee?* This refers to the priest who rebelled [and violated] the statutes of God, thereby causing himself to be

---

* Literally, 'Behold, his soul is swollen, not levelled therein'. In the Hebrew, the contrast is between a protuberance and level ground. But it is virtually impossible to reproduce this effect in English.

smitten with the judgments of wickedness. The horrors of
evil diseases acted upon him and he paid the price of his
misdeeds in the body of his flesh.[38] And as for the phrase,
*because thou hast plundered nations aplenty, all the rest
of the peoples will plunder thee,* this refers to the final
priests of Jerusalem who will amass for themselves
wealth and gain by plundering the people, but whose
wealth and plunder will ultimately be delivered into the
hands of the army of the Kittaeans, i.e. 'the rest of the
peoples'.

(8) *Because of human bloodshed and the violence done
to land and city and to all that dwell therein.* This refers
to the wicked priest. Because of the mischief which he had
done to him who taught the Law aright and to the men
associated with him, God delivered him into the hands of
his enemies, that they might torture him with scourging
and wear him out with bitterness of spirit for acting un-
righteously against His elect.

(9–11) *Woe unto him who gets evil gain for his house,
setting his nest on high, to be safe from the reach of harm!
Thou hast planned but shame for thy house—the cutting off
many peoples, and thou hast sinned against thine own self!
For the stone shall cry out from the wall, and the beam
from the woodwork respond!* This refers to the [   ]
who planned to build himself a mansion in such a way that
its very stones would be furnished through oppression and
the beams of its woodwork through robbery.[39] And as for
the phrase *the cutting off of many peoples and thou hast
sinned against thine own self,* this refers to the House of
Judgment where God will render His judgment in the
midst of many peoples. Thence will he in turn transport
him for the execution of sentence, and in their midst He
will condemn him and sentence him to the fire of brim-
stone.

(12, 13) *Woe unto him who builds a city by bloodshed
and founds a town by wrongdoing! Behold, will it not
come from the Lord of hosts that peoples shall labor only
for fire, and nations weary themselves for naught?* This
statement refers to the preacher of lies who misled many
people into building a worthless city by bloodshed and into

establishing a community by falsehood,[40] directing their
efforts[41] to the service of vanity and instructing them in
deeds of falsehood. The result will be that all their labors
will prove in vain, since they will encounter the judgments
of fire for having abused and defamed God's elect.

(14) *For the earth shall be filled with the knowledge
of the glory of the Lord as waters cover the sea* This
statement refers to the fact that when God eventually
restores them to their former glory, [   ] falsehood
[will] [   ], and thereafter knowledge will be revealed
to them, abundant as the waters of the sea.

(15) *Woe unto him that plies his neighbor with drink,
that pours out his flask [ḥematho], yea, makes him drunk,
in order to gaze on their festivals!*[42] This refers to the
wicked priest, who chased after the true exponent of the
Law, right to the house where he was dwelling in exile,[43]
in order to confuse him by a display of violent temper
[ḥamatho], and who then, on the occasion of the rest-day
of Atonement, appeared to them in full splendor in order
to confuse them and trip them up on the day of the fast,
the day of their sabbatical rest.[44]

(16) *Thou art sated with disgrace instead of with
honor. The cup in the Lord's right hand will come around
unto thee, and basest disgrace will fall upon thine honor.*
This refers to the priest whose disgrace exceeded his honor,
because he did not circumcise the foreskin of his heart,
but kept walking in the ways of drunken debauch in order
to slake his (insatiable) thirst. The cup of God's wrath will
confound him, so that all he will really increase will be
[shame, disgrace] and anguish.

(17) *The violence of Lebanon shall overwhelm thee and
the assault of wild beasts shall crush you, because of human bloodshed and of violence done to land and city and
to all that dwell therein.* The statement refers to the
wicked priests and means that God will mete out to him
the treatment that he meted out to the needy. 'Lebanon'
stands here for the Communal Council,[45] and 'wild beasts'
for the simple-minded Jews who carry out the Law
[*Torah*]. God will condemn him to annihilation, even as
he plotted to annihilate the needy. And as to the state-

ment, *because of bloodshed in the city and violence in the
land,* the 'city' refers to Jerusalem wherein the wicked
priest wrought his abominable works and wherein he defiled the sanctuary of God; while the 'violence in the land'
refers to the cities of Jewry[46] wherein he plundered the
property of the needy.

(18) *What value has a graven idol, when its maker has
graven it, or a molten image, or teachers of lies? For the
maker is but trusting in his own creation, is simply making
dumb idols!* This statement refers to the idols which the
heathen make to serve and worship. On the day of judgment these will not deliver them.

(19) *Woe unto him that says to a stock, awake: to a
dumb stone, arise!* This refers to [   ].

(20) *Hush before the Lord, all the earth!* This refers
to all the heathen who have been worshipping stock and
stone. On the Day of Judgment God will annihilate all
who worship idols and all the wicked from the earth.

. . . .

8 Cease from anger, and forsake wrath:
Fret not thyself, *it tendeth* only to evil-doing.

9 For evil-doers shall be cut off:
But those that wait upon the LORD, they shall inherit the land.

10 For yet a little while, and the wicked shall not be:
Yea, thou shalt diligently consider his place, and he shall not be.

11 But the meek shall inherit the land;
And shall delight themselves in the abundance of peace.

. . . .

14 The wicked have drawn out the sword, and have bent their bow,
To cast down the poor and needy,
To slay such as are upright in the way.

15 Their sword shall enter into their own heart,
And their bows shall be broken.

. . . .

18 The LORD knoweth the days of the perfect:
And their inheritance shall be for ever.

19 They shall not be ashamed in the time of evil:
And in the days of famine they shall be satisfied.

20 But the wicked shall perish,
And the enemies of the LORD shall be as the excellency of the pastures:
They shall consume; in smoke shall they consume away.

21 The wicked borroweth, and payeth not again:
But the righteous dealeth graciously, and giveth.

22 For such as be blessed of him shall inherit the land;
And they that be cursed of him shall be cut off.

23 A man's goings are established of the LORD;
And he delighteth in his way.

24 Though he fall, he shall not be utterly cast down:
For the LORD upholdeth him with his hand.

25 I have been young, and now am old;
Yet have I not seen the righteous forsaken,
Nor his seed begging *their* bread.

26 All the day long he dealeth graciously, and lendeth;
And his seed is blessed.

. . . .

32 The wicked watcheth the righteous,
And seeketh to slay him.

33 The LORD will not leave him in his hand,
Nor condemn him when he is judged.

Commentary on Psalm 37

(Fragment A: col. i)

(8, 9) *Refrain from anger and abandon wrath; fret not thyself, it tendeth only to evil-doing. For evil-doers shall be cut off.* This applies to those who return to the Law [*Torah*] and do not refuse to repent their evil-doing. Those, however, who are defiant about repenting their iniquity will be cut off.

But they that wait upon the Lord—those shall inherit the earth. The reference in the word 'those' is to the congregation of God's elect, the men who do His will.

(10) *Yet a little, and the wicked shall not be. Though I[1] look well at his place, he shall not be.* This refers to all [who practise][2] wickedness. At the end of the forty years[3] they shall cease to exist, and no wicked man shall be found on earth.

(11) *But the meek shall inherit the earth and delight in peace abounding.* This refers to the poor[4] who accept the time of affliction (penury), but who will eventually be delivered from all the snares of [want.] It refers also to the meek[5] of the earth who [endure] all manner of. . . .

(Fragment B)

(14, 15) *The wicked have drawn out the sword and bent their bow, to cast down the poor and needy and to*

*slay such as walk the straight road. Their sword shall enter
their own heart, and their bows shall be broken in pieces.*
This refers to the wicked men of Ephraim and Manasseh[5a]
who seek to assail* the priest and the men of his counsel
when the time of trial is come upon them. God will rescue
the latter out of their hand, and thereafter they themselves
will be delivered into the hands of the violent men of the
heathen, to execute judgment upon them.†

*   *   *   *

(Fragment A: col. ii)

(18, 19) [*The Lord knows the days of the blameless,
and their heritage will abide for ever. They shall suffer
no hurt[6] through evil times.*] [This refers to the 'men of
blameless conduct' and to the congregation of God's elect]
who will [eventually] come back from the wilderness[7] and
live in safety[8] for a thousand generations.[9] The land [shall
be theirs] and their seed's for ever.[10]

(20) *And in the days of famine they shall be satisfied.
But the wicked shall perish.* This means that God will
sustain them when they hunger in the time of their affliction (penury); whereas the wicked—that is, all who do
not do [their duty]—will perish of hunger and plague.

*But they that love[11] the Lord shall be as him who is
the glory of the lambs.[12]* This refers to the congregation
of God's elect, who will become leaders and princes
[among His people] like [rams][13] among their flocks.

They shall vanish one and all like smoke.[14] This refers
to the princes of the [heathen] realm who have oppressed God's holy people. They shall vanish like the
smoke of a hearth [in the wind].

(21, 22) *The wicked borroweth and doth not repay,
but the righteous is gracious and giveth. Verily, they that
are blessed of God shall inherit the earth, but they that
are cursed of Him shall be cut off.* This refers to that
congregation of poor men who [make over] their entire

* Literally, 'to put forth hand against'.
† Literally, 'for judgment'.

estate to the [common fund.][15] These shall inherit the
'mountain of the height of Israel',[16] and delight in its
holiness. But as to the 'cursed' who are to be 'cut off—this
refers to those tyrants among the [nations] who have
acted wickedly against Israel. They shall be cut off and
[destroyed] for ever.

(23, 24) *The goings of a man are ordered by the Lord,*
and He busieth himself[17] *with his every step. Though he*
fall, he shall not be flung headlong, for the Lord graspeth
his hand in support. This refers to the priest, the man
who expounds the Law correctly[18] [and who has always
been instructing the people in the statutes of God, so that]
they have built for Him a congregation[19] of [truth] resting
on a firm foundation.

(25, 26) *I have been young, and now am old; yet have*
I not seen the righteous forsaken, nor His seed begging
bread. All the day long He is gracious and lendeth, and
His seed becometh a blessing.

*   *   *   *

(Fragment C)

(32, 33) *The wicked watcheth out for the righteous,*
and seeketh [*to slay him. But the Lord will not abandon*
him into his hand, nor] *suffer him to be condemned when*
he is arraigned. This refers to the wicked [prie]st who has
p[ut forth his hand against him who was teaching the Law
aright] in order to have him put to death [and to make an
end of the Covena]nt and the Law [*Torah*]. Yet, though
he assail him, God will not ab[andon him into his hand,]
nor [suffer him to be condemned when] he is arraigned,
nor [   ]. He [will] heap [re]tribution upon that man
by giving him into the hands of the violent men of the
heathen, to execute [judgment] upon him.[20]

NOTES

Commentary on the Book of Micah

1. This interpretation is based on the fact that the Hebrew words rendered *a place for the planting of a vineyard* could also be translated (purely formally), *them that lead the vineyard astray*. Since Israel is described in Scripture as God's vineyard (Isa. 5.1; 27.2), our author fancifully took the verse to mean that God would eventually 'dump' the false teachers who misled His people.

2. What the prophet meant, of course, was that Jerusalem had been turned into the equivalent of a pagan 'high place' or sanctuary. But our author took the words to imply the converse of what had previously been said. Israel, he declares, has turned to idolatry; but the true 'high place' of the Jews is the temple in Jerusalem. His further interpretation is based on the fact that the name Jerusalem can be fancifully explained as containing the two elements, *y-r-h*, 'teach', and *shalom*, 'peace'. The true sanctuary, he suggests, is that built by the righteous teachers who ensure peace and security on the Day of Judgment!

3. This is a tentative restoration, seeking to recover what may have been our author's way of interpreting the Scriptural text. It is based on the fact that the Hebrew word rendered *roll down* resembles that which means *sojourn*, while the word rendered *uncover* is identical in form with that meaning *drive into exile*. The 'stones'

and 'foundations' of idolatry would readily have been identified with the venal priests of Jerusalem.

4. The basis of this interpretation is that the gate of the city was the place of judgment.

5. This interpretation is suggested by the fact that the Hebrew word for 'gate', viz. *sha'ar*, resembles the name Seir, and thus calls to mind Deut. 33.2: 'The Lord came from Sinai, and rose from Seir unto them'. Cp. also Judges 5.4.

Commentary on the Book of Nahum

1. The interpretation is based on Pss. 26.8; 68.6; 76.3; II Chron. 36.15, where Jerusalem (Zion) is designated as God's 'abode'; and on Jer. 2.15, where the adversaries of Israel are described as 'young lions'.

2. The comment alludes to an incident described by Josephus (*Ant.*, XIII, 14. 1–2) in connection with an uprising of the Jews against the cruelty of Alexander Jannaeus, around 88 B.C.: 'They sent also to Demetrius Eucerus [king of Syria] and besought him to make common cause with them in their defense. So Demetrius came with an army and took those that had invited him, and pitched camp near Shechem. Thereupon, Alexander, with his 6,200 mercenaries and about 20,000 Jews who were of his party, went forth against Demetrius, who had 3,000 horsemen and 40,000 foot soldiers . . . (Eventually) they joined battle. Demetrius won, and all of Alexander's mercenaries were slain . . . Alexander took to the hills'. (The story is told also in *War*, I, 4.4–5.) Evidently, after his victory, Demetrius sought to enter Jerusalem and claim the throne.

3. Evidently, Antiochus IV Epiphanes (175–164 B.C.).

4. The 'Kittians' are here evidently identified with the Romans, as later in the Aramaic Version (Targum) of Num. 24.24 and in the Vulgate.

5. The comment shows that the author read the Hebrew

word *BeDê,* 'sufficient for', as *BaDDê,* 'limbs' (cf. Job 18.13).

6. Warriors or heroes are called 'mighty lions' in II Sam. 23.20; Isa. 33.7—according to a traditional interpretation—and 'whelps' (Ez. 32.2). A similar expression is frequent in Arabic (e.g. Yaqut, III. 437, 17; 615, 13). Comparable also is Aeschylus, *Choephori,* 939, where Orestes and Pylades are so described. Cp. also Euripides, *Orestes,* 1401.

7. Cp. Josephus, *loc. cit.:* 'Some 6,000 Jews, moved to pity by the change in Alexander's fortune, gathered together and joined him. At this, Demetrius grew alarmed, and withdrew from the country. The Jews then turned on Alexander, but were defeated and slain in great numbers. When he had shut up the most powerful of them in the city Bethone, he besieged them therein; and when he had captured the city and brought those men into his power, he had them transported to Jerusalem and perpetrated upon them one of the most barbarous acts in the world. For while he was carousing with his concubines, in full view of the citizenry, he ordered some eight hundred of those men to be crucified; and, while they were still alive, he ordered the throats of their children and their wives to be slit before their eyes. This was by way of revenge for the injury they had done him' (Whiston's translation, slightly revised).

8. The Mishnah (*Sanhedrin,* 6.4) records the opinion of the sages that 'none is hanged save the blasphemer and the idolator'. This is an interpretation of the Scriptural text (Deut. 21.23) that 'he that is hanged is a curse (reproach) to God', in the sense that hanging presupposes blasphemy.

9. The comment shows that our author read *RBKH,* 'thy multitude', not *RKBH,* 'its chariotry', as in the traditional (Masoretic) text. His reading agrees with that of the Greek (Septuagint) and Syriac (Peshitta) Versions.

10. Cp. *Commentary on Habakkuk* 2.5–6 (above, p. 253).

11. 'Ephraim' and 'Israel' denote the Samaritans, who claimed to be the remnant of the Northern Kingdom and to be descended from Ephraim and Manasseh.

Commentary on the Book of Habakkuk

1. The traditional (Masoretic) text reads, 'Look ye among the nations' (Heb. *BaGoYiM*). Our author read, by a slight change, *BoGeDiM*, 'traitors'—a reading also found in the ancient Greek (Septuagint) Version.

2. Cp. *Zadokite Document*, vi, 19; viii, 21; xx, 12–13; and see General Introduction, pp. 4, 24.

3. These words have been inserted to bring out the basis of the author's interpretation.

4. See Introduction to *The War of the Sons of Light and the Sons of Darkness*, below, pp. 277f.

5. The traditional (Masoretic) text reads, 'Its judgment and its dignity proceed from itself', i.e., 'it is a law to itself'. It is apparent, however, from his subsequent comment that our author construed the Hebrew word *se'tho*, usually rendered 'his dignity', as somehow connected with the verb *hishi'*, 'deceive'.

6. This is obviously intended as an interpretation of the words, 'His judgment [standard of justice] proceeds from himself'.

7. The traditional text reads, '[are turned] eastwards' [or, 'look straight ahead'].

8. All of the terms used in the Hebrew can refer either to temper or to tempest; and this is the basis of the interpretation.

9. This has been thought to refer to standard *Roman* methods of laying siege to a city.

10. Literally, 'this one', which the author construed as meaning 'so-and-so'.

11. The traditional text reads, 'and becomes guilty'—Heb.

ve-ashem. Our author read *ve-yashem*, 'and devastates'.

12. This has been thought to allude to the Roman Senate.

13. The allusion may be general rather than specific. In any case, it would fit several different historical situations, so that, in the absence of further information, attempts to precise it would seem both premature and futile.

14. The prophet's words are usually construed differently. viz. 'Thou hast set him, O Rock, for judgment, and established him, O Rock, for correction. [Thou art] purer of eyes than to behold evil, and canst not look on perverseness'.

15. The Hebrew word [*bl'*] means both 'swallow up' and 'confound'. It is evident that our author understood it in the latter sense.

16. Not to be taken literally as referring to a particular person called Absalom. The expression means simply, 'conspirators like the associates of the Biblical Absalom'.

17. See General Introduction, p. 25.

18. The traditional text reads, 'Which have no ruler over them'.

19. This is thought to refer to the Roman practise of worshipping military standards. This, however, is not definitely attested before Imperial times.

20. Josephus tells us (*Ant.*, XIV, 4.5) that, until its capture by Pompey in 63 B.C., the city of Jerusalem had often to pay more than 2,000 talents annually in tribute to its foreign masters.

21. The traditional (Masoretic) text reads, 'His net' (Heb. *ḥermô*). Our author, by a change of one letter, read *ḥarbô*, 'his sword'.

22. The meaning of the Hebrew word is uncertain.

23. This seems the only way of reproducing the author's interpretation of the words, 'That he who runs may read' (literally, 'that he who reads may run').

24. The Hebrew word (*YAFIaH*) is usually rendered 'pants, hastens' or possibly 'depones'. But from his subsequent interpretation it seems that the author connected it with a like-sounding root, preserved in Syriac and Arabic, meaning 'be feeble, debilitated, laggard'.

25. Literally, 'for the mysteries of God are destined to be performed wondrously'.

26. King James' Version: 'Behold, his soul [which] is lifted up is not upright in him'. American Jewish Version: 'Behold, his soul is puffed up, it is not upright in him'. The Revised Standard Version resorts to conjectural emendation and renders: 'Behold, he whose soul is not upright in him shall fall'. This, however, is patently wrong, because it misses the contrast between the two Hebrew words in question, the one of which means 'swollen, protuberant' and the other 'low-lying, level'.

27. The interpretation is based on a play on words: the term rendered 'swollen' is *'fl*, which the author fancifully identifies with the like-sounding *kfl*, 'be double', and this at once suggests to him Isaiah 40.2.

28. Heb. *Judah*.

29. The Hebrew ('Masoretic') text has *hayayin*, 'wine'. By a slight change, our author read *hôn*, 'wealth'.

30. The Hebrew word *yahir* is usually derived from a root *yhr* which is assumed to mean 'be proud' and is therefore rendered 'grows insolent'. But our author may well have connected it with the Syriac and late Heb. *hrhr*, 'be prurient'.

31. The Hebrew word *ynvh* is usually connected with *naveh*, 'dwelling', and rendered 'and abides not at home'. But our author evidently identified it with an homophonous *nvh* (=*n'h*), 'be comely, seemly'.

32. I.e., the netherworld.

33. King James' Version: 'Woe to him that increaseth [that which is] not his! how long? and to him that ladeth himself with thick clay!' (The 'thick clay' is here compounded out of ancient ignorance of what the

relevant Hebrew word meant. We now know that it signifies 'pledge(s)'.

34. Literally, 'who was called (renowned) for truth'. The assumption that this refers to his actual name, which he subsequently changed, is quite erroneous and overlooks a common Hebrew idiom.

35. See above, n. 13.

36. This colloquialism seems the only way of reproducing the effect of the Hebrew, which lies in the fact that the word for 'creditor, usurer' derives from a verbal root meaning 'bite'!

37. The Hebrew word (*yakişu*), usually rendered 'awake', is fancifully construed by our author as if it were the very similar *ya'kişu*, 'sting'. Once again, an English colloquialism best conveys the point.

38. A. Dupont-Sommer has suggested that the reference is to the wicked priest Aristobulus II who was arrested and imprisoned and finally died of poison in prison at the hands of Pompey's supporters. But to die of poison is not to die of loathsome diseases, and what our author is trying specifically to interpret is Habakkuk's reference to 'bites' and 'stings'. Besides, this whole business of looking for precise historical allusions seems grossly overdone; the passages in question may have in mind *typical* rather than *actual* cases. The use of the perfect tense is not against this; we may render; 'This refers to the kind of wicked priest who, in the past, was invariably exposed to this and this suffering', etc.

39. Here again the reference may be typical rather than actual.

40. H. H. Rowley (*The Zadokite Fragments and the Dead Sea Scrolls*, 1952, p. 67) makes the ingenious suggestion that this refers to the rebuilding of the city of David in the time of Antiochus Epiphanes, mentioned in I Maccabees 1.33. The wicked priest, he thinks, was Menelaus. But once again we may be chary of precise identifications.

41. Literally, 'making them weary themselves in'.

42. The traditional (Masoretic) text reads, 'in order to gaze on their nakedness' (*me'orêhem*). In the ancient Hebrew script, the letters *r* and *d* are often barely distinguishable, and our author evidently read *me'odêhem*, 'their festivals'. However, I believe that he saw in this reading a subtle *double-entendre*, for *me'odêhem* can also mean 'their totterings'. Hence, he interpreted the Scriptural text as referring to an occasion when the congregation was made to totter (or stumble) in the observance of a holy day.

43. See General Introduction, p. 19. The Hebrew expression (*ABYT GLUTÔ*) has been read differently (viz. *ABÔT GLUTÔ*) and rendered 'desiring his exile', i.e. aiming to drive him into exile. Other considerations apart, however, it should be observed that the verb *A-B-H* (from which *ABÔT* would derive) means properly 'assent to, comply with', rather than 'desire, aspire to, aim at'.

44. Cp. Lev. 16.31; 23.32.

45. The name Lebanon means 'white' (referring to the white cliffs). The point of the interpretation lies in the fact that the members of the Brotherhood wore white—as do the modern Samaritans and Mandaeans.

46. Heb. *Judah*.

Commentary on Psalm 37

1. The received (Masoretic) text reads: 'Though thou look'.

2. A word (Heb. *'ôsê*) has dropped out.

3. In accordance with the common Jewish tradition that the 'Messianic' ministry will last for forty years and then be followed by the Golden Age.

4. The Hebrew word is *ebyônîm*, and this has inspired the theory that the Qumran Covenanters were really the Ebionites, rather than the Essenes. But the infer-

ence is unnecessary, for it is difficult to see what other word the writer could possibly have used in the normal sense of 'poor, needy'.

5. The Hebrew word is *'aniyîm*, and it is interesting to note that in the Aramaic dialect of the early Palestinian Christians, the cognate term is used specifically in the sense of 'ascetic'. The writer, whose native language was Aramaic, probably had this in mind.

5a. The interpretation is inspired by Ps. 78.9: 'The children of Ephraim were as archers handling the bow'. The reference is to the Samaritans; see note 10 to *The Commentary on Nahum*.

6. The Hebrew word is usually rendered 'be shamed', but in Aramaic (and in Arabic) it has the sense of 'suffer misfortune' or even 'be ill', and the subsequent comment shows that the writer so understood it. (The actual quotation from Scripture is missing in the manuscript; it was written at the foot of the preceding column, which is now lost.)

7. To be understood metaphorically as well as literally; see Introduction, pp. 4, 24.

8. Restoring *beyesh[a']* rather than *beyosh[er]*, which is suggested by Allegro. Cf. Jer. 23.6.

9. In fulfillment of the Scriptural promise, Deut. 7.9.

10. Cf. Gen. 12.7; 15.8; 17.7–8; 28.13; Deut. 1.8.

11. The received (Masoretic) text and all the Ancient Versions read 'But the enemies of the Lord'. In the Hebrew, there is a difference of only one letter.

12. RSV: 'The enemies of the Lord are as the glory of the pastures', i.e., as grass that quickly withers. But the Hebrew word rendered 'pastures' (viz. *karîm*), if derived from a different verbal root, can mean 'lambs', and this is how the ancient Jewish interpreters understood it. (The true meaning is in any case obscure, and various emendations of the text have been suggested.)

13. The text is defective, and reads simply, '[   ] sheep'; I supply 'rams' (Heb. *êlê*) for the sense.

14. The traditional text reads, by a different vocalization of the same consonants, 'They shall vanish like smoke, yea vanish'.

15. See *Manual of Discipline*, 1, 11–12.

16. The expression is borrowed from Ez. 17.23.

17. Usually rendered 'delighteth', but the word is also used in the sense of 'be preoccupied', and it is evident that the writer so understood it.

18. The expression usually rendered, 'Teacher of Righteousness'.

19. The word rendered 'congregation' came in Syriac to mean 'church'. It is extremely interesting to find it associated here with the verb 'build', for this usage—foreign to the Old Testament—at once recalls the New Testament's 'building the church'. Indeed, if one wishes to indulge fancy, one may even suppose that the imperfectly preserved phrase actually spoke of 'building a church [congregation] firmly on a rock', for the verb 'set firm', which is here employed, is actually used, in Ps. 40.3(2), of 'planting firmly on a rock'. In that case, we should have here a striking parallel to Jesus' famous words to Peter (Mat. 16.18).

20. The reference may be typical, not specific. It is therefore hazardous to seek a precise identification.

THE TRIUMPH OF GOD

OF GOD

Descriptions of the Final Age

There shall be a time of trouble, such as never was since there was a nation even to that same time; and at that time thy people shall be delivered, every one that shall be found written in the book.

DANIEL 12.1.

INTRODUCTION From time immemorial, it has been the custom in many parts of the world to usher in the New Year or a new season by staging a pantomimic combat in which the New defeats the Old, Fertility discomfits Drought, Summer ousts Winter, or Life subdues Death. Traces of such primitive ritual survive to this day in the European Mummers' Plays, which are acted out on crucial calendar dates (e.g. Mid-summer) and which portray the conflict of the seasons or the triumph of a valiant 'Saint George' over a grisly dragon which threatens to engulf the earth.

In ancient Babylon, an essential element of the New Year ritual was the recital (possibly also the enactment) of a time-honored myth relating the victory of Marduk, the patron god of the city, over Tiamat, a draconic marplot who sought to overthrow the authority of the gods. In Canaan, a similar story rehearsing the defeat of Yam, the God of the waters, and Mot, the god of death, by Baal, lord of fertility, is preserved on clay tablets of the fourteenth century B.C. discovered, since 1929, at Ras Shamra on the north coast of Syria; and it is probable that this was recited in connection with the New Year festival, celebrated at the time when the drought broke and the early rains began. Moreover, vestiges of a similar myth, in which Yahweh (Jehovah) is portrayed as having conquered the draconic Leviathan in a primordial battle-royal, may also be detected in sundry poetic passages of the Old Testament (Psalms 74.13–14; Job 9.13; 26.12–13).

What is deemed necessary to restore the world-order from year to year is deemed necessary *a fortiori* in order to bring in the New Age which will succeed the present Era of Corruption. The seasonal battle thus becomes projected into eschatology—that is, into the standard picture of the Last Things. In Jewish folklore, as represented by numerous references in pseudepigraphic literature and in the Talmud, the adversaries of God in this final conflict were identified not so much with demonic or cosmic powers as with the unrighteous elements among men—the heathen and the recalcitrant who served the Prince of Darkness (Belial) and constituted his 'army'. In accordance with a celebrated prophecy in the Book of Ezekiel (chaps. 38–39), these earthly antagonists were in turn identified more especially with 'the children of Gog and Magog'—originally, remote northern peoples from 'the back of the beyond', but now regarded, in a purely metaphorical sense, as symbolic of all who denied the God of Israel and oppressed His chosen. Moreover, in line with what the prophet Zechariah had foretold (14.3–5), it was held that the Lord Himself would come with His heavenly legions and fight on behalf of His people.

The war against Gog and Magog formed the more militant complement to that process of inner regeneration and repentance that was to secure the advent of God's Kingdom on earth. If Israel itself might ensure its continuance and the restoration of its fortunes by a sincere return to the Law and the Covenant, it was nevertheless essential that the wicked should be finally and irretrievably put to rout.

To men who believed that the Final Age was indeed at hand, preparations for this war were a matter of imminent and urgent concern. They had to have a detailed Plan of Campaign. *The War of the Sons of Light and the Sons of Darkness* (inscribed on one of the scrolls discovered by the bedouin boys in 1947) is such a plan—a kind of G.H.Q. manual for the guidance of the Brotherhood at 'Armageddon'.

Not the least interesting feature of this document is that it is far from being a mere fanciful lucubration, something spun out of thin air. On the contrary, as General Yigael Yadin has pointed out, it very largely conforms to standard Roman patterns of military organization, procedure and strategy. A few examples (drawn from the present writer's independent observations) must here suffice:

(1) The troops are to be drawn up in three lines [viii, 6]; this is the Roman *triplex acies* (Sallust, *Jugurtha*, 49). (2) The soldiers who initiate the attack are to hurl javelins *seven* times into the enemy ranks [vi, 1]; this recalls the fact that the front-line *velites* of the Roman army were armed with seven javelins (Livy, xxiv, 34). (3) The attack is to be launched to the accompaniment of a united war-cry destined to strike terror in the heart of the foe [viii, 9–10]; the same practice obtained among the Romans (Caesar, *Bell. Civ.*, iii, 92, Livy, vii, 36; Sallust, *Catiline*, 60). (4) The high priest exhorted the troops before they went into action, and addressed them as 'warriors' [xii, 10]; this is simply an adaptation of the *allocutio* delivered by a Roman general. He, too, was expected to call them *milites;* when Caesar once addressed them as *Quirites*, this aroused indignation (Suetonius, *Caes.*, 70; Dio, xlii, 53). (5) The 'trumpets of assembly' answer to the Roman *tuba concionis;* (6) the inscriptions on the standards are in accordance with Roman usage (Veget., ii, 13), though cleverly adapted in accordance with the Biblical phrase, 'In the name of our God will we set up our banners' (Psalm 20.6).

We cannot yet tell when this document was written. A clue to the date has been recognized by some scholars in the fact that two of the prime enemies of Israel are identified as 'the Kittians of Assyria' and 'the Kittians of Egypt'. Since the Biblical term 'Kittians'—originally denoting the inhabitants of Kition in Cyprus—was used in Hellenistic Jewish literature to denote the 'Macedonians' of the Alexandrian Empire, it has been supposed that this refers to the Seleucids of Syria and the Ptolemies of Egypt, which would mean—in the words of its original editor, the late Professor E. L. Sukenik—'that this scroll was composed after the partition of Alexander's empire among the Diadochi'. This, however, is not an absolutely necessary inference. Assyria and Egypt were, after all, the classic foes of Israel, and their ultimate downfall bulks very largely in Old Testament prophecies of the Final Age, while the term 'Kittians' came in time to lose any precise signification and to be used—like 'Hun' or 'Tartar'—to denote 'barbarians' in general. Hence, the reference to 'Kittians' of Assyria and Egypt may have been made, like that to Moabites, Edomites, Ammonites and Philistines [i, 1–2], merely out of deference to tradition.

The war against Gog and Magog would mark the end of the present Era of Wickedness, but not the end of the world. It would last forty years—the period of so-called 'Messianic travail', and would pave the way for the 'Era of (Divine) Favor'. This too needed its blueprint, and a small portion of that blueprint is preserved in what has generally been called *The Two-Column Fragment*.

This tantalizing document, found in the same cave as the main scrolls, is really a Manual of Discipline for the future Restored Congregation of Israel. It has excited especial interest because it describes the protocol for a banquet attended by 'the Messiah'. This has led to the belief that it deals with the Messianic Banquet (on the flesh of Leviathan) often described in rabbinic literature, and also that it prefigures, albeit in a limited degree, the Christian Eucharist.

The plain fact is, however, that the term 'Messiah'—or, more specifically, 'Messiah of Israel'—means no more than 'the duly anointed king'. This text, as we have said, is concerned with the administration of the future ideal community of Israel. After describing the rules that are to obtain regarding education, eligibility for public office, and military service, the author takes up the question of rank and precedence. The high priest, he affirms, is to occupy the supreme position and to be superior to any layman. He then gives a pertinent illustration. If, he says, the anointed king himself (expressly described as 'the Messiah [anointed] of Israel', in implied contrast with 'the Messiah of Aaron', i.e., the high priest) should attend a communal banquet, the high priest is nevertheless to be seated first, and it is to be the high priest's duty and privilege to pronounce the Grace before Meals. Moreover, in order to make the point even clearer, our author lays it down explicitly that this rule is to be observed even at smaller gatherings, when there may be no more than ten persons present—the minimum religious quorum [*minyan*] in traditional Jewish law!

The interpretation of this document as referring to a 'Lord's Supper' has been bolstered by a daring but unfortunate conjecture, whereby a faint and damaged passage of the text is made to read: 'When God begets the Messiah, he [i.e., the Messiah] is to enter with them'. It may therefore be pointed out that the crucial word 'God' is here simply an arbitrary restoration, and that the word read as 'begets' (viz. *YW[LI]D*) is more probably to be read 'is present' (viz. *YW['']D*), while that rendered 'he is to enter' means properly 'he is to come' and belongs to the next sentence. What is actually said, therefore, is that 'if the anointed (king, i.e. [*hmlk*] *hmših*) happens to be present (*yw[']d*) with them, the priest, as head of the entire Congregation of Israel is (nevertheless) to come . . . and take his seat (first)'.

A pendant to these more important texts about the Future Age is afforded by the two small fragments here named *The New Covenant* and *The Coming Doom*.

The former is quite obviously part of an homiletic exposition of the famous prophecy in Jer. 31.31–33; 'Behold, the days come, saith the Lord, that I will make a new covenant with the house of Israel, and with the house of Judah . . . I will put my Law in their inward parts, and in their heart will I write it; and I will be their God, and they shall be My people'.

The latter may perhaps best be explained as part of a 'sermon' or discourse [Hebrew, *derashah*] based on a string of similes relating to the Last Day.

The War of the Sons of Light
and the Sons of Darkness

·   ·   ·   ·   ·   ·   ·   ·   ·   ·   ·   ·

The first engagement of the Sons of Light against the Sons
of Darkness—that is, against the army of Belial—shall be
an attack on the troop of Edom, Moab, the Ammonites and
the Philistine area and upon that of the Kittians of Assyria,
and of those violators of the Covenant who give them aid.
When the Sons of Light who are now in exile return from
the 'desert of the nations' to pitch camp in the desert of
Judah, the children of Levi, Judah and Benjamin, who
are now among those exiles, shall wage war against these
peoples—that is, against each and every one of their troops.

After that battle they shall advance upon the [king of]
the Kittians of Egypt. In due time, he will sally forth in
high fury to wage war against the kings of the north, being
minded in his anger to destroy his enemies and cut down
their power.² This, however, will be the time of salvation
for the people of God, the critical moment when those that
have cast their lot with Him will come to dominion,
whereas those that have cast it with Belial shall be doomed
to eternal extinction. [Great] havoc shall then beset the descendants of Japheth:³ Assyria shall fall, with none to help
her, and the dominion of the Kittians shall depart. Wick-

edness will thus be humbled and left without remnant, and no survivor shall remain of the Sons of Darkness.

[Streaks of lightn]ing will flash from one end of the world to the other, growing ever brighter until the era of darkness is brought utterly to an end.[4] Then, in the era of God, His exalted grandeur will give light for [evermore,][5] shedding on all the Sons of Light peace and blessing, gladness and length of days.

On the day the Kittians fall, there shall be mighty combat and carnage in the presence of the God of Israel, for that is the day which He appointed of old for the final battle against the Sons of Darkness. Thereon the company of the divine and the congregation of the human shall engage side by side in combat and carnage, the Sons of Light doing battle against the Sons of Darkness with a show of godlike might, amid uproarious tumult, amid the war-cries of gods and men, in a veritable day of havoc. It will be, indeed, a 'time of [   ] tribulation'[6] for 'the people redeemed of God', but, unlike all their previous tribulations, this one will come to a speedy end in a redemption which shall last for ever.

When they engage the Kittians, [amid all the combat and car]nage of battle, the Sons of Light shall have luck three times in discomfiting the forces of wickedness; but three times the host of Belial shall brace themselves to turn back the tide. At this, the squadrons of the infantry shall become faint-hearted, but the power of God shall strengthen their hearts, and on the seventh occasion the great hand of God shall finally subdue [the army of Belial. For will He summon] all the angels of His dominion and all the humans [that are bound to His communion] [   ] [and amid] the Holy Beings He Himself will appear* to give aid [   ], [and He will make] the truth [to shine forth,] bringing doom upon the Sons of Darkness [   ] [and] they shall surrender. . . .

---

* Restored after Zechariah 14:3,5: "Then shall the Lord go forth and fight against those nations, as when He fighteth in a day of battle . . . And the Lord my God shall come, and all the Holy Ones with Him (LXX text)."

[*Of religious offices during wartime*]

(ii, 1–6)

[   ] fathers of the community, fifty-two in number.[7]
After the high priest and his deputy they shall appoint
an order of major priests, twelve in number, to serve constantly before God. Furthermore, twenty-six major officials
duly assigned to service shall serve in their appointed
offices;[8] and after them there shall be twelve major levites,
one for each tribe, to serve constantly. The major officials
charged with service shall serve in rotation, but subordi-
nate to them shall be the chiefs of the tribes and the
fathers of the community stationed constantly at the gates
of the sanctuary.

The major officials assigned to service shall take up their
positions, in discharge of their duties, on the festivals,
new moons, sabbaths or weekdays duly assigned to them.
They shall be fifteen years of age and upwards.[9] Their
function shall be to attend to the burnt-offerings and the
sacrifices, to set out the incense of 'pleasant savor' for God's
acceptance, to perform rites of atonement in behalf of all
His congregation, and constantly to clear away the fat
ashes which lie before Him on the 'table of glory'.

[*Of recruitment*]

(ii, 6–9)

All of these dispositions, however, are to apply only to
the year of release. For the remaining thirty-three years
of the War,[10] the dignitaries appointed to the Assembly
and all the chiefs of families in the community are to select
the soldiers for service in the various foreign countries.
They are to draft them annually out of all the tribes of
Israel in accordance with the established conventions of
warfare.[11] Only in the year of release is there to be no
draft, for that is a year of sabbatical rest for Israel.

[*Of the sequence of campaigns*]

(ii, 9–14)

Of the thirty-five working years, the first six are to be devoted to mobilization, the entire community collectively taking part in it. During the remaining twenty-nine years, the war is to be conducted in a series of separate campaigns. In the first year, they are to fight in Mesopotamia; in the second, against the Lydians; in the third, against the rest of the Syrians, against Uz, Hul, Togar and Masha,[12] which are across the Euphrates; in the fourth and fifth, against Arpachshad;[13] in the sixth and seventh, against all the Assyrians, Persians and Easterners as far as the Great Desert; in the eighth, against the Elamites; in the ninth, against the descendants of Ishmael and Keturah.[14] For the next ten years the campaign shall be concentrated against all the Hamites,[15] wherever they dwell; and for the remaining decade against all the [   ] throughout their habitations.

*   *   *   *

Concerning the Battle Dispositions and the Trumpets of Assembly at the time when the gates of war are opened for the infantry to go forth, and concerning the trumpets for signaling the first onslaught, the ambush, the pursuit after the defeat of the enemy, and the recall

(iii, 1–11)

On the trumpets of assembly for the entire community, they shall write: *The Enlisted of God.*[16]

On the trumpets of assembly for officers, they shall write: *The Princes of God.*

On the trumpets of enrollment they shall write: *The Rank of God.*

On the trumpets of the dignitaries they shall write: *The Heads of the Families of the Community.*

When they assemble at the general meeting-house, they shall write: *Enactments*[17] *of God for the Sacred Council.*

On the trumpets of the camps they shall write: *The peace of God be in the camps of His saints.*

On the trumpets of advance they shall write: *The Power of God is able to scatter the enemy and to put to flight all who hate righteousness. And he recompenses the loyalty [of them that love God, but requites]*[18] *them that hate Him.*

On the trumpets for marshalling the battle they shall write: *The marshalled squadrons of God are able to wreak His angry vengeance upon all the Sons of Darkness.*

On the trumpets of assembly for the infantry, when the gates of war are opened for them to go out to the enemy line, they shall write: *A reminder*[19] *of the vengeance to be exacted in the Era of God.*

On the trumpets of carnage[20] they shall write: *The force of God's power in battle is able to fell all the perfidious as slain men.*

On the trumpets of ambush they shall write: *The hidden powers*[21] *of God are able to destroy wickedness.*

On the trumpets of pursuit they shall write: *God has smitten all the children of Darkness. He will not turn back His anger until He has consumed them.*

And when they return from the battle to rejoin the ranks they shall write on the trumpets of recall: *God hath taken back* (gathered in).[22]

And on the trumpets which signal the route of return from the war against the enemy and the way back to the community in Jerusalem, they shall write: *Joy of God at the return of peace.* * [23]

* Or, 'at a safe return'.

*This is the order
of the standards for the entire community
when they are enrolled*

(iii.12–iv, 2)

On the great standard which precedes the entire army [lit. 'people'] they are to write *People of God* together with the names Aaron and Israel and those of the twelve tribes of Israel according to their pedigrees.

On the standard of the camp commanders of the three tribes (of Levi, Judah and Benjamin) they are to write [   ].

On the standard of each separate tribe they are to write: *Banner of God,* together with the name of the chieftain of the [   ], the name of the chieftain of the ten thousand and those of the [   ].

On the standard of Merari[24] they are to write: *Offering unto God,*[25] together with the names of the chiefs of the Merarites and those of the commanders of its thousands.

On the standard of the thousand they are to write: *God's anger is vented*[26] *in fury against Belial and against all that cast their lot with him, that they have no remnant;* together with the name of the commander of the thousand and of its hundreds.

On the standard of the hundred they shall write: *From God*[27] *comes the power of battle against all sinful flesh,* together with the names of the commander of the hundred and of its tens.

On the standard of fifty they shall write: *Finished is the stand of the froward through the mighty acts of God,*[28] together with the names of the commanders of the fifty and of its tens.

And on the standard of ten they shall write: *Paeans of God on the ten-stringed harp,* together with the names of the commander of the ten, and of the nine men under his command.

When they go out to battle, they shall write upon their several standards: *Truth of God, Righteousness of God,*

Glory of God, Justice of God, and thereafter the specific name of each division. And when they draw near the battle, they shall write upon their standards: *Right Hand of God, Battle-Array of God, Tumult of God, Slain of God,* and thereafter their specific names.[29]

And when they come back from the battle, they shall write upon their standards: *Grandeur of God, Greatness of God, Praises of God, Glory of God,* together with their specific names.

Order of the standards of the community.

When they go out to battle, they shall write on the first standard: *Community of God;* on the second, *Camps of God;* on the third, *Tribes of God;* on the fourth, *Families of God;* on the fifth, *Squadrons of God;* on the sixth, *Assembly of God;* on the seventh, *Recruits of God;* on the eighth, *Armies of God;* and they shall write also the specific names, with all their ranks.

And when they draw near to the battle, they shall write upon their standards: *War of God, Vengeance of God, Feud of God, Requital of God; Strength of God; Recompense of God; Might of God; Annihilation by God of all vain nations;* together with all their specific names.

And when they return from the battle, they shall write on their standards: *Salvation of God, Triumph of God, Help of God, Support of God, Praise of God, Thanksgiving to God, Acclaim of God, Peace of God.*

(A fragmentary passage follows, giving the measurements of the standards.)

[.] On the [standard?] of the leader of the entire community they are to write his name and the names of Israel and Levi and Aaron, and the name of the twelve tribes of Israel according to their pedigrees, and the names of the twelve commanders of those tribes.

*Order of deploying the
battle-squadrons when their full
force is mustered*

(iv. 3–vi, 6)

To form a complete front. The line is to consist of a thousand men. Each front-line is to be seven deep, one man standing behind the other. All of them are to hold shields of polished bronze, resembling mirrors. These shields are to be bordered by a wreath-like rim wrought artistically by a skilled smith out of [   ]30 gold, silver, bronze, and precious stones, blended in a variegated arrangement as on a woman's breastplate.

Each shield is to be two and one half cubits long and two and one half cubits wide. The men are to hold in their hands a spear and a lance. The length of the spear is to be seven cubits, of which one half-cubit is to consist of the blade and the point. (*There follows a highly technical description of the spears. Since, however, we do not yet know the precise meaning of many of the terms employed, it is impossible to translate the passage with confidence.*)

*   *   *   *

[   ] seven times and then return to their positions. After them three squadrons of the infantry shall go forth and take up positions between the lines. The first squadron shall fling seven war-darts into the enemy line. On the blade of each dart they shall write: *The flash of the spear*31 *evinces the Power of God.* And on the second javelin they shall write: *Spurtings*32 *of blood, causing men to fall slain through the anger of God.* And on the third dart they shall write: *Flame of the sword devouring the evil-doing slain by the judgment of God.* They shall hurl such darts seven times in all, and then return to their positions. After them shall go forth the two other squadrons of the infantry and take up positions between the two lines. The one shall hold spear and shield and the other spear and lance, to

fell the slain in the judgment of God and to subdue the
enemy line by the might of God, to the end that every
vain nation may reap the fruit of its evil. Then shall the
sovereignty belong to the God of Israel, and He will evince
His power among the sacred hosts[33] of His people.

[Of the cavalry]

(vi, 7–17)

The seven battle lines shall be flanked in turn, on the
left and on the right, by cavalry. Each line shall be ac-
companied by two hundred light horsemen, so that there
will be in all seven hundred of the latter on the one side
and seven hundred on the other.

These horsemen shall occupy a similar position in the
camp, though in that case they shall be disposed on all
(four) sides.

There shall be four thousand and six hundred of them,
all told. In addition, there shall be fourteen hundred heavy
horse accompanying the general ranks—fifty for each line
of troops.[33a] The light and heavy horse that accompany the
troops shall therefore amount in all to six thousand.

All the cavalry that go out to battle with the infantry
shall consist of stallions swift of foot, non-biters,[34] long in
the wind, full-grown and mature, trained for battle and
used to hearing all kinds of sounds and facing all kinds of
sights. Their riders shall be stout-hearted warriors, trained
in horsemanship; and their ages shall range between thirty
and forty-five.[35] Those, however, who are assigned to line
duty shall be from forty to fifty years old. They shall [be
equipped with] [   ] and helmets and greaves, and
shall hold in their hands round shields and spears [   ],
long [   ] and a bow and arrows and war-darts. And
all of them shall be primed in [   ]. [It shall be their
duty to] [   ] and to shed the blood of those who
are destined to be slain in consequence of their guilt.

*   *   *   *

[*Of age and health requirements*]

(vii, 1–7)

The line troops are to be forty to fifty years of age.[36]
Those who arrange the camps are to be from fifty to
sixty.[37] The officers too are to be from forty to fifty years
of age; and all who strip the dead and collect the spoil
and clean up the terrain and keep the weapons and prepare the food are to be between twenty-five and thirty.
No toddling child or woman is to enter their camps from
the moment they leave Jerusalem to go to war until they
return; neither is anyone that is lame or blind or halt, or
that has a long-standing blemish in his flesh or that is
afflicted with any manner of bodily contagion, to go with
them to war. All of them are to be men willing to face the
hazards of battle, unimpaired in spirit and flesh and ready
for the day of vengeance. Moreover, any man who is not
yet cleansed from a bodily discharge on the day of battle
is not to go down with them; for holy angels march with
their hosts.

A distance of about two thousand cubits is to be set in
every case between the camp and the latrine, and no un-
cleanliness is ever to be in evidence in the precincts of the
camp.

[*Of the battle signals*]

(vii, 8–ix, 9)

When the lines of battle are drawn up to face the foe, line
in front of line, then out of the center gap in the ranks[38]
there shall come into the lines seven priests of the descendants of Aaron, clothed in robes of white silk, wearing
the linen tunic and the linen breeches, girt with the linen
girdle of silk twined artistically with blue and purple and
deep scarlet thread, after the model of broidery, and with
mitred turbans on their heads—garments of war which
they are not to bring into the sanctuary. The one priest

shall walk about before all the troops of the line to encourage them in the battle, while in the hands of the other six shall be the trumpets for calling to arms, and the trumpets for sounding the charge, and the trumpets for recall. And when these priests go out between the lines, seven levites shall go out with them, and in their hands shall be seven trumpets made out of rams' horns. And three officers selected from the levites shall walk ahead of these priests and levites. And the priests shall sound a blast on the two [*or:* two of the] trumpets used for call[ing to arms]. [   ] fifty shield-men;[38a] and fifty infantrymen shall go out from the one gap, [and fifty from the other,] and the levitical officers [shall go out with them.] And they shall go out with every line in this manner. [   ]. The men of the infantry shall go out from the gaps and [take up posi]tion between the two [lines.]

*   *   *   *

The trumpets shall keep sounding for the slingers until they have hurled a full seven times. Then the priests shall blow the recall for them, and they shall return (lit. come) to the first line to take their stand in their assigned position. Thereupon the priests shall sound a blast on the trumpets of assembly, and the squadron of infantry shall go forth from the gaps and take up position between the lines, and on their flanks shall be horsemen to the right and to the left. The priests shall then sound upon the trumpets a quavering (?) blast for the drawing up of the line of the battle. The columns shall disperse to their several ranks, each to his assigned position. And when they have taken up position in three lines, the priests shall sound a second blast—a low, subdued note for advance to the enemy line. Thereupon they are to grasp their weapons. Then the priests are to sound blasts on the six trumpets used for rousing to the slaughter—a sharp insistent note for directing the battle. And the levites and all the people with ram's horns are to sound a single blast—a great warlike trump to melt the heart of the enemy. At the sound of that blast, the war-darts are to issue forth to fell the slain. Then they are to accelerate the notes of the ram's horns, and the priests are to blow upon the trumpets a sharp, insistent sound to direct the wings of the battle, until they have hurled their darts into the enemy line seven times. Thereupon the priests are to sound upon the trumpets the signal of recall—a low, quavering (?) subdued note.

In such fashion are the priests to blow the signals for the three squadrons. And when the first squadron begins to hurl its darts, the [priests] are to blow [   ] [on the trump]et a great blast to direct the bat[tle] [   ]; the priests are to sound a blast for them on the trumpets [   ] their assigned positions in the ranks [   ], and [   ] shall take up position.

*   *   *   *

[   ] they shall engage in felling the slain. And all the people shall silence their war-cries, while the priests keep blowing the trumpets for carnage, to direct the battle, until the enemy are discomfited and turn tail. The priests shall go on blowing to direct the battle, and when the enemy are being discomfited before them, the priests shall sound on the trumpets of assembly, and all the infantry troops stationed between the front lines shall go out to them, and six squadrons shall take up positions. The force of the total squadrons then entering the combat shall consist of seven lines comprising in all twenty-eight thousand troops, and the cavalry shall number six thousand. All of these shall pursue the enemy to annihilate him in the battle of God unto his eternal extinction. And the priests shall blow for them on the trumpets of pursuit, and they shall fall upon the enemy to pursue him unto destruction. And the horsemen shall keep chasing them back into the thick of the battle until utter destruction is achieved. And while the enemy are falling slain, the priests shall go sounding the signals from a distance; they shall not go into the midst of the slain lest they be defiled by their impure blood; for the priests are holy and they are not to defile the oil of their priestly anointment with the blood of vain heathen.[39]

*Order of disposing the troops
in various battle-formations:*[39a]

(a) in a straight line[40] *flanked by so-called
'(human) towers';* [41]
*(b) in a curved line resembling the lower
half of a circle,*[42] *similarly protected;*
*(c) in a curved line resembling the upper
half of a circle,*[43] *similarly protected;*
*(d) in a slight curve with center foremost,
protected by spearhead columns advancing
from the flanks;*[44]
*(e) in a slight curve with ends foremost, pro-
tected by wings (of cavalry)*[44a] *advancing on
both flanks, in order to strike terror in the
enemy.*

(ix, 10–15)

(In all such cases,) the shields of the men constituting
the '(human) towers' are to be three cubits long, and their
spears eight cubits. The 'tower' is to consist of two side-
lines each made up of a hundred men carrying shields, and
of a front line similarly composed. It is to be a three-sided
affair, and thus to comprise three hundred shields in all.
It is to have two gaps, one on the [right and] one on the
left. All of the shields of the 'towers' are to bear inscriptions. Those of the first 'tower' are to carry the legend,
MICHAEL; [those of the second, GABRIEL; those of the
third,] SARIEL; and those of the fourth, RAPHAEL[45] . . .

*   *   *   *

[*Of the exhortation
of the troops*]

(x, 1–xii, 18)

[   ] our[46] camp, and to guard ourselves from all
unclean things, and Thou art He who told us aforetime

that Thou wouldst be in our midst, a great and awful God, to make spoil of our enemies before us. Thou also art He who taught us from of old for all our generations saying: When ye draw near unto the battle, the priest is to stand and speak to the people saying: 'Hear, O Israel, ye are drawing near this day onto battle against your enemies. Fear not, neither let your hearts grow soft, neither be dismayed nor affrighted before them, for your God is marching with you to do battle for you against your foemen to the end that He may save you'.[47]

Then shall the officers thus address all that are ready for the battle, stout-hearted men, to encourage [them] with the power of God and to restore all whose hearts melt and to encourage altogether all the soldiers of the army: 'To this didst Thou refer when Thou spakest through Moses saying: "When thou goest to war in your land against a foeman that assails you, sound ye the trumpets [Num. 10.9]. Then shall ye be called to remembrance before your God and ye shall be saved from your enemies." Who is like Thee, O God of Israel, in heaven or on earth, that can do the like of Thy great deeds and of Thy mighty power? And who is like Thy people Israel whom Thou didst choose for Thyself out of all the nations of the lands, a people of men hallowed by the covenant and schooled in the Law, men enlightened with un[derstanding], men who [   ], who heard the glorious voice and saw the holy angels, men whose ears are opened and who hear deep things. [Thou art He who ordained] the outspreading of the heavens; the host of the luminaries; the several duties of spirits and the spheres of dominion of holy beings; the treasuries of ha[il and snow; and the balance of] the clouds.

'Thou art He who created the earth and the rules whereby parts thereof are assigned to desert and wasteland; likewise all that issues from it and all the fruits of its [yield]; the bounds of the seas also and the reservoirs of the rivers; the cleavage of the deeps; all manner of beasts and fowl; the fabric of man and his offspring; the confusion of tongues and division of peoples; the settle-

ments of [all] the families [of men], and the apportion-
ment of the earth as inheritances [among them].

'[Thou art He who decreed the day of sabbath rest and]
the holy festivals, and the turning-points of the years[48]
and [all] the appointed seasons. [   ].

'These things have we come to know through Thine
understanding which [Thou hast planted within us].

'[Thou hast bent] Thine [ear] to our cry; for [   ]'

*   *   *   *

'[To none] but Thee belong the [issues of] war, and it is
by the strength of Thy hand that their corpses have been
flung forth, with none to bury them.

'Goliath the Gittite, a man of mighty strength, didst
Thou deliver into the hand of thy servant David, because
David trusted in Thy great name and not in sword or
spear.[49] For Thine is the battle. The Philistines also didst
Thou humble time after time by Thy holy name; and
Thou didst also deliver us many times through the hands
of our kings by virtue of Thy mercies and not of our deeds
which we did evilly commit, nor of our acts of transgression.

'Thine is the battle; from Thee comes the power; and
it is not ours. It is not our strength nor the might of our
hands that achieveth this valor, but it cometh through
Thy strength and through Thy great valorous might. So
didst Thou tell us of old, saying: "There shall step a star
out of Jacob; there shall rise a rod out of Israel, and it
shall smite the brow of Moab and undermine all the children of pride. And it shall proceed from Jacob and destroy
every remnant from the city; and the enemy shall be dispossessed, but Israel shall triumph" [Num. 24.17–19].
Moreover, by the hands of Thine anointed, the men who
had vision of things foreordained, Thou hast related unto
us the warlike triumphs of Thy hand—how Thou hast
waged battle against our foes and caused the troops of
Belial—the seven vain nations[50]—to fall into the hands of
the pauper folk whom Thou didst redeem by wondrous
might [and set] in [safe]ty and peace.

'Now is the heart that was melting turned to a wellspring

of hope. Thou hast done unto these as Thou didst unto
Pharaoh and the captains of his chariots at the Red Sea.
The base[51] of spirit wilt Thou burn up like a flaming brand
in a hayrick, a brand that devours wickedness and that
will not turn back until guilt is destroyed.

'Of old didst Thou tell us of the time when Thy mighty
hand would prevail against the Kittians, in that Thou didst
declare: "Assyria shall fall by the sword of no human, and
the sword of no man shall devour him".

'Into the hands of the needy hast Thou delivered the
foemen in all lands, and into the hands of them that were
bowed to the dust. So hast Thou humbled the mighty of
the peoples; brought their deserts upon the wicked; vindi-
cated among all men the truthfulness of Thy judgments;
won for Thyself eternal fame among the people [whom
Thou hast redeemed; revealed to those whom Thou hast
worsted that Thou art indeed the Lord] of Battles;[52] shown
forth Thy great and holy Being[53] in the sight of the rest
of the nations, that [   ] may know [   ], when
Thou wreakest judgment upon Gog[54] and upon all his
throng and takest vengeance upon [   ], that Thou
wilt wage battle against them from heaven [   ]'.

*   *   *   *

'For [with Thee] in heaven are a multitude of holy
beings,[55] and armies of angels are in Thy holy abode, to
[serve as] Thy [legionaries];[56] and down on earth Thou
hast [likewise] placed at Thy service the elect of an holy
people.[57] The roster of all their host is with Thee in Thy
holy habitation, and the [   ] in Thy glorious abode.
And the benefits[58] of Thy blessings and Thy covenant of
peace hast thou inscribed for them in a charter[59] of
[Eternal] Life—an assurance that through all the epochs
of time Thou wilt be their king, and that when Thou con-
tendest in judgment Thou wilt muster an army of (these)
Thine elect, in their thousands and tens of thousands, side
by side with Thine holy beings and Thine angels, and that
they shall prevail in battle and, along with the heavenly
elect [be triumphant.]

'O God, Thou, resplendent in Thy sovran glory, and the

congregation of Thy holy beings are indeed in our midst as a perpetual help. We have [poured] contempt upon kings, scorn and contumely upon mighty men. For the Lord [*Adonai*] is holy, and the King of Glory is with us, along with the holy beings.[60] Warrior angels are in our muster, and He that is Mighty in War[61] is in our throng. The army of His spirits marches beside us. Our horsemen come like clouds or like banks of dew, to cover the earth, or like torrential showers, to rain judgment on all that grows in it.

'Arise, O warrior![62]
Take thy captives, thou man of glory;
and reap thy spoil,[62a] O valiant![62b]
Set thy hand upon the neck of thy foemen,[62c]
and thy foot upon mounds of the slain.[63]
Smite the nations that assail thee,[63a]
and let thy sword devour guilty flesh.[64]
Fill thy land with glory
and Thine inheritance with blessing.[65]
Be a multitude of possessions[65a] in Thy fields,
silver and gold and precious stones in Thy palaces.
Zion, rejoice exceedingly,[65b]
and shine forth, O Jerusalem, with songs of joy,
and let all the cities of Judah exult![66]
Let thy gates be continually open,
that the wealth of the nations may be brought unto thee;[67]
and let their kings minister unto thee,
and all that oppressed thee make obeisance to thee,
and lick the dust of thy feet![68]
    O daughter of my people,
ring out your songs of joy![68a]
Put on your finery,[69]
step forth [   ]
[   ] Israel, to rule for evermore!
[   ] the warriors, O Jerusalem!
Be exalted, O Lord, above the heavens!'[70]

*   *   *   *

[Of the priestly benediction]

(xiii, 1–xiv, 1)

And his brethren the priests and the levites and all the elders of the ranks that are with him, standing each in his assigned position, shall bless the God of Israel and all His unerring works, and shall curse the name of Belial and all the spirits associated with him. And they shall take up word and say:

'Blessed be the God of Israel for all His holy plan and for His unerring works; and blessed be all that serve Thee in righteousness and acknowledge Thee in faithfulness. But cursed be Belial for his invidious schemes, and damned be he for his guilty dominion; and cursed be all the spirits of his ilk for their wicked designs, and damned be they for all their filthy acts and unclean. For they are of the portion of darkness, while the portion of God is everlasting light.

'And now, O God of our fathers, we will bless Thy name for ever. For we are the people [of Thine inheritance.] With our fathers didst Thou make a covenant, and Thou hast confirmed it with their seed throughout the epochs of time. In all the evidences of Thy glory among us there hath always been the memory of Thy covenant. Therefore hast Thou granted help to the remnant and ever renewed that covenant, and therefore hast Thou ever vouchsafed unto us Thy deeds of truth and Thy wondrous acts of justice. Thou hast made us unto Thee an eternal people, and hast cast our lot in the portion of light, that we may evince Thy truth; and from of old hast Thou charged the Angel of Light[71] to help us. In his hand are all works of righteousness, and all spirits of truth are under his sway. But for corruption thou hast made Belial, an angel of hostility. All his dominion is in darkness, and his purpose is to bring about wickedness and guilt. All the spirits that are associated with him are but angels of destruction. They follow only the laws of darkness, and all their craving is directed toward it. But we—we are in the portion of Thy truth.[72]

We will rejoice in the might of Thy hand and be glad
in Thy salvation and exult in the strength of [Thy right
hand and in the gift] of Thy peace.

'Who is like Thee in strength, O God of Israel? Thy right
hand is with the needy.

'And what angel or [prince of heaven] can give such
help as Thou givest with Thy redemption?

'Of old hast Thou set for Thyself a day of warfare against
wic[kedness], to triumph in truth and to destroy guilt; to
bring darkness low and raise light on high;[73] [   ] [to
ensure that the Sons of Light] stand for ever, and to
destroy all the Sons of Darkness; to bring joy to [all
        ]. Hast Thou not appointed us for [that time?].'

*   *   *   *

'[   ] as when the fire of His fury was kindled
against the idols of Egypt.'

[Of the hymn of victory]

(xiv, 2–17)

When they come up from gathering in the fallen and
return to the camps, they shall all of them sing the hymn
of return. Next morning, they shall launder their garments
and wash themselves clean of the blood of the guilty
corpses and return to their assigned positions at the place
where the line was drawn up before the slain of the enemy
fell. And there they shall all of them bless the God of
Israel and extol His name together in joy and take up
word and say:

'Blessed be the God of Israel
Who keeps the loyalty of His covenant
and constantly evinces salvation
to the people whom He redeemed.
He has summoned those that were stumbling [   ],[74]
but has gathered the horde of the heathen for extermina-
        tion without survival,

exalting the melting heart by [His] justice,
opening the mouth of the dumb for joyful song,
endowing with strength hands that were slack,
teaching them arts of war;
giving firm stance to tottering knees
and vigor to the shoulders of the bowed;
and [   ] to the lowly spirits;
firmness to the melting heart,
and [   ] to those whose way is blameless.
All wicked nations are come to an end
and all their heroes have no standing.
But we— [Thou hast granted us] a remnant;
[therefore will we bless] Thy name.

'O God of mercies,
Who keepest the covenant sworn unto our fathers,
and Who, throughout all our generations,
hast wondrously shown forth Thy mercies unto our remnant.
[Thou hast caused us to prevail] against the dominion of Belial
that, for all His covert hostility,
he has not thrust us away from Thy covenant.
Thou hast rebuked the spirits of His lot
[   ] the [   ] of his sway.
Thou hast preserved the life
of [the people] whom Thou didst redeem;
hast upholden the falling by Thy strength,
but cut down all the proud of stature.
Their warriors have none to deliver them;
their fleet men[75] have no escape;
their honored men Thou turnest to contempt;
and every creature of vanity [thou reducest to nau]ght.
But we—we are Thy holy people;
For Thy holy works we will praise Thy name,
and for Thy deeds of power we will extol [Thy]
    [   ],
at all the stated times, and at all the foreordained
    moments of nature:

at the coming of day and night,
and the outgoing of evening and morning;[76]
for great is [   ] of Thy [   ]
and Thy mysterious wonders in the heights.
For Thou raisest up unto Thee out of the dust,
and castest down from the angels.
Be exalted, be exalted, O God of gods,[77] and lift thyself
    up in Thy wrath! [   ]
[Let destruction befall] the Sons of Darkness,
but let Thy great light shine [for the Sons of Light
    ].'

*   *   *   *

B[78]
[Preparations for battle]

(xv, 1–2)

*   *   *   *

[For it is a 'time of trouble for Israel',][79] and of the
[visita]tion of war upon all the nations. They that have
cast their lot with God shall [be blessed] with everlasting
redemption, but annihilation shall overtake all the wicked
nations. All who have been making preparations for the
war shall go and pitch camp against the king of the Kittians and against all the army of Belial that are destined
along with him [for the day of vengeance] by God's sword.

[Of the exhortation
of the troops]

(xv, 3–xvi, 1)

The high priest shall stand up with his brethren the
priests and the levites and all the men of the ranks beside
him, and shall recite in their hearing the prayer of the
battle line and shall rehearse to them the full order of
regulations for the occasion together with all the words
of their thanksgivings, and he shall there marshal all the

lines according to [   ]; and the priest that is chosen
by the unanimous decision of his brethren to officiate at
the moment of vengeance[80] shall walk about and encourage all the troops and say:

'Be strong and stouthearted and acquit ye as men of
valor. Be not afeared neither dismayed [neither terrified
before] them; and be not a-quail neither awe-struck before them, and turn not back, neither [   ], for they
are a wicked horde, and all their deeds are in darkness,
and for darkness is all their craving. But all their refuges
and strength shall be as smoke that dissolves, and all their
multitudinous throng [   ]. None of their [   ]
shall be found any more, and all their ruinous structure[81]
shall be speedily cut down [   ]. Be of good courage
for the battle of God; for this day has been determined as
the day of battle [   ] against all [   ] and as the
day of combat against all flesh. The God of Israel lifts up
His hand with wondrous power [against] all the spirits
of wickedness [   ]. And the warrior angels gird themselves for battle; they are marshalled in serried ranks and
[mustered] for the day [of combat] [   ], to remove
[   ] in his destruction.'

*　　*　　*　　*

'The God of Israel has [summoned] a sword against all
the nations,[82] but with the saints of His people He will do
a work of power.'

[Of the order of battle]

(xvi, 2–9)

This is the order of their operations [   ] when they
stand over against the camps of the Kittians. After the
priests have sounded a blast for them on the trumpets of
[memorial,][83] they shall open gaps [in the ranks], and the
infantry shall go forth, and their columns shall stand between the lines; and the priests shall sound for them the
signal for drawing up the lines, and at the sound of the
trumpets the chiefs shall disperse and each take up his

position at his assigned place. Then the priests shall blow
a second time, and when they stand over against the line
of the Kittians, within hurling distance, each man shall
raise his hand with the weapon in it. Six [times] shall the
priests sound on the trumpets the signal for carnage—a
sharp, insistent sound, to direct the battle. And the levites
and all the people with ram's horns shall sound a loud
blast. And as the sound goes forth, they shall start lashing
out and felling the Kittians. All the people shall silence
their blasts while the priests are sounding on the trumpets
the signal for carnage. And the battle shall be waged vic-
toriously against the Kittians.

*[Of encouragement
in moments of reverse]*

(xvi, 11–xvii, 15)

In the event that Belial girds himself to help the Children of Darkness, so that through God's inscrutable will
and as a means whereby he may 'put the gold to the test',[84]
the corpses of the infantry begin to fall, the priests shall
sound the signal of assembly for the second line to go out
as a relief to the battle. They shall stand between the lines,
and as the relief approaches the original line, they shall
sound the signal for the former to retire. Then the high
priests shall come near and stand before the second line
and encourage them [   ] in God's war. And he shall
take up word and say:

'[Blessed be He who] strengthens the heart of His people; who "tests [the gold"]. He will not suffer your slain
[to be many]. For ye have heard of old of the mysterious
ways of God.'

*   *   *   *

'[   ] and He hath appointed their retribution, hotly
pursuing them; and [He will come to the rescue] of those
tested in the trial, [   ]. And He hath sharpened His
weapons, and they shall not be [blunted] until the wicked
is [consumed.] And as for you, remember the judgment

passed upon Nadab and [Abih]u, the sons of Aaron. By passing judgment upon them God also shewd His holiness before the sign of the people, in that he [at once] chose [Eleazar] and Itamar to confirm the covenant of eternal [priesthood].[85]

'And ye—be of good courage and fear them not. For they are but vanity. All their craving is for emptiness and futility, and that in which they rely shall be as though it had never been. But as for the God of Israel, all that has been and is and shall be throughout the vicissitudes of all time are in His hand.

'This is the day which He hath appointed for abasing and humbling the [Prince] of the Dominion of Wickedness. But He will send perpetual help to those who have a share in His redemption through the power of Michael,[86] the mighty, ministering angel; and He will send also an eternal light to light up the children of Israel with joy.[87] They that have cast their lot with God shall enjoy peace and blessing. In this way, the rule of Michael will be exalted among the angels, and the dominion of Israel among all flesh. Righteousness shall flourish in heaven, and all who espouse God's truth shall rejoice in the knowledge of eternal things. And ye, the sons of His covenant, be of good courage in the trial which God visits upon you, until He gives the sign[88] that He has completed His test. His secret powers will always support you.'

After these words, the priests shall blow a blast to deploy the various divisions of the line; and at the sound of the trumpets, the columns shall break up and take up positions in their assigned places. Then the priests shall sound a second blast on the trumpets to bid them draw near. And when the men of the line draw near the lines of the Kittians, and are within hurling distance, everyone shall raise his hand with his weapons in it, and the priests shall sound on the trumpets the signal for carnage, and all the people with ram's horns shall sound a blast, and the infantry shall start to launch out against the army of the Kittians, and to fell them. Then all the people shall silence

the sound of the blast, while the priests keep on blowing
[   ] to attacks before them.

*   *   *   *

[Of thanksgiving for victory]

(xviii, 1–15)

When the great hand of God is raised against Belial
and against all the forces under his dominion, inflicting on
them an eternal discomfiture, and when the war-cry of
Israel and of the holy beings rings out, as they pursue
Assyria; and when the sons of Japhet fall never to rise,
and when the Kittians are cut off without [survivor]; then,
[   ] when the hand of the God of Israel has indeed
prevailed against all the multitude of Belial, the priests
shall sound the blasts of memorial, and all the lines of
battle shall rally unto them, and all shall receive their
portion of the spoil [   ] to 'devote' it.[89] And when
the sun is hasting to set on that day, the high priest shall
stand up, and the priests and the levites that are with him,
and he shall look upon the [   ] battle array and
there bless the God of Israel. And they shall take up and
say:

'Blessed be Thy name, O God [of merci]es, for Thou hast
done great and wondrous things. From of old hast Thou
kept Thy covenant unto us; and Thou hast opened for
us gates of salvation time after time so that [Thy power]
might be revealed] through us. And Thou, O God, hast
done righteously, for Thy name's sake.

'[Verily, Thou hast wrought] wondrously, and the like of
this hath not been from of old. Thou it is who determined
[this] time for us, and this day [Thy glory] hath shone
upon us, [   ] and Thy [   ] is with us, ensuring
perpetual redemption, removing the enemy from us, that
he be no more. And Thy mighty hand [   ] felleth
our foemen until final discomfiture. And now the day is
pressing upon us to chase after their horde, for Thou [hast]
[   ] and chilled the hearts of [their] mighty men,

that they cannot stand. Thine is the power,[90] and in Thy hand lies [the issue of] war, and there is none [can withstand Thee]'.

*   *   *   *

(Column 19, the concluding column, is largely a duplicate of the high priest's exhortation in Column 12. It is preserved in fragmentary fashion.)

Manual of Discipline for
the Future Congregation
of Israel

*This is the rule for the whole body of Israel
when, in the future, they lead their lives in the
manner of the sons of Zadok, the priests, and
of those associated with them—the men who
declined to follow the popular trend, who constituted the true community of God, who went
on keeping the Covenant in the midst of general wickedness and so made atonement for
the land:*

All that present themselves are to be assembled together,
women and children included. Then, all the provisions of
the Covenant are to be read out aloud to them, and they
are to be instructed about all its injunctions, so that no one
may fall into error through ignorance.

*And this is the rule for all that make up the
complement of that body—that is, for every individual who is an Israelite by birth:*

Every person is to be trained from childhood in the
Book of Study, to be enlightened (so far as his age per-
mits) in the various provisions of the Covenant and to be
schooled in its various injunctions for a period of ten
years; after which he is to be liable to the regulations
regarding the several degrees of purity.

At twenty, he is to undergo an examination preparatory to his admission by vote, as a constituent member of his family, to the council of the holy community. He is not to have carnal knowledge of woman until he is twenty years old and has reached the age of discretion. Furthermore, it is only then that he is to be eligible to give testimony in matters involving the laws of the *Torah* or to attend judicial hearings.

At twenty-five, he is to take his place in the formal structure of the holy community and be eligible for communal office.

At thirty, he may take part in litigation and in rendering judgments and may occupy a position on the staff of the militia—that is, as the captain of a battalion, company, squadron or platoon or as one of the tribal commissioners or officers selected from the various families by the Aaronid priests.

All heads of families within the community who are chosen by lot for communal service, 'to go in and come out before the congregation', are to receive their assignments in accordance with their intellectual ability and their moral integrity. Everyone is to respect the rank of his fellow, and in case of dispute between any two men, each is to be given his commission according to his capacity.

No one who is feeble-minded is to take part in litigation or in rendering judgments in any matter affecting the community as a whole, nor is he to occupy any communal office or to serve in the armed forces in wars against the heathen. His family, however, is to be duly registered in the military roster, and he is to be drafted [instead] for compulsory labor in the line of his usual occupation.

The levites are to serve as local adjutants to the Aaronid priests in formally admitting to the armed forces all members of the community selected for service as commissioners or officers in accordance with the total military requirements to be laid down by the sons of Zadok, the priests and the heads of the various families. Ditto in the matter of granting releases. The draft status of every man is to be determined by the heads of the families.

If public notice is posted for a juridical or consultative assembly, or if notice of war be posted, everyone is to observe a three-day period of personal sanctification, so that any one who presents himself on any of these occasions may come duly prepared. This refers to men over twenty who are eligible for summons to the council and likewise to all the sages, scholars and learned men of the community—the so-called 'irreproachables'—and again to all men serving in the armed forces, including the commissioners and officers and the captains of battalions, companies, squadrons and platoons, as well as to the levites in the several departments of their office. These together constitute the so-called 'dignitaries'—that is, the laymen who sit in the presence of the sons of Zadok, the priests, at all deliberative assemblies.

No one who is afflicted by any form of human uncleanness is to be admitted to the community, nor is anyone who becomes so afflicted to maintain his position within it. Similarly, no one who is afflicted with a bodily defect, who is stricken in hands or feet, who is lame or blind or deaf or dumb, or who has any visible bodily defect, is to be admitted to a place among the 'dignitaries' for 'holy angels are in the congregation'.

If any such person has something to say to the sacred council, an oral deposition is to be taken from him, but he himself is not to come, seeing that he is afflicted.

> *This is the protocol for a session of the dignitaries, the men eligible for summons to the consultative council, in the event that the anointed (king) should be present among them:*

The (high) priest, as head of the entire community of Israel, is to come first, and the heads of the Aaronid priestly families and the dignitaries—that is, the men eligible for summons to meetings of the general council—are to take their seats before him in order of rank. After that, the anointed (king), being a layman, is to come, and the chiefs of the armed forces are to take their seats before him in order of rank, each occupying the same position as he does in camp or on the march. Then, in turn, the heads of the families of the community, together with the sages, [scholars and learned men], are to take their seats before them.

If they happen to be foregathering for a common meal or to drink wine together, when the common board has been spread or the wine mixed for drinking, no one is to stretch out his hand for the first portion of the bread or wine prior to the priest. It is he who is to pronounce the blessing over the first portion of the bread or wine, and it is he that is first to stretch out his hand to the bread. After that, the anointed (king), a layman, is to stretch out his hand to the bread; and after that the members of the community in general are to pronounce the blessing, in order of rank.

This rule is to obtain at all meals where there are ten or more men present.

The New Covenant

(Col. 1)

.   .   .   .

[but   wilt Thou] allot unto the righteous.

The portion of the wicked shall be [to be afflicted with pain]s in their bones and to be a reproach to all flesh;
but the righteous [shall be destined to en]joy the rich delights[1] of heaven and to be [glut]ted[2] on the yield of the earth.

[Thou wilt distinguish between the right]eous and the wicked.
Thou wilt give the wicked as our [ran]som, and the faithless [in exchange for us].[3]

[Thou wilt make] an end of all that oppress us;
and we shall give thanks unto Thy name for ever, [and bless Thee alway;]
for this it is for which Thou hast created us,
and that it is that [beseemeth] Thee.

     BLESSED . . .

(Col. 2)

[and Thou hast appointed] the greater luminary for the season of [day and the lesser luminary for the season of night],[4] and there is no overstepping their bounds.

They all [minister unto Thee, and defy not Thy word],[5] and their sway is over all the world.

But the seed of man hath not understood all of which Thou hast made it heir, neither have men known Thee whensoever Thou hast spoken;
but they have done more wickedly than all things else, and have not perceived[6] Thy great power.
And Thou hast rejected them, because Thou delightest not in wrongdoing, and wickedness hath no standing in Thy presence.

Howbeit, in the time of Thy good pleasure,[7] Thou wilt (again) choose unto Thyself a people, for Thou hast remembered Thy covenant; and Thou wilt make them to be set apart unto Thee as an holy thing distinct from all the peoples; and Thou wilt renew Thy Covenant unto them with a show of glory[8] and with words of Thy holy [spirit,] with works of Thy hand and with a script of Thy right hand, revealing unto them both the basic roots[9] of glory and the heights of eternity; [; and Thou wilt appoint] for them a faithful shepherd,[10] one who will [   ] the lowly and [   ] the [   ].

The Coming Doom

*   *   *   *

[They pay no heed to the] real hidden [meaning of things, but divert themselves instead with all] kinds of iniquitous arcane lore. [   ] They do not know the hidden meaning of what is actually taking place, nor have they ever understood the lessons of the past. Consequently, they have no knowledge of what is coming upon them and have done nothing to save their souls from the deeper implications of present events.

This, however, will symbolize things for you. What is going to happen is, as it were, that all iniquity is going to be shut up in the womb and prevented from coming to birth. Wrong is going to depart before Right, as darkness departs before light. As smoke disappears and is no more, so will Wrong disappear for ever. But Right will be revealed like the sun. The world will rest on a sound foundation. All who cling to rarefied arcane lore will cease to exist. The world will be filled with knowledge, and ignorance exist no more.

The thing is certain to come. The prophecy is true, and by this you may know that it will not be revoked:

Do not all peoples hate wrongdoing? Yet, is it not rampant among them all? Are not the praises of truth sung by all nations? Yet is there a single race or tribe that really adheres to it? What nation likes to be oppressed by a stronger power? Or who wants his property plundered unjustly? Yet, is there a single nation that has not oppressed its neighbor? Or where in the world will you find a people that has not plundered the property of another?

*   *   *   *

NOTES

The War of the Sons of Light and the Sons of Darkness

1. Since Cols. xv–xix largely repeat what has been said previously, it is apparent that our present text of this document really represents a compilation out of two different recensions. They are here distinguished as A and B respectively.

2. Literally, 'cut off the horn'. For a similar idiom, cp. Lam. 2.3.

3. I.e., the Greeks and their associates; cp. Gen. 10.2–5.

4. *The Third Book of the Sibylline Oracles* (334–40)—a basically Jewish work written around 140 B.C.—predicts a comet before the final disaster.

5. Cp. Isa. 60.20.

6. Jer. 30.7.

7. I.e., for the weeks in the year.

8. This diverges from normal Jewish usage, which recognized only 24 courses.

9. According to Num. 1.3, the minimum age for military service was 20 years; in Roman usage, it was 17. In *The Manual of Discipline for the Future Congregation of Israel*, twenty is regarded as the age of majority.

10. The war is to last forty years. The release occurs at the end of every seventh year, and lasts for one year.

11. Cp. Num. 1.3–4.

12. I.e., the children of Aram (Syria), mentioned in Gen.

10.23. (*Togar* is an error for *Gether* of the Scriptural text.)

13. Cp. Gen. 10.23.

14. I.e., the South Arabians; cp. Gen. 25.1–5.

15. Cp. Gen. 10.6–20.

16. The Heb. word for 'enlisted' comes from the same root as that for 'assembly'. For the military sense, cp. Isa. 13.3, etc.

17. In Hebrew, the word rendered 'enactments' (viz. *te'udoth*) resembles that for 'meeting' (viz. *mo'ed*).

18. These words have evidently fallen out of the text.

19. A play on the Biblical expression, 'memorial of the trumpet'; Lev. 23.24. Cp. also Num. 10.10.

20. Literally, 'of the slain', i.e., for giving the signal for slaughter.

21. Literally, 'the mysteries'. The idea is suggested, of course, by the mention of *ambush*.

22. I.e., withdraws (His troops).

23. A pun on the name Jeru*salem*, the Hebrew for 'peace' being *shalom*.

24. Merari was a son of Levi (Ex. 6.16, 19). According to rabbinic legend, the sons of Merari were entrusted with the transportation of the heavy portions of the Tabernacle, when Israel was wandering through the wilderness (cp. L. Ginzberg, *Legends of the Jews*, vol. iv [1911], p. 194). In line with this tradition 'Merari' may here denote the ordnance corps.

25. A crude pun on the name Merari, the Heb. for 'offering' being *terumah*. If the last two syllables are read backwards (in Hebrew) they somewhat resemble the first two of Merari!

26. Again a crude pun: 'thousand' is *elef*; 'God's wrath' is *af el*.

27. Another pun: 'hundred' is *meah*; 'from' is *meeth*.

28. Certain letters of the motto, when combined, spell out the Hebrew word for 'fifty'. I have tried to reproduce this in the translation.

29. The ensign of a Roman manipulus included a shield, usually of silver, on which were represented the images of such warlike deities as Mars or Minerva; and, in Imperial times, of the emperors (Tacitus, *Annals*, i.43; *Hist.*, i.41; iv.62) or of their favorites (Suetonius, *Tiberius*, 48; *Caligula*, 14). The specification in our text may have the earlier Roman usage in mind, but it is clearly influenced also by Psalm 20.6: 'In the name of our God will we set up our banner(s)'.

30. We do not yet know what the Heb. term employed here really means.

31. The word for 'blade' also means 'flash'.

32. The Heb. for 'javelin' comes from a root which also means 'spurt'.

33. Literally, 'the holy ones'. But the point is that this was also a term for 'warriors', who were consecrated for war; cf. Jer. 22.7; 51.27f.

33a. Note that later (ix.4) the total attacking force is said to comprise 28,000 men.

34. Literally, 'mild-mouthed'.

35. In the Roman army, service in the cavalry was the privilege of the upper class.

36. In Num. 4.3, fifty is the maximum age for military service; in Roman usage, it was 46.

37. These would correspond to the *fabri* and similar technicians of the Roman army.

38. Literally, 'gates', but what are meant are the spaces (*intervalla*) between the massed lines—a regular feature of Roman military formations.

38a. These would correspond to the Roman *scutati*, opposed to the cavalry (*equites*); cp. Livy, xxviii, 2.

39. It has been contended that in the days of the Second Temple, priests were not in fact anointed. But no deductions as to the date of our document should be drawn from that fact, for the expression is purely metaphorical and may therefore be a survival in language from earlier usage. Exactly comparable is our

own expression, 'a blot on the scutcheon'; no one carries a scutcheon today.

39a. In this section, the author employs a number of technical terms derived from Roman military strategy. Since these would be unintelligible to the layman, I have reproduced them by paraphrase. In identifying them, I have leaned heavily on Yigael Yadin's masterly interpretation.

40. Literally, 'rectangle', i.e. the Roman *agmen quadratum*.

41. I.e. the Roman *testudo*, a compact mass of troops advancing under cover of their uplifted shields joined together in the form of a *testudo*, or tortoise, to protect themselves from the shafts of the enemy. This formation was also called 'tower' (*turris*).

42. I.e. the Roman *forfex*, or 'scissors-formation'.

43. I.e. the Roman *cuneus*, or 'wedge-formation'.

44. Literally, 'slight flexing of the bow'.

44a. I.e. the Roman *alae* (*equitum*).

45. Cp. Enoch 40.9–10.

46. This is part of the exhortation ('pep-talk') delivered to the troops before battle, i.e. the Roman *allocutio*.

47. Deut. 20.3–4.

48. I.e., solstices and equinoxes.

49. Cf. I Sam., ch. 17.

50. I.e., the seven nations dispossessed by the Israelites when they conquered Canaan.

51. The Hebrew words (*nekha'e ruah*) are usually rendered 'crushed in spirit' (cp. Isa. 66.2). But it is apparent that our author interpreted them rather from a like-sounding word (*nechim*) which occurs in Psalm 35.15 and which the ancient Aramaic version (*Torgum*) indeed understood to mean 'base, impious'. (The expression is similarly employed in the *Hymn of the Initiants*.)

52. The restoration is based on Isa. 42.13. Cp. also Ex. 15.3.

53. Literally, 'Thou magnifiest and hallowest Thyself'. The

phrase is especially significant because it echoes the opening words of the famous *Kaddish*-doxology, one of the earliest elements of the Jewish liturgy. It derives from Ez. 38.23.

54. Ezekiel, ch. 38. See the General Introduction, p. 23.

55. The point lies in the double meaning of the word rendered 'holy beings', viz. (a) angels, (b) warriors; cf. above, note 33.

56. The restoration is based on the necessity of finding a heavenly counterpart to the earthly election of God's people as His fighting army.

57. The word rendered 'elect' also means 'picked troops' —a usage which occurs already in documents of the eighteenth century B.C. from Mari, on the Upper Euphrates.

58. Literally, 'lovingkindnesses'. What the writer has in mind, I think, is something like a Roman Imperial decree imposing peace and promising prosperity.

59. The writer uses the rare Hebrew word *heret*, which occurs only in Ex. 32.4 with the here inappropriate sense of 'graving tool'. Perhaps he chose this recondite term to suggest the Latin *charta*, somewhat in the sense of 'charter'.

60. Ps. 24.7f.; Zech. 14.5.

61. *Ibidem;* in both passages God is called 'the Mighty One'.

62. Judges 5.12.

62a. Ez. 39.10.

62b. Num. 24.18.

62c. Gen. 49.8.

63. II Sam. 1.19, 25.

63a. Cf. Num. 24.8.

64. Deut. 32.42.

65. Ecclesiasticus, 36.14.

65a. Jer. 49.32.

65b. Cf. Zech. 2.14(10).

66. Ps. 48.12.

67. Isa. 60.11.

68. Isa. 49.23.

68a. Isa. 42.11 (read as in the Qumran Scroll of Isaiah, with a slight variation from the standard [Masoretic] text).

69. Isa. 52.1; Psalms of Solomon, 11.8.

70. Ps. 57.6, 12; 108.6.

71. Cp. *Manual of Discipline,* iii, 13 ff.

72. I.e., Thy Law.

73. For the word *u-lehagbir* in the manuscript, I emend *u-lehagbiⁱah.*

74. E.g., to renewed vigor. (There is a small gap in the text.)

75. The word is perhaps an imitation of the Latin *velites* (as if from *velox,* 'swift'), the light-armed front-line troops.

76. Compare the beginning of the *Hymn of the Initiants.*

77. Cp. Ps. 7.7.

78. See above, n. 1.

79. Cp. Jer. 30.7.

80. This is 'the priest anointed for leading in war'. The office is mentioned in Mishnah, *Sotah,* VIII, 2, where he is described as addressing the troops in Hebrew (rather than Aramaic or any other vernacular). Cp. also Talmud, *Yomâ,* 72b, 73a.

81. Or, 'all the structure *of their being'.*

82. Cp. Jer. 25.29.

83. Cp. Num. 10.10.

84. There is perhaps a pun in the original, for the word rendered 'gold' could also mean 'diligent'. The sense will thus be that the truly adept are tested like gold against dross.

85. Cp. Lev. 10.1 ff.

86. Michael guards Israel; cp. Dan. 12.1 ff.

87. Cp. Isa. 60.19.

88. Literally, 'wave his hand'.

89. I.e., to destroy everything unacceptable and offensive to the God of Israel.

90. Cp. I Chron. 29.11.

The New Covenant

1. The word B'DY of the original text is clearly an error for B'DNY (or B'DN).

2. Restoring *le-he*[*rawô*]*th*; cf. Isa. 34.7; Ps. 23.5.

3. Cp. Isa. 43.3.

4. Cp. Gen. 1. 14–18.

5. Cp. Ecclesiasticus 42.23; 43.10.

6. Literally, 'understood'.

7. A technical expression for the future age, corresponding to the *Rahuta* ('Era of Favor') of Samaritan belief.

8. Cp. Ex. 24. 16–17.

9. Literally, 'fundaments, rudiments'. The word is used in Samaritan to denote the elemental hosts that were believed to be present at the revelation on Mount Sinai. Our author, however, employs the term in a somewhat different sense, implying that the essence of God's glory and the lofty eminences of eternity were then made manifest to Israel. (We must read *YeSODê*, not *YiSSuRê*, since the word is contrasted with *Ma'aLê*, i.e., 'foundations' with 'heights'.)

10. I.e., a new Moses. The lawgiver was known in later Jewish literature as 'the faithful shepherd'; cp. Ex. 3.1. Cp. also John 10.14.

SOURCES

1. THE MANUAL OF DISCIPLINE

Burrows, Millar, ed., *The Dead Sea Scrolls of St. Mark's Monastery*, vol. ii, fasc. 2. New Haven: American Schools of Oriental Research, 1951.

Habermann, A.M. *'Edah we-'Eduth*. (Jerusalem 1952), pp. 57-88. (Hebrew)

2. THE ZADOKITE DOCUMENT

Rabin, Chaim, *The Zadokite Documents*. Oxford, 1953.

Rost, L., ed., *Die Damaskusschrift*. (Kleine Texte fuer Vorlesungen and Uebungen, ed. Hans Lietzmann, No. 167.) Berlin, 1933.

Zeitlin, S., ed., *The Zadokite Fragments*. (Jewish Quarterly Review Monograph Series, No. 1.) Philadelphia: The Dropsie College, 1952. (Facsimiles of the original manuscripts.)

3. A FORMULARY OF BLESSINGS

Barthélemy, D. and Milik, J. T., *Qumran Cave I. (Discoveries in the Judaean Desert I)*. Oxford, 1955; No. 28b, pp. 118-29. Plates xxv-xxix.

4. THE HYMN OF THE INITIANTS

Manual of Discipline, cols. x-xi.

5. THE BOOK OF HYMNS or PSALMS OF THANKSGIVING

Sukenik, E.L., ed., *The Dead Sea Scrolls of the Hebrew University*. Jerusalem: The Magnes Press, 1955. Plates xxxv-lii.

6. THE ORATION OF MOSES

Barthélemy-Milik, *op. cit.*, No. 22, pp. 91-96. Plates xviii-xix.

7. COMMENTARY ON NAHUM

J. M. Allegro, in *Journal of Biblical Literature*, 75 (1956), 89-93.

8. COMMENTARY ON HABAKKUK

Burrows, *op. cit.*, Plates lv-lxi.
Habermann, *op. cit.*, pp. 39-56.

9. **COMMENTARY ON MICAH**

Barthélemy-Milik, *op. cit.*, No. 14, pp. 74-77. Plate xv, lines 8-19.

10. **COMMENTARY ON PSALM 37**

J. M. Allegro, in *Palestine Exploration Quarterly*, 1954: 69-75; supplemented by further fragments published by the same scholar in *Journal of Biblical Literature*, 75 (1956), 94-95.

11. **THE WAR OF THE SONS OF LIGHT AND THE SONS OF DARKNESS**

Sukenik, *op. cit.*, Plates xvi-xxxiv.

Yadin, Yigael, *Megillath Milhamath Bne Or bi-Bne Hoshech*. Jerusalem: The Bialik Institute, 1956.

12. **MANUAL OF DISCIPLINE FOR THE FUTURE CONGREGATION OF ISRAEL**

Barthélemy-Milik, *op. cit.*, No. 28a, pp. 108-18. Plates xxiii-xxiv.

13. **THE NEW COVENANT**

ibid., No. 34, ii.

14. **THE COMING DOOM**

ibid., No. 27, col. i, pp. 102-05. Plates cii-cv.

FOR FURTHER READING

Readers of this volume may wish to delve further into the scholarly controversy that is now raging around the date of the Scrolls and the identity of the Dead Sea Brotherhood. They may also be interested in exploring the various and ingenious attempts that have been made to peg such characters as the Teacher of Righteousness, the Wicked Priest, and the Man of Lies to specific historical characters; and they may like to hear more about such relatively arcane matters as Hebrew palaeography and radiocarbon dating. They will find admirable digests of the information they are seeking in Millar Burrows' *The Dead Sea Scrolls* (New York 1955) and in H. H. Rowley's *The Zadokite Fragments and the Dead Sea Scrolls* (Oxford 1952). Among periodical articles written in English, the following will probably suffice to provide general orientation and a broad coverage of the divergent views:

Brownlee, W. H., "A Comparison of the Covenanters of the Dead Sea Scrolls with Pre-Christian Jewish Sects." *The Biblical Archeologist,* 1950: 50-72.

Burrows, M., "The Discipline Manual of the Judaean Covenanters." *Oudtestamentische Studien,* VIII (1950), 156-72.

Cross, F. M., "The Scrolls from the Judaean Dessert." *Archaeology,* V (1956), 41-53.

Driver, G. R., *The Hebrew Scrolls from the Neighborhood of the Dead Sea.* Oxford 1951. (Driver denies the high antiquity of the Scrolls.)

Grossouw, W., "The Dead Sea Scrolls and the New Testament." *Studia Catholica,* 1951: 289-99; 1952: 1-8.

Kahle, P., "The Age of the Scrolls." *Vetus Testamentum,* 1951: 38-48. (Kahle prefers a date in the second century C.E.)

Lieberman, S., "Light on the Cave Scrolls from Rabbinic Sources." *Proceedings of the American Academy for Jewish Research,* 1951: 395-404.

Rabinowitz, I., "A Reconsideration of 'Damascus' and the '390 Years' of the Damascus (Zadokite) Fragment." *Journal of Biblical Literature,* 1954: 11-35. (Argues that the sojourn of the Brotherhood in 'the wilderness of Damascus' is to be understood figuratively.)

Teicher, J. L., "The Dead Sea Scrolls: Documents of the Jewish-Christian Sect of the Ebionites." *Journal of Jewish Studies,* 1951: 67-99.

id., "Jesus in the Habakkuk Scroll." Ibid., 1952: 53-55.

The 'Essene theory' may best be studied in A. Dupont-Sommer's fascinating, if sometimes erratic, study, *The Jewish Sect of Qumran and the Essenes* (London 1954). This theory, now increasingly accepted, forms the basis of Edmund Wilson's *The Scrolls from the Dead Sea* (New York 1955), but Wilson's deductions concerning the bearing of the Scrolls on Christianity have been seriously challenged by specialists.

ANALYTICAL INDEX

This index consists of a list of the major themes and concepts which appear in *The Dead Sea Scriptures*. They are arranged in the following categories:

A. THE COMMUNITY
B. GOVERNMENT OF THE COMMUNITY
C. LAWS AND PRACTICES
D. OPPONENTS OF THE BROTHERHOOD
E. THE LAST THINGS (Eschatological Doctrines)
F. ANGELOLOGY

Within each category the reader will find listed the topics relevant to it and where references to these topics occur in the scrolls themselves and elsewhere in ancient literature. The abbreviations used are as follows. These same abbreviations are used as well in the following index entitled BIBLICAL QUOTATIONS AND PARALLELS.

CD   The Coming Doom

H   The Book of Hymns

HC   The Commentary on Habakkuk

HI   The Hymn of the Initiants (= Manual, cols. x-xi)

M   The Manual of Discipline

MFC   The Manual of Discipline for the Future Congregation

NC   The New Covenant

W   The War of the Sons of Light and the Sons of Darkness

Z   The Zadokite Document

A. THE COMMUNITY

1. *The Brotherhood as a whole was called 'the Congregation,' i.e. of Israel, of God* (cf. Num. 27.12; 31.16, etc.)

M v.20; Z ix.15,42; xi.1-2; xv.7; xvii.7; W ii.1,3,7; iii.4,11, etc. The Heb. term is *'edah*. This is usually rendered 'synagogue' by the Septuagint. The cognate Syriac word was the technical term for 'the Church'; see Nestle, ZNTW, 1901: 263.

2. *The Community was distributed over several 'encampments.'*

Z vii.6; xii.22; xiii.4,7,13,20; xiv.3,8-9; xix.2-3

The term not only described the actual situation of the brethren in the Desert of Judah, but also defined them as the 'army of God' about to fight the apocalyptic war against the forces of evil.

The building at Qumran is best regarded as the headquarters of the entire Brotherhood, possibly the place where it met for those annual conventions described in *The Manual of Discipline*. Its library would thus have comprised the literature of the entire movement, and not simply of a local 'chapter.'

3. *The several 'chapters' were called 'communes' or 'cenobies' (Heb. yahad).*

M i.12,16; ii.22,24; vi.15,24,26; vii.6,17,18,20,23; viii.10,11, 12,16-17,19,22; ix.2,5-6,7,10,18-19; Z ix.39-40,52-53,70-71.

R. Marcus has pointed out that Philo uses the comparable Greek term *koinonia* in speaking of the Essenes.

4. *Another term was 'the corporation' (Heb. hibbur).*

Z xii.8

Such corporations (Heb. *haburôth*) of Pharisees are often mentioned in Talmudic literature.

5. *The Brethren styled themselves 'the Elect.'*

M viii.6 ('elect of favor'); H ii.13 ('elect of righteousness')
The title expressed the fact that they were indeed the 'chosen' of God, pledged to the Covenant (cf. Isa. 65.9; Ps. 105.43, etc.). The title was adopted also by the early Christians: Mat. 24.22, 24; Mark 13.20,22,27; II Tim. 2.10; I Peter 1.1. Cp. also 'the elect of God,' Luke 18.7; Rom. 8.33; Col. 3.12; Titus 1.1.
The Mandaeans likewise call themselves 'the Elect': Lidzbarski, *Mandäische Liturgien*, 75, 106f.; id., *Johannesbuch*, ii, 69,102, 221. So, too, among the Manichaeans, the true followers of Mani are termed 'the Elect' *(vičidagan).*

6. *They also called themselves 'those in the lot (portion) of God.'*

M.ii.2

Cp. Ignatius, *Ad Eph.*, 3.8: 'that I may be found in the lot of the Christians at Ephesus.'
The opposite was 'those in the lot (portion) of Belial.'

7. *They claimed special 'illumination' and adopted the name of 'Sons of Light.'*

M i.9; iii.13,24; W i.3, etc.

The title was adopted also by the early Christians: Luke 16.8; John 12.36; I Thes. 5.5.

Among the Mandaeans, 'sons of light' meant 'angels,' with whom, indeed, the *illuminati* claimed association: Lidzbarski, *Mand. Lit.*, 18.24,36. Cp. also Montgomery, *Aram. Incantation Texts from Nippur* (1913), i.9. Men predestined to eternal life were called likewise: Brandt, *Mand. Schriften*, 13.9.

(a) *The illumination was an 'enlightenment of the countenance'*

H iv.5,27; ix.26-27

Cp. *Odes of Solomon* 41.6, 'Let our faces shine in His light.' (cp. also ib., 36.3)

(b) *It was called 'Light-Perfection' (Heb. Ôr-Tôm).*

H iv.6,23; xviii.29

An imitation of the Biblical Urim and Thummim, interpreted as 'lights and perfections.'

The idea may have come to the Brotherhood from its precursors, the Assidaeans (*Hasidim*, 'pious ones') of the Maccabean age, and have been based on Deut. 33.8-9.

On the concept of divine illumination, cp. John 1.19; Eph. 1.18; 3.9; Heb. 6.4; 10.22; II Cor. 3.4,6.

For the idea in mysticism, cp. Jacopone da Todi, *Lauda* xci: 'Lume fuor di mesura Resplende nel mio core' (A light immeasurable Shines in my heart); see Underhill, *Mysticism*, 249-50.

8. *The Brotherhood called themselves 'Sons of Truth.'*

M iv.5-6; H vi.29; vii.30; ix.35; x.27; xi.11

8a. *The ideal Community was described as 'the House of Truth.'*

M v.6; viii.9

9. *Forms of Revelation:*

(a) *the Brethren were recipients of God's 'truth.'*

H i.27; ii.10; v.9,26; vii.24; ix.4,9,10; W xiii.9-10,12

In Jewish tradition, this 'truth' is often identified directly with the Torah (Law). So, too, in Mandaean thought, 'truth' (Kushta) is, virtually, mystic revelation; see W. Sundberg, *Kushta* (1953). In Samaritan, 'the Verity' (Qushtah) is a common term for the Law.

See also: Romans 15.8; Gal. 2.5.

(b) *this 'truth' was an esoteric doctrine.*

    H v.11,25; ix.24

Cp. Odes of Solomon 8.11: 'Keep My secret, ye who are kept by it.'

(c) *God 'opened the ears' of the faithful.*

    H i.21; vi.4

(d) *God engraved the 'truth' on their hearts.*

    H xviii.27

(e) *they were especially 'schooled' by God.*

    H ii.39; vii.14

Derived from Isa. 54-13. Cp. John 6.45; I Thes. 4.9.

(f) *they had the 'vision' of knowledge (or understanding).*

    H iv.18

On vision in mystic experience, see Underhill, *op. cit.*, 279ff.

(g) *they drank from the fountain of knowledge.*

    H ii.18; iv.11; v.26; 'fount of light,' H vi.17

Derived from Ps. 36.10. Cp. *Odes of Solomon* 6.7f.; 30.1-2.
St. Francis of Assisi gives the mystic chalice to John of Parma and other brethren: *Fioretti*, cap. 48. Mechthild of Magdeburg speaks of 'drinking for a space of the unmingled wine': *Flieszende Licht der Gottheit*, pt. i, ch. 43. Blake declares, 'I am drunk with intelletcual vision': *Letters*, ed. Russel (1906), 171. See Underhill, *op. cit.*, 235.

(h) *they share the transcendental knowledge of God and angels.*

    M iv.22 ('knowledge of the Most High'); cf. H ii.3

Cp. *Odes of Solomon* 23.4: 'Walk ye in the knowledge of the Most High.'

(i) *they have direct access to God, need no intermediary.*

    H vi.13 (but the text is not altogether certain)

(k) *they ascend to the 'height of eternity.'*

    H iii.20

Cp. the familiar mystic symbol of the 'ascent'; W. R. Inge, *Mysticism in Religion* (1948), 80-82.

(l) *God's 'power' is manifested in them (Heb. higbir).*

    H i.34; iv.8,23,27,28; v.15; W xvi.1.

'Power' (Heb. *geburah*) is a common synonym for God in Rabbinic literature.

10. *The Brethren are 'volunteers' (Heb. mithnadebim).*

M v.1,6,8,10,21,22; vi.13

The term has a military connotation (cp. Ju. 5.9) and thus suggests the idea of an 'army of God'—the 'Onward, Christian soldiers' concept.

Cp. I Macc. 2.42 (of the Hasidim); *Didascalia Apostolorum*, init.

11. *Community is called 'God's (eternal) plantation.'*

H vi.15; viii.6,10

Based on Isa. 66.1. Cf. Mishnah, Sanhedrin 1; *Psalms of Solomon*, 14.3-4; *Odes of Solomon* n.15-16; 38.18-21. Mandaean: *Right Ginza*, II.iv. init.; *Mand. Liturg.*, 149.,190,179ff., Apostolic Constitutions, init. Analogous is 'neophyte' in I Tim. 3.6.

12. *Community forms one congregation with celestial hosts ('communion of the saints').*

M ii.25; xi.7-8; H iii.21; vi.14; xi.11-12; frag. ii.10

Cp. Enoch 43.104; Ephes. 2.19.

13. *Brethren are driven from native soil.*

H iv.8-9 ('like a sparrow from its nest')

Cp. *Psalms of Solomon* 17.15-16.

14. *Brethren dwell in desert or in 'land of Damascus.'*

Z vi.15,19; vii.19; viii.21a; xx.12; W i.2-3

Based on Amos 5.25-27; hence, not to be taken literally. See General Introduction, pp. 4,24.

Like all mystics, the brethren oscillated between a keen sense of God's nearness and a despair at His seeming remoteness. Cp. John of the Cross, *The Dark Night of the Soul*, I ii,ch. 6: 'That which this anguished soul feels most deeply is the conviction that God has abandoned it . . . cast it away into darkness . . . It has also the same sense of abandonment with respect to all creatures, and that it is an object of contempt to all, especially to its friends' (cp. H. v.25f.).

15. *The brethren feel that they are being tested and proven.*

M viii.4; H. v.16f.; W xvii.1,9

exposed to 'snares of wickedness,' H v.8; to 'snares of corruption,' H iii.26.

Cp. Underhill, *op. cit.*, 385: 'Trials, taken *en bloc,* mean a disharmony between the self and the world with which it has to deal.'

B. GOVERNMENT OF THE COMMUNITY

1. *The formal Deliberative Council (Heb. 'esah).*

M i.8,10; ii.25; v.7; vi.12; vii.22; viii.5,22; Z xx.24; MFC i.26,-27; ii.2,9,11.

In the Syriac dialect of the early Christians of Palestine, the cognate term serves as the equivalent of Greek *synhedrion;* cf. F. Schwally, *Idioticon* (1893), 41f. A. Dupont-Sommer (*The Jewish Sect of Qumran and the Essences,* 63) thinks that '*esah* denoted the sect as a whole and that it may be the origin of the name Essenes!

2. *Officers:*

(a) '*Leader (Prince) of the Entire Congregation.*'

Z viii.17,20; Blessings; MFC; W v.1

Cp. I Macc. 14.27 (of Simon). Yadin thinks this is the equivalent of the term *ethnarch.* Obviously, however, it would have been only the Brotherhood itself that conferred such a 'loaded' title on its supreme official; the leader of a religious splinter group would not formally have enjoyed that status in the ryes of the civil administration.

(b) '*Overseer of All the Camps.*'

Z xiv.8-9

Virtually, 'archbishop'—albeit in a primitive sense.

The 'leader of the entire congregation' and 'the overseer of all the camps' would have been officers of the entire fraternity.

(c) *high priest*

It is noteworthy that the high priest is mentioned only in texts concerned with the eventual state of the Restored Community, e.g. in the *War of the Sons of Light and the Sons of Darkness* and in *The Manual of Discipline for the Future Congregation.* This would suggest that the Brotherhood, while it condemned the venality of the hierarchy at Jerusalem, did not appoint its own 'antipope.' In Z xiv.7 there is, to be sure, mention of a 'priest who supervises the general membership,' but this is not a high priest in the accepted sense, and it is significant that in M vi.14 the same officer is described simply as 'the supervisor' without reference to priestly status.

(d) *priests*

M i.18,21; ii.1,19; v.2; vi.3-4,5,8,19; vii.2; viii.1; Z iii.21;
iv.2; vii.1; ix.13,15; xiii.2,5,7; xiv.3; xvi.44; W *passim*

(e) *priests were called 'sons of Zadok'*

M v.2; ix.14; Z iv.1

It is at least arguable that it is not the community as a whole
but solely its priests that are described in the Scrolls as 'sons
of Zadok,' even though the title may later have been given
an extended meaning. In that case, it would derive directly
from Ez. 40.46; 43.19; 44.15; 48.11, and there would be no
need to look for a 'righteous teacher' named Zadok as the
'founding father' of the Brotherhood in the days of the Second
Commonwealth.

(f) *courses of priests*

W ii.4

(g) *'the priest anointed for war'*

W xv.16

Cp. Mishnah, Sotah VIII, 2.

(h) *the 'teacher of righteousness' (Heb. môreh zedeq).*

Z i.11; vi.11; vii.20a; xx.1,28,32; MC ii.5 (on 1.5); Comm.
on Ps. 37.24; HC i.13 (on 1.4); ii.2 (on 1.4-5); v.10 (on
1.13); vii.4 (on 2.2); viii.3 (on 2.4); ix.10 (on 2.8); xi.5
(on 2.15)

The term means really 'the right guide', i.e. the true expounder of the Law; see General Introduction, p. 5.
There is no need to assume that all references refer consist-
ently to a single historical figure.
Note that in Pal. Targum to Dt. 18.18, the Future Prophet is
called expressly 'the prophet of righteousness.'
The title was later adopted by the Karaites.

(i) *teacher acts as 'father' to the brethren*

Z xiii.9; H vii.20

Cp. *Apostolic Constitutions* ii.6,7.

(k) *three priests at head of community*

M viii.1 ff.

Cp. the three 'pillars' of the Church; Gal. 2.9.

(l) *presbyters; the 'twelve perfect men'*

M viii.1; Z [vii.5]; xx.25,7

Cp. the comparison of the presbyters with the twelve apostles in *Didascalia* 45.23; 46.16 and in Ignatius, *Ad Trall.*, ii.2-3; *Ad Magnes.*, vi.1; *Ad Philad.*, v.1.

Note also that among the Waldenses, advanced members of the brotherhood were called 'the perfect.'

(m) *judges*

    Z x.1,4; xiv.13; xv.4,16; xvi.19

Ten in number (Z x.4). Hence, cp. the courts of ten in Temple law: Mishnah, Sanhedrin I,3.

(n) *levites*

    M i.19,22; ii.4,11; Z iii.21; iv.3; x.5; xiii.3; xiv.4; W *passim*

(o) *'messiahs' (anointed)*

    M ix.11; Z vi.10; vii.21a; xii.23; xiii.20; xiv.19; MFC

The usual expression is 'messiahs (or, messiah) of Aaron and Israel.' This has led to all kinds of wild speculation. But all it means is simply 'the anointed high priest and the anointed king.' (For 'messiah' as applied to the high priest, op. Lev. 4.3; Mishnah, Shebu'oth i.7; Horayoth ii.1, etc. As the title of the king, cp. Ps. 18.51, etc.).

(p) *'overseer, inspector'*

    M vi.19-20; Z ix.18,22; xiii.16,17; xiv.11,13; xv.14

Such 'overseers' served as financial executives of religious brotherhoods in Hellenistic times. Josephus mentions a similar officer among the Essenes.

(q) *'overseer of the camp'*

    Z xiii.7,13

(r) *'overseer of the general membership* (lit. *the many).'*

    M vi.12; Z xv.8

(s) *'inspector'* (Heb. paqid)

    Z xiii.11; xiv.6

It is not quite clear whether the 'overseer' *(mebaqqer)* or the 'inspector' *(paqid)* more closely answers to the *episkopos* or 'bishop' of the early Church, for the Septuagint uses the Greek term to translate both of the Hebrew words.

(t) *'interpreter'*

    H ii.13

Cp. I Cor. 14.28.

(u) *'expositor'* (Heb. doresh)

    M vi.6; Z vii.18

Cp. Mishnah, Yomâ i.6; Josephus, *BJ* II, viii.6,19; *Ant.*, XIII, v.9, on 'expositors' among the Essenes.

C. LAWS AND PRACTICES

ablutions	M iii.4f.,9; iv.21; v.13; Z x.10-13
atonement	M viii.6-9; ix.4-14; H. col.iv.
blasphemy	M v.19; Z xv.1-5
calendar	HI (=M x) 1-7
contamination	Z xii. 15-18
demoniacal possession	Z xii.2-3
dietary laws	Z xii.11-15
fraud	M vii.6f.
lost property	Z ix.11ff.
marriage	Z iv.21-v.6
name of God	M ii.6-7; Z xv.1-5
oath	M v.8; Z ix.9-16
oath, abrogation of	Z xv.6ff.
purity	M vi.16-22,25; vii.3-16; viii.24
revenge	M i.11; ii.6-9; iv.11; v.2-25; Z.ix.2-8
sabbath	Z x.14-xi.18
sacrifices	M ix.4-5
sanctuary, defilement of	Z xi.18-xii.2
slaves (servants)	Z xii.11
testimony	Z ix.17-x.3
vows	M v.8; Z xvi.13

D. OPPONENTS OF THE BROTHERHOOD

1. *Belial and his forces*

M i.18,23-24; Z iv.13,15; v.18; viii.2; xii.2; W *passim*

Cp. Or. Sib., ii.165f.; Jubilees i.20; Testament of Reuben ii, of Levi, iii; of Zebulun, ix; of Naphtali, ii; of Benjamin, vi; Called 'spirit of darkness': Test. Levi xix; Joseph vii, xx. Cp. also Mat. 24.5-12; II Tim. 3.1f.; *Didache* 21.3; II Cor. 5.15.

2. *'Children of Corruption'*

M ix.16; x.19; Z vi.15; xiii.14

Cp. Jub. 10.3; 15.26. John 17.12; II Thes. 2.3; *Gospel of Nicodemus* 20.
The expression may have been derived from Deut. 32.5. (Cf. also Isa. 1.4)

2a. *'Men of Corruption'*

M ix.22

3. *'Sons of Darkness'*

M i.10; [W i.6]

Cp. Montgomery, *Aram. Incantation Texts from Nippur* (1913), 16.7, where the epithet characterizes *demons* (like Arabic *jinn*).

4. *'Builders of a rickety wall.'*

Z iv.19; viii.12,18

Derived from Ez. 13.10.

5. *'Prophets of deceit (delusion).'*

H iv.10,20.

6. *'False prophets.'*

H iv.16

Cp. Mat. 7.15; 24.11,24; Mark 13.22; Luke 6.26; Acts 13.6; II Peter 2.1; I John 4.1. Mandaean: *Right Ginza* II.i, 107.

H v.26: 'They that alter the works of God by propounding sinful mysteries.'

By 'prophets' the writers meant simply 'teachers,' as in I Cor. 12.28; 14.29.

7. *'Lying (deceitful) interpreters.'*

H ii.31; iv.9-10. Cf. also H ii.14.

8. *'Seekers after smooth things'*

H ii.32.

9. *'The froward'* (*Heb.* helka'im).

H iii.25-26; iv.25,35

Derived from Ps. 10.10 (where, however, the meaning is uncertain).

10. *'Furtive men, dissemblers'* (*Heb.* na'alamim)

H iii.28; iv.13; vii.34

Derived from Ps. 26.4.

11. *Specific Opponents:*

   (a) *'Man of lies'*

   Z xx.15; HC ii.1; v.11

Rabin cps. II Thes. 2.3.

   (b) *'Preacher of Lies'*

   Z viii.13

The Heb. means properly, 'Dribbler of lies,' in reference to Micah 2.6,11.

(c) 'Man of Scoffing'

    Z i.14; xx.11 (pl.)

Cp. Isa. 28.14; Prov. 29.8.

(d) 'House of Absalom'

    HC v.9

For the interpretation, see above, p. 25.

(e) 'House of Peleg'

    Z xx.22

A concocted name. Heb. *p-l-g* means 'divide.' Hence, the meaning is, 'divisive elements.'

E. THE LAST THINGS
(Eschatological Doctrines)

1. *History divided into 'Era of Wrath (Sin, Wickedness)' and 'Era of Favor.'*

    (a) 'Era of Wrath'

        Z i.5; H iii.28

Cp. Zeph. 1.5 ('Day of Wrath'), and cp. Talmud, B.B. 10a, Shab. 11a; Ab.Zar. 18b, for 'Wrath' as an eschatological term. Cp. also Ecclesiasticus 48.10.

    (b) 'Era of Wickedness'

        Z vi.10,14; xii.23; xiv.19; xv.7,10; xx.23 ('Era of Perfidy')

Cp. Enoch 22.12; 80.2.

    (c) 'Era of Favor'

        H xv.15; frag. ix.8; NC

Cp. Isa. 61.2 ('Year of favor'). The Samaritans likewise divide history into the 'Era of God's Turning Away' (*Fanutah*) and that of His 'Favor' (*Rahutah*).

REQUITAL:

1. *'The Final Era'* (Heb. qes).

    M iii.23; iv.18,25; Z iv.9,10; xix.10; xx.15; HC vii.2

2. *'Time of Visitation Inquisition'* (Heb. pequdah)

    M iii.18; iv.18-19,26.

3. *Final Judgment*

    M iv.20

4. *'Day of Requital'*

M ix.23

Based on Deut. 32.35, read as in LXX and Sam.

5. *Spirits and angels also will be judged*

H vii.29

6. *'Messianic Travail'*

Hymn No. 5, *passim*

For the expression 'pangs of the Messiah,' cf. Talmud, Shab. 118a; Sanh. 98b; Mat. 24.8; Mark 13.8-9; I Thes. 5.3.

Described: Jubilees 20.11-25; Or. Sib. ii.154f.; II Esdras v-vi; Mat. 24.6-29; Rev. chs. 6-9; Talmud, Sanh. 96b-97a.

7. *Conflagration (Ekpyrosis)*

H iii.29ff.; W xiv.17. Cf. also M ii.8.

Cp. Dan. 7.10f.; Psalms of Solomon 15.14f.; Or. Sib., ii.253f., 296; iii.542,689; iv.176; Luke 17.28; II Peter 3.6ff.; II Thes. 1.7f.; Rev. 19.20; 20.10,14f.; 21.8.

Berosus (quoted in Seneca, *Nat Qu.* ii.29,1) predicted a final conflagration.

On non-Semitic parallels, cp. C. Clemen, *Primitive Christianity and its Non-Jewish Sources* (1912), 161f.; M. Eliade, *The Myth of the Eternal Return* (1954), 87-88; R. Mayer, *Ist die biblische Vorstellung vom Weltenbrand eine Entlehnung aus dem Parsismus?* (1947).

8. *Messianic Era of Forty Years*

Cp. Apoc. Esdras xiii.23-25; Talmud, Sanh. 99a; Midrash Tehillim xc, §393. Possibly based on Ps. 95.10 (cf. Yalqut Shime'oni *in loc.*).

9. *War against Belial, Gog, etc.*

H iii.35f.; vi.29ff.; x.34-35; W *passim* (especially, i.10, 13-14)

Cp. Test. Levi, v.27; of Dan, ii.10-11; John 12.31; II Cor. 6.15.

Gog and Magog: Isa. 25.6; Zech. 14.2. Cp. Or. Sib. iii.319, 519,632f.; v.101; Syriac Apoc. Baruch 70.7-10; Pal. Targum to Num. 9.6; 24.17; Enoch 56; 90.16; Assum. Mosis 8.1ff.; II Esdras 5.6; 13.33f.; Mishnah, 'Eduyoth ii.10. The basic notion occurs already in Theopompus quoted by Plutarch, *De Is.*, 47.

ablution after victory	W xiv.3
cavalry	W vi.8-17
exhortation before battle	W xv.6ff.

REWARDS:

Cp. Test. Abraham; Jubilees i.29; Enoch 72; Mat. 19.28; Jewish 'Burial Kaddish'; *Manichaean:* F. W. K. Müller, *Handschriften-reste,* ii.15 (employing the Iranian term *frasagard*).

Renewal (rebirth) is also an element of mystical experience; cp. George Fox, *Journal,* ed. N. Penny (1911), I, ch. ii. 'Now was I come up in spirit through the Flaming Sword into the Paradise of God. *All things were new.*'

Cp. Talmud, Sanhedrin 91b (sevenfold Messianic sun); Midrash Konen 24–25 (based on Isa. 30.26). Cp. also Isa. 60.19; Rev. 21.23,25; 22.6; *Odes of Solomon,* 21.5.

Based on Deut. 18.18 and Mal. 3.23ff. (Cf. Ecclesiasticus 48.10.) Samaritans identify him with Moses Redivivus; Jews, with Elijah (Talmud, Menahoth 45a; B.M. 3a; Aboth de Rabbi Nathan 24.4).

Cp. Mat. 11.14; 17.10ff.; Mark 9.11f.; John 1.45; 5.46; 6.14; 7.40; Acts 7.37; Rev. 11.3ff.

Often alternates with *priestly* forerunner. (Note that both Moses

and Elijah were priests.) Cp. Test. Levi, v.13-20; Heb. 3.1;
4.15ff.; 5.4,10; 6.20.

5. *Messianic 'Star'*
    Z vii.18

Based on Num. 24.17. Cp. Test Levi, v.15; Judah, iv.20; Samaritan Liturgy, ed. Cowley, ii.88 Heh 10; 92.17; 96.32; (all
by Abisha b. Pinehas, d. 1376).

6. *'Faithful Shepherd' will arise*
    NC

Based on Isa. 63.11. Cp. Heb. 13.20. 'Shepherd of souls':
I Peter 2.25. Cp. also John 10.11,14; I Peter 5.4.
Enoch 90.17-27 speaks of God as the Master Shepherd who
will deliver his flock from the seventy evil shepherds.

7. *New Covenant will be concluded*
    NC

Based on Jer. 31.32-33. For the true meaning, see above, pp. 4,24.
The Covenant will be inscribed on human hearts: H xviii.27.
Cp. Jer. 31.33; Rom. 2.14f. (Stoic parallel adduced in Feine,
Der Römerbrief [1903], 95ff.)

8. *God records deeds of men for reward or punishment*
    H i.23-24; xvi.10

Cp. Slav. Enoch 50.1; *Odes of Solomon* 9.12. Rabbinic parallels in L. Ginzberg, *Legends of the Jews*, v.128, n.141.

9. *Righteous will acquire crown of glory*
    M iv.7; H ix.24

Cp. Wisdom of Solomon 6.16; Odes of Solomon 9.11; I Peter
5.4 *Mandaean:* Lidzbarski, *Mand. Lit.*, 4f.,29,108,177,243,267.

10. *Righteous will acquire robe of majesty*
    M iv.8

11. *Future Community will be the true temple of God.*
    M viii.5f.

Cp. I Cor. 3.16-17; Ephes. 2.20-22. Cp. also Heb. 8.2.

F. ANGELOLOGY

1. *General names for angels:*
    (a) *'divine beings'* (Heb. elim)
        H x.8; frag. ii.3,10; W i.10,11; xiv.15,16; xv.14; xvii.7

(b) '*host of heaven*'
>H iii.35

(c) '*host of the holy ones*'
>H iii.22; x.34-35

(d) '*eternal host*'
>H xi.13

(e) '*communion of the holy ones*'
>H iv.25

Derived from Ps. 89.8(7).

(f) '*sons of heaven*'
>H iii.22

(g) '*stalwarts*' (*Heb.* gibbôrê kôᵃh)
>H viii.11; x.34-35. (Cp. 'wondrous stalwarts,' H v.21; 'stalwarts of heaven,' H iii.35-36)

Derived from Ps. 103.20.

(h) '*glorious ones*'
>H x.8

Cp. Slav. Enoch 22.9

(i) '*holy ones*'
>Z xx.8

2. *Particular angels:*

(a) Prince of Lights	M iii.20
(b) Angel of Darkness	M iii.20-21
(c) Angel of Truth	M iii.24
(d) Angel(s) of the Presence	Blessings
(e) Angels of Destruction	M iv.12; Z ii.6; viii.2
(f) Mastemah, Angel of Adversity	Z iv.13; v.18; viii.2; vxi.5

The 'angels of destruction' are likewise mentioned in Talmudic literature (e.g. Shab. 88a) and in Enoch 53.3; 56.1. Cowley (*Jewish Quarterly Review,* viii, 571) states that an angel of similar name is known also to the Samaritans, but I have found no trace of him in the whole of Samaritan literature. Mastemah recurs in Jubilees 49.2. The name is related philologically to Satan.

3. *Guardian angels*
>H v.21f.

4. *Protective angels:*

    (a) Gabriel   W ix.16
        Cp. Ginzberg, *Legends*, v.21. Origen, *De Princip.* i.81, says that
        Gabriel is the angel of war.

    (b) Michael
        Cp. Dan. 10.21; Rev. 12.7; Jude 9; Ginzberg, *op.cit.*, v.4.

    (c) Raphael   M ix.15

    (d) Sariel (or Uriel)   W ix.15

5. *Angels participate in final eschatological war*

    H iii.35f.; vi.29f; x.34-35; W xv.14.

BIBLICAL QUOTATIONS AND PARALLELS

This index is intended to serve as a tool for those who may wish to trace the main Biblical parallels to the Scrolls. It is therefore geared to the columns and lines of the original texts, even though these have been indicated in the translations only *by sections.*

In the case of the Old Testament, the parallels are *verbal,* representing direct quotations woven into the texts. In that of the New Testament, however, what is usually involved is a correspondence of *ideas and concepts,* though in certain instances verbal identity is also to be found.

An interesting feature of the Old Testament parallels is that there is no quotation from the Book of Esther, the one book of Scripture that has not yet turned up among the Qumran fragments.

EZEKIEL		JONAH	
4.5	Z i.6	2.6	H iii.18
7.17	H iv.33-34	2.8	H viii.29
11.19	H xviii.26	4.8	H vii.5
14.3,4,7	M ii.12; H iv.15		
20.35	W i.3	**MICAH**	
21.3 (20.47)	H iii.29-30	1.4	H iv.34
21.12 (7)	H iv.33-34	2.10	H iii.8
23.46	M ii.6	6.8	M iv.5; v.4; viii.2
31.6	cf. H viii.8	7.2	Z xvi.15
31.14	H viii.5-6	7.19	H xvii.15
35.8	W xv.1		
36.3	H ii.1	**NAHUM**	
36.26	H xviii.26	1.2	Z ix.5
38.9	W xii.9	1.6	H iii.28
38.16	W xii.9	1.11	H vi.21
38.23	W xi.15	2.2	H ii.6
39.10	W xii.10		
44.15	Z iii.21-iv.2	**HABAKKUK**	
		1.4	H iv.25
DANIEL		2.1	H vii.29
4.9	cf. H viii.8	2.3 (LXX)	H v.27
9.27	H iii.36	2.15	H iv.10-11
10.5 (16)	H iii.7		
		ZEPHANIAH	
HOSEA		1.15	H v.30; ix.6
2.17	W x.9		
3.4	Z xx.16	**ZECHARIAH**	
4.14	H ii.19; iv.7	2.17	W xii.2
4.16	Z i.13	3.8	H vii.21
5.10	Z v.20; viii.3	12.6	W xi.10
6.3	H iv.5		
10.8	H viii.25	**MALACHI**	
12.15	H xi.19	1.4	H ii.7; iii.24
14.3 (LXX)	H i.28	1.10	Z vi.13
14.5	H xiv.26; xv.10		
		MATTHEW	
AMOS		3.3	M viii.14
2.14	W xiv.11	3.11	M iii.7-8
3.9	H iii.25	5.33-37	cf. M v.8
5.16 (adapted)	H xi.14	11.14	M ix.11
5.26-27	Z vii.14	17.10	M ix.11
9.11	Z vii.16	18.8	M ii.7
		19.28	M iv.25
OBADIAH		24.8	H v. *passim*
21	W vi.6	24.22,24	M viii.6; H ii.13